Management Basics
for Veterinarians

Management Basics
for Veterinarians

Lowell Ackerman DVM DACVD MBA MPA

ASJA Press
New York Lincoln Shanghai

Management Basics for Veterinarians

ASJA Press
an imprint of iUniverse, Inc.

For information address:
iUniverse
2021 Pine Lake Road, Suite 100
Lincoln, NE 68512
www.iuniverse.com

The authors have made every effort to ensure the accuracy of the information herein. However, appropriate information sources and professionals should be consulted where appropriate. It is the responsibility of every veterinarian to evaluate the appropriateness of a particular opinion in the context of actual clinical and financial situations, and with due consideration to new developments.

ISBN: 0-595-28711-5 (Pbk)
ISBN: 0-595-74905-4 (Cloth)

Printed in the United States of America

To my wonderful wife Susan, my three adorable children–Nadia, Rebecca, and David–and our beloved canine companion, Marilyn

TABLE OF CONTENTS

PREFACE

Much has changed in the last several years in the way that veterinarians have regarded business and management topics. At one time, it was almost anathema for veterinarians to accept profit and the art of practicing medicine as being part of the same mission. But, times have indeed changed.

There are now several studies that have shown that veterinarians' salaries lag far behind those of similarly trained professionals, and that this dramatically impacts the ability of new graduates to service their educational debt. It also suggests that unless changes are made, the profession will not attract the best and the brightest due to the poor return on investment of time and money.

Those changes that are needed in the profession are reflected within the pages of this book. And while studies show that the profession is lagging, there have never been more opportunities for the advancement of veterinary medicine and profitable practice. However, such changes require a paradigm shift from practicing in a retail model with relatively unskilled staff, to practicing in a professional model, with well-trained paraprofessional staff. Note that our human counterparts in medicine and dentistry do fine financially, without the sale of pharmaceuticals and retail markups on laboratory testing. We can be there as well, while practicing the highest quality veterinary medicine at the same time.

While many veterinarians choose to believe that expertise in medicine necessarily precludes having business sense, nothing could be further from the truth. In fact, business and medicine are both evidence-based disciplines with much in common. When a patient is sick, we use standard algorithms to determine the most likely causes, and run appropriate diagnostic tests. We do the same thing with a business that is in failing health. We might run an inventory audit instead of a radiograph, or look at financial statements rather than laboratory results, but the problem-solving approach is the same.

Once a medical problem is unearthed, we prescribe appropriate treatment. The same holds for businesses. A practice may not need an antibiotic injection, but an infusion of capital might be just what the doctor orders for an outdated facility. Finally, once the problem is corrected, we periodically monitor the patient with wellness exams, assuring continued health. Businesses are no different. We continue to take their vital signs, benchmark them against established "normals" and make sure that they continue on a healthful trend. What could possibly be a more natural extension of expertise than applying the same care to practice management as patient management?

This book includes information on the management skills important in practice, from understanding customer service to developing appropriate promotional tools. Chapters cover human resources, operations, implementing profit centers, measuring performance, and even some legal elements of successful practice.

While veterinary graduates may not need to apply specific details related to accounting, economics, or other such topics, understanding the basic premises of business disciplines is no different than the notion of learning physiology, anatomy, histology and embryology as a prelude to a better understanding of clinical veterinary medicine. This information was covered in much detail in *Business Basics for Veterinarians* and it is strongly recommended that this book be read for more details on these subjects. The chapters in *Business Basics for Veterinarians* included:

- The Veterinary Marketplace
- Leadership
- Planning
- Budgeting
- Economics
- Accounting
- Money Matters
- Marketing
- Financial Management
- Operations Management
- Business Plans

The information from these chapters is important to a solid understanding of the basic business tenets inherent in all ventures. The chapters in the book you are now reading were selected based on the applicability of material for actual veterinary practice, including developing profit centers, providing exceptional customer service, measuring your progress on the path to profitability, effectively managing staff, and much more.

The goal of this work is to provide veterinarians with a basic foundation in practice management. I would like to thank everyone who helped to make this book a reality, including the contributing authors and all of the individuals and organizations that have contributed to the body of knowledge encompassing business and veterinary medicine.

Lowell Ackerman DVM DACVD MBA MPA

Acknowledgements

I would like to thank Elizabeth Bellavance DVM MBA, Mark Davis, Tracy Dowdy CVPM, Karen Felsted CPA MS DVM CVPM, Jim Humphries BS DVM, Thomas Lynch MA, Frank Muggia JD, and Kurt Oster MS SPHR, for their chapter contributions to this book. Also, I would like to acknowledge the contribution of those who allowed themselves to be photographed for inclusion in this book. This includes: Nadia, Rebecca & Marilyn Ackerman, Susan Abbott, Erin Crowley, Theresa Gamache, and Kathleen Vaclavik.

LIST OF ABBREVIATIONS

AAHA	American Animal Hospital Association
AAVMC	Association of American Veterinary Medical Colleges
ACT	Average Client Transaction
APPMA	American Pet Products Manufacturers Association
ATC	Average Transaction Charge
AVMA	American Veterinary Medical Association
BARK[sm]	Business Assessment Report Kard
CBC	Complete Blood Count
COT	Costs of Transaction
CPA	Certified Public Accountant
Cr	Credit
CV	Curriculum vitae
DLH	Direct Labor Hours
Dr.	Debit
EOQ	Economic Order Quantity
GAAP	Generally Accepted Accounting Principles
GAO	General Accounting Office
GDP	Gross Domestic Product
FV	Future Value
MACRS	Modified Accelerated Cost Recovery System
MBA	Master in Business Administration
Megastudy	The Current and Future Market for Veterinarians and Veterinary Medical Services in the United States, 1999. KPMG LLP Economic Consulting Services
OCBOA	Other Comprehensive Basis of Accounting
PDCA	Plan, Do, Check, Act
PDP	Personal Development Plan
PPF	Production Possibilities Frontier
PV	Present Value
ROI	Return on Investment
SMART	Stretching, Measurable, Appropriate, Realistic, Time-limited
SWOT	Strengths, Weaknesses, Opportunities, Threats

TQM	Total Quality Management
VMDS	Veterinary Management Development School
VMI	Veterinary Management Institute
VTE	Veterinary Time Equivalents

WEB SITE RESOURCES

Entity	URL
Bizvet	www.bizvet.com
Brakke Consulting	www.brakkeconsulting.com
Consultants & Advisors	www.avpmca.org
Consultant Directory (AAHA)	www.aahanet.org/web/consultants_directory.html
Economic Research Service	www.ers.usda.gov/statefacts/
Inflation Tracker	www.westegg.com/inflation
Internal Revenue Service	www.irs.ustreas.gov/
MassVet	www.massvet.com
National Commission on Veterinary Economic Issues	www.ncvei.org
Scorecard	www.balancedscorecard.org
Small Business Administration	www.sba.gov
Veterinary Healthcare Consultants	www.vhc.biz
Veterinary Management Institute	www.aahanet.org/web/vmi.html
Vet-Zone	www.vet-zone.com

LIST OF CONTRIBUTORS

Lowell J. Ackerman DVM DACVD MBA MPA

 *Dr. Lowell Ackerman is a Diplomate of the American College of Veterinary Dermatology and in addition holds an MBA from the University of Phoenix and an MPA from Harvard University. He is involved in clinical practice as a clinical assistant professor at Tufts University School of Veterinary Medicine as well as helping to develop the business skills curriculum there. In addition, Dr. Ackerman is affiliated with Veterinary Healthcare Consultants, LLC–a national consulting firm dedicated to providing innovative and resourceful business solutions for veterinary professionals and humane organizations. His primary business interests include leadership, team building, customer relationship management, strategic planning, Total Quality Management, profit center development, veterinary fee issues, marketing, promotion, action planning, and performance measurement. Dr. Ackerman developed the BARK^{sm} system for performance evaluation of veterinary practices.*

Dr. Ackerman is the author/co-author of 75 books to date (including Business Basics for Veterinarians) and numerous book chapters and articles. He lectures extensively, on an international basis. Dr. Ackerman is a member of the American Animal Hospital Association, the American Veterinary Medical Association, the Association of Veterinary Practice Management Consultants & Advisors, the American Society of Journalists and Authors, and the Association of Veterinary Communicators.

Elizabeth Bellavance DVM MBA

Dr. Bellavance graduated from the Ontario Veterinary College in 1991 and returned to school in 1995 to complete an MBA. She has several years experience in mixed animal practice. Currently, Dr. Bellavance provides project management and consulting services to the veterinary industry while completing a CMA (Certified Management Accountant) designation.

Mark Davis

Mark Davis has been a veterinary practice manager and a practice management consultant for the last eight years in general, specialty and emergency settings. He is a graduate of the AAHA Veterinary Management Institute and has worked in California, Hawaii, Maryland, the District of Columbia and Virginia. He currently resides in Norfolk, VA

Tracy Dowdy, CVPM

Tracy Dowdy is a career consultant who is dedicated to helping veterinarians and all those who work with them reach new levels of success in all aspects of their business. She gained experience in the personnel industry working with Fortune 500 companies before entering the veterinary field. Since Tracy's father is a veterinarian, she has had years of opportunities to gain knowledge about the profession throughout her life. In 1995, Tracy joined Advanced Animal Care Centre located in Bedford, Texas. Within three years of leading the practice in a new, client and service oriented direction, the practice tripled in gross revenues and received a Hospital Design Merit Award (June 1998) and the Practice of Excellence Award (June 2000) from Veterinary Healthcare Communications, the publishers of Veterinary Economics magazine.

In March of 1998, Ms. Dowdy started Veterinary Management Solutions to help veterinarians and practice owners achieve the same success she was able to provide to

Advanced Animal Care Centre. Ms. Dowdy has consulted with over 100 practices nationwide in the areas of financial growth, staff retention, client service and many other aspects of practice management.

Ms. Dowdy has built on her management and training experiences to create her own, unique hands-on approach. By working alongside veterinary teams and their leaders, she helps them develop a practice that is service and client centered by setting and training to standards of service, empowering the healthcare team, building effective and efficient workflow systems, improving communications, conduct, and appearances, creating a culture of emotional wealth sharing, and ultimately moving the entire practice to higher levels of personal and collective enjoyment as well as improved financial success.

Tracy has been published in local and national veterinary journals and has spoken at local, regional and national veterinary meetings. She is available to speak on topics such as leadership, client service and staff training at national and regional conferences. Ms. Dowdy is a Certified Veterinary Practice Manager and a Charter Member of the Association of Veterinary Practice Management Consultants and Advisors.

Karen Felsted CPA MS DVM CVPM

Dr. Felsted graduated from the University of Texas at Austin with a degree in marketing. She spent 12 years in accounting and business management, six of it with the "Big-8" accounting firm of Arthur Young (now Ernst & Young.) During this time, she also obtained an MS degree in Management and Administrative Science (concentration: accounting) from the University of Texas at Dallas.

After graduating from the Texas A&M University College of Veterinary Medicine, Dr. Felsted began her career as a veterinary practitioner in both small animal and emergency medicine while maintaining her existing veterinary accounting and consulting practice. In 1999 she opened and became Manager-in-Charge of the Dallas office of Owen E. McCafferty, CPA, Inc., a national public accounting firm specializing in tax, accounting and practice management services for veterinarians. During this time she received her Certified Veterinary Practice Manager certificate. In 2001, she joined Brakke Consulting, Inc., where she continues to offer practice management consulting services to veterinarians. She also runs her own accounting firm specializing in financial services for veterinarians.

Dr. Felsted has been published in numerous national and international veterinary journals including Veterinary Economics and Texas Veterinarian. She has spoken at many local, national and international veterinary meetings.

Jim Humphries BS DVM

Dr. Jim Humphries is a veterinarian, media spokesperson and communications consultant in Colorado Springs, Colorado. He was the animal health reporter for NBC Dallas-Ft. Worth for 10 years, and has been a contributor to CBS The Early Show for over 13 years. Jim has given over 4,000 interviews and completed 23 national media tours for the animal health industry. He now consults with a variety of businesses and industries in the area of media relations and training. He is the author of a new web resource for small business and medical practice promotions and publicity, www.Publicity123.com.

Thomas A. Lynch MA

Thomas A. Lynch, MA is the founder of Veterinary Healthcare Consultants, LLC—a national consulting firm dedicated to providing innovative and resourceful business solutions for veterinary professionals and humane organizations. Earlier in his career, Tom served as Hospital Administrator for a large, 24-hour, full-service, veterinary hospital. Additionally, he served as a member of the adjunct faculty at a private New England college where he taught business courses including Principles of Management, Principles of Marketing, and Small Business Management. Tom holds undergraduate degrees in business management and marketing, and a master's degree with a specialization in management and a concentration in veterinary practice administration. He has been published in the Journal of the American Veterinary Medical Association, Journal of the Veterinary Emergency and Critical Care Society, Veterinary Product News, Veterinary Economics, Veterinary Practice Staff, and DVM Newsmagazine.

Frank Muggia JD

Mr. Muggia is a graduate of Middlebury College and Boston University School of Law. For the past 13 years, he has been serving the veterinary community with representative clients across the country. Mr. Muggia's national practice has him trying cases in State and Federal Courts throughout the country including New York, Massachusetts, Georgia and Florida, and advising clients throughout the country.

Mr. Muggia has become one of the most well respected attorneys in the United States in the field of veterinary law; whether buying or selling a practice, resolving partner and employee conflicts, effectuating a solid and comprehensive business plan, or litigating restrictive covenants. He is well published in the area and lectures nationally within the veterinary industry, in addition to being listed as an approved consultant by the American Animal Hospital Association. He can be reached at www.MuggiaLaw.com

Kurt A. Oster MS SPHR

Kurt A. Oster, MS, SPHR is a practice management consultant with Veterinary Healthcare Consultants, LLC–a national consulting firm dedicated to providing innovative and resourceful business solutions for veterinary professionals and humane organizations. Kurt is certified as a Senior Professional in Human Resources (SPHR), the highest level of certification offered by the Society for Human Resource Management. Prior to consulting, Kurt served as Hospital Administrator for a 16-doctor, 24-hour, full-service, veterinary hospital for six years. Additionally, he worked as an educator for a veterinary software firm for nine years. During this time he educated the staffs of over 325 veterinary practices on all disciplines of practice management. Kurt is the finance instructor for the American Animal Hospital Association's (AAHA) Veterinary Management Development School (VMDS) Level One and Advanced. He is a frequent lecturer and he has been published in the Veterinary Practice News and is regularly featured in AAHA's Trends Magazine. He may be reached via e-mail at kurt@vhc.biz

GIVING CLIENTS WHAT THEY WANT MOST

Lowell Ackerman DVM DACVD MBA MPA

Dr. Lowell Ackerman is a Diplomate of the American College of Veterinary Dermatology and in addition holds an MBA from the University of Phoenix and an MPA from Harvard University. He is involved in clinical practice as a clinical assistant professor at Tufts University School of Veterinary Medicine as well as helping to develop the business skills curriculum there. In addition, Dr. Ackerman is affiliated with Veterinary Healthcare Consultants, LLC–a national consulting firm dedicated to providing innovative and resourceful business solutions for veterinary professionals and humane organizations. His primary business interests include leadership, team building, customer relationship management, strategic planning, Total Quality Management, profit center development, veterinary fee issues, marketing, promotion, action planning, and performance measurement. Dr. Ackerman developed the BARK^{sm} system for performance evaluation of veterinary practices.

Dr. Ackerman is the author/co-author of 75 books to date (including Business Basics for Veterinarians) and numerous book chapters and articles. He lectures extensively, on an international basis. Dr. Ackerman is a member of the American Animal Hospital Association, the American Veterinary Medical Association, the Association of Veterinary Practice Management Consultants & Advisors, the American Society of Journalists and Authors, and the Association of Veterinary Communicators.

You might think that clients come to you because of your perfect suture lines or the expert way in which your technicians place a catheter–but you'd be wrong! Like all consumers, clients have their own way of valuing veterinary service, and it often has little to do with medical practices. Of course, all clients want excellent medical care for their pets. It's just that they often don't use the same barometers of care that veterinarians do.

What is value?

All consumers look for exceptional value, receiving at least as much product or service as they are paying for, and preferably a little more. It is this concept of value that is critical to veterinary practice (and to all businesses), to satisfy and exceed the needs of clients.

The new paradigm in veterinary practice is not related specifically to fees, or even to customer service alone. It is predicated on customer relationship management, and leveraging that relationship to achieve exceptional results. This new paradigm pervades most industries today. A bank as a place to keep your money is a commodity that inspires little loyalty. The financial institution that integrates your banking, investment, home loans, and credit card activities is a valued partner. So it goes in veterinary medicine. By adding functionality, convenience, aesthetics, branding and so forth, value is added that makes the final product or service more valuable to the consumer. The "added value" of a product or service is the value to the client after your intervention less the value before you were involved. Just as the credit card commercials suggest, some activities are "priceless" when compared to others that are a sum of their costs. It is this differential that allows veterinarians to earn a respectable livelihood by delivering true added value to clients–the good health and longevity of their pets.

Value-added analysis is an important concept in Total Quality Management (TQM) and in Client Relationship Management (CRM) and was covered in "Business Basics for Veterinarians". The analysis helps to determine where value is added to a process and where it is not. We divide these activities into three categories:

- Real value-adding activities (RVA) that are important to clients
- Medical value-adding activities (MVA) that don't add value for clients, but are necessary from a medical or hospital perspective
- Non value-adding activities (NVA) that neither add value from the perspective of the client nor the hospital

The goal of such an exercise is to see how much of the total cost is attributable to each category, and ideally to eliminate non-value-adding activities and minimize medical value-adding activities (since that value is not appreciated by clients).

For example, in evaluating the processes involved in something as routine as an ovariohysterectomy (spay), the clients value most the safe use of anesthesia, gentle and individualized care, pain management, lack of trauma, and getting their pets back quickly. These are valued even more than the premise for having the surgery–making sure the pet doesn't produce offspring. From a medical perspective, there is value in safe anesthesia, having the surgery completed in a reasonable period of time, and discharging the patient, without incident, back to the client. In reviewing the processes, a practice could make some bold changes to highlight the real value-adding activities, minimize the medical value-adding activities, and hopefully eliminating the non value-adding activities.

Clients value virtually any part of the process that provides individualized care for their pets, including anesthetic monitoring, pain management, and nursing care. On the other hand, using sutures versus staples or selecting isoflurane versus sevoflurane is a medical value-adding activity that has only marginal value for clients; they expect veterinarians to select what would be medically appropriate for their pet. Sometimes there is a crossover point and this can lead to controversy. That is one of the reasons that adding pain management as an elective procedure (pay for service) has sometimes elicited unexpected comments from clients. Many clients find it troublesome that pain management would be optional and just expect that veterinarians already do everything in their power to alleviate suffering. Why would they not provide pain management for such procedures–surely not just because a client didn't elect to pay extra for it? Pain management should be included in every veterinary practice and most clients perceive it not only as real value-added, but clearly providing medical value as well.

As far as non-value-adding activities, this sometimes involves questioning protocols and processes and challenging convention. For example, with today's anesthetic regimens, why are elective surgical patients kept overnight in the hospital? This is especially troubling in hospitals that do not have an attendant supervising the animals during the night. In this scenario, would it not be better to discharge the pet to the care of the owners, with instructions to monitor closely overnight and go to the emergency clinic if there were any problems? Clients may even pay a premium for such a "day surgery", would invariably more closely monitor their pets than would be the situation in an unstaffed hospital, and this is turn would reduce costs for the practice.

What a client values

Doing a value-added analysis is always a good exercise for a practice, but there are some basic guidelines to follow to meet the needs of most clients. I refer to these as the 6 Cs of Customer Relationship Management:

- Concept/Conformance
- Compassion
- Customer Service
- Convenience
- Competence
- Cost

Concept/Conformance

According to Gerald Zaltman, a marketing professor at Harvard Business School and author of "How Customers Think", at least 95% of all cognition occurs below the level of conscious awareness. In addition, most human communication (as much as 80%) occurs through nonverbal means. Therefore, the most important aspect of giving clients what they want most has nothing to do with surgical technique, marketing programs, or customer discounts. It has most to do with meeting their unconscious expectations for a top-quality veterinary facility. That includes clean, well-maintained facilities (without any offensive odors), a well-dressed, courteous, and professional-appearing staff, and evidence of official stature (e.g., premise certification, diplomas, etc.).

The impression starts when a client telephones the practice to book an appointment. Their expectations are that the telephone will be answered by someone who is courteous and professional, and while that person might not be able to answer questions best posed to the doctor, that person is nonetheless assuring that booking an appointment is the most appropriate step to best meeting the pet's health care needs. The client does not want the impression that the person answering the telephones was asking "do you want fries with that?" the week before. The expectation is that being a receptionist in a veterinary office is a career. Veterinarians should keep this in mind when hiring staff and be prepared to pay the going wage of receptionists in other health care fields.

Since receptionists hold such critical positions in veterinary practices, a lot of effort should be taken to find the right individuals, train them properly, and give them incentive to stay. In many ways, the receptionist is a more stable anchor for the practice than are associate veterinarians. The receptionist is often the most important liaison with clients, and an important reason why clients stay with a practice. After all, the receptionist may greet them by name, knows their animals, and all their preferences (e.g., late afternoon appointments are needed). Turnover in this position can be disastrous for a practice.

It is worth the time and expense to properly select a receptionist with good "people skills", professional deportment, a love of animals, and proper use of language. Remember that the receptionist is the practice ambassador, so an inability to communicate professionally, or poor spelling or syntax in the medical records, sends the wrong message to the public.

Veterinary technicians are an important part of the veterinary health care matrix, and yet current models of veterinary health care practice often do not reflect this importance. In too many settings, veterinarians play the role of technicians, collecting blood, holding animals for radiographs, placing catheters, etc. As such, there is a dangerous situation in this country in which paraprofessionals are terribly underpaid and undervalued and there is little incentive for them to remain in veterinary practices. For the position to be a career it is necessary to pay technicians their worth and this requires refining the models of how veterinarians practice. This is a topic for another chapter, but technicians only remain in practice an average of 6-7 years, so that can't be considered a very good career option. I only mention this here, because in the human health care system, nurses are what keep hospitals running cost effectively. We need that in veterinary medicine.

Remember that clients, while asking the doctor for a best medical opinion, often also consult with the technician and receptionist about what they would do. You better be sure that staff can afford to follow practice recommendations regarding vaccination, heartworm prevention, flea/tick control, dental prophylaxis, geriatric evaluations, etc. If not, expect compliance to be less than you would like. Consider offering pet health insurance as a perk for veterinary employees. You might be surprised at how much it improves your bottom line. Clients want to believe that the staff practices what you preach and honestly believes and implements the practice recommendations for their own pets.

Like all other staff, doctors must present themselves to clients in a professional manner. They should be well groomed, professionally dressed, and provide an air of authority and accessibility. Clients have come to expect the image of the doctor in a white lab coat (no blood stains or fur accumulation, please), stethoscope stuffed in the pocket, and a friendly but authoritative demeanor. Don't disappoint them! Wearing surgical scrubs is fine when you are emerging from surgery to inform them about how the operation went, but otherwise, stick to the expected uniform.

Throughout the practice, all team members should endeavor to present themselves in a professional manner. This includes referring to the veterinarian as "doctor" at all times, even if first names are used elsewhere. Clients expect this level of respect, and the same benefits can be seen when staff use proper terminology, such as "vaccinations" instead of "shots" and "clinical re-evaluation" instead of "recheck". Endeavor to ensure that everybody in the practice walks the walk, and talks the talk. Being professional in the practice should be infectious, and the professional practice team should not tolerate unprofessional conduct, attitude, or even indifference. More on that in the chapter on breakthrough performance, but don't underestimate the power of the professional practice team. That's what clients want, and that is what they are paying for.

It is also important to remember why clients seek veterinary services in the first place. It is not because of the building, the equipment in it, or even how nice the doctor and staff are. The reason that people come to a veterinary practice is because they are seeking "solutions" to their animal-care issues. Provide those solutions and your clients will come back time and again, and they'll tell their friends.

Compassion

Next to appearances, clients want to know that the people in the practice love animals and are capable of loving, or at least appreciating, the uniqueness of their animal(s). Once again, this doesn't require an expensive marketing campaign. It does require having staff that do love animals and are not inhibited about fussing over animals presented to the practice.

This can be accomplished in a number of ways and is one of the least expensive forms of external marketing available. Have a "Welcome to the Practice" book in the reception area, with photos of all staff members, their pets, and some biographical information on each, including their specific training and certification and how long they have been with the practice. A group photograph with all the practice staff and their pets is another nice touch. The same type of material should appear on the practice web site.

Clients are very appreciative when people fuss over their pets. Even in a professional setting, there is room for petting and displays of affection for animals. Standardize the process by having staff take photos of clients' pets frequently. Some should appear in the medical record as identifiers, some on the web site (if clients give permission, which they almost always do), and others in photo books or on bulletin boards. You might also take pictures of pets happily giving a blood sample (from the cephalic vein, not the jugular) or similar procedures, because clients are often unaware of what goes on "behind closed doors" in a veterinary practice. It is also important to share images that are medically important, but that don't show the pet in distress, such as a photomicrograph of a *Demodex* mite, an image from a radiograph, a photo of the pet's gingival condition, etc. But, most importantly, clients want to know that their pets are in the hands of individuals who care about pets in general, and theirs in particular. Pets are extensions of their owners, and it should not be surprising that people want to be liked, and want their pets to be liked.

Even in the examination room, it is important early on to "lay hands" on the pet and make some form on contact before starting or continuing discussions with the client, and before the clinical examination. There needs to be some form of pet "acknowledgement", so that owners can relax and proceed. After the initial contact, it can be very comforting for pet and owner for attention to be focused on the owner. In that brief period of time, the owner can express their concerns and the pet can relax. Then the examination can proceed. It doesn't take much to show how much you care.

Customer Service (relationship building)

People love their pets and are prepared to pay what is necessary to keep them healthy, but clients are also consumers and are looking for all the qualities they value most in retail outlets. Veterinary medicine is not about a one-time sale to a faceless client. It is about actively cultivating a relationship with that client that may span the lifetimes of several pets. Accordingly, practices need to concentrate not only on excellent veterinary medicine, but exceptional customer service as well.

When customers are paying a lot of money for a service, whether for veterinary medicine or a cup of gourmet coffee, they have certain expectations of the value they will receive for their money. If your customer service can consistently meet those expectations, then you will have a profitable practice indeed and clients will be getting their money's worth in the transaction.

The interesting thing about customer service is that clients rarely voice their concerns in this regard but it is the main reason why they go elsewhere. Clients want desperately to be loyal to your practice, and they will be if given the opportunity. The reason that clients don't consciously cite customer service as the reason they leave practices, is that it is often due to the 95% unconscious decisions made in this regard. Here's a common example. Ms Smith buys a large bag of prescription food but even after repeated attempts, her dog Poochie refuses to eat it. As a business, you might think that it is in your best interest to tell the client that you can't provide refunds on opened packages, but is this really in your best long-term interests? If you do this, you may have kept the proceeds from the pet-food sale, but you may have also antagonized and lost the client as well (i.e., operation succeeds, patient dies). That could cost you years and years of future revenues, all for the cost of a bag of dog food. According to an AAHA newsletter (November 2002), it costs five times more to get a new customer than to keep an existing one and 16 times more to get a new customer to the same level of profitability as an existing customer. A better response–"Ms Smith, I'm so sorry that Poochie didn't like the food. Of course, we'll take it back. Let me talk with the doctor and see if there isn't something else that we might try." Whether you use the food for in-hospital use or throw it away, you protected your most valuable asset–your client. Remember where your true revenues are coming from; you are in the retail serv-ice sector, not product sales.

While it not possible to meets the needs of 100% of clients, it is important to set definitive standards for aspects of the practice in which you intend to have a com-petitive advantage. While a satisfied customer will tell 2-3 people about their pos-itive experience, a dissatisfied customer is likely to tell 8-10. Fortunately, if you fix the complaint quickly and respond fairly, 80% of those unhappy customers will become loyal satisfied customers. Therefore, don't look at client complaints as inconveniences. Look at them as opportunities to retain a loyal client, and you can take that to the bank a lot easier than finding a replacement client. Even if the client does not get everything that they think they want, you can retain them if they believe that they were treated fairly, and that you made an honest attempt to quickly remedy the situation.

The easiest way to deal with customer service issues before they become real problems is to give authority to front-line staff to resolve problems and keep clients happy. Contrary to popular belief, staff do not "give away the store" when given this authority. Customers want on-the-spot solutions for their problems. The worst thing that a veterinary practice can do is force the front-line staff to enforce client unfriendly policies, only to have the veterinarian then give in to the client. This not only demoralizes the front-office staff, but it reinforces the notion that clients should go straight to the doctor when there is a problem. Bad idea!

One final note on customer service (given that there is a whole chapter on it else-where in this book). You probably don't know how well you are doing in cus-tomer service unless you ask your customers. Customer satisfaction surveys are great, but periodically just asking clients how well the practice is meeting their needs is always a good idea. When clients request that their medical records be sent elsewhere, take the time to find out why. Perhaps they won't give candid rea-sons on a telephone call, but they might be willing to fill out a survey. If they appreciate how important it is to your practice to have satisfied clients, they might even consider returning at some point. Sometimes, just knowing that the practice cares to ask about them is enough for clients to question whether they will get that level of caring and commitment elsewhere.

Convenience

Convenience is a key issue in providing exceptional customer service. Ideally, your veterinary practice is in a convenient location, and clients have easy access to avail themselves of your services. Location may not be as critical to veterinary medicine as it is to real estate, but it is a concern for many pet owners. Sometimes just being on the other side of a geographic landmark (bridge, highway, town line) is enough to conjure up images to the client that you are too far away to be convenient. The farther you are from your preferred client base, the more important the other aspects of customer service, to compensate. Similarly, parking can be an issue, especially in urban practices. Since most people will not be traveling with their pets on public transit, being able to park and access the veterinary practice easily is very important for most pet owners.

Convenience also applies to hours of operation. As family demographics have changed over the years, there are fewer and fewer stay-at-home moms available to take the pet to the veterinarian during regular business hours. And yet, according to surveys, women are responsible for pet health care in about 70% of cases. This has increased the need for drop-off capabilities, and for seeing patients after traditional business hours. In fact, there is a whole range of concierge-type services that clients would pay for if it didn't mean that they had to take time off work for pet health care. Think about it.

Convenience of payment options is not the same as extending credit to clients. While no doubt there is a market niche for providing veterinary care on credit terms, this should be discouraged in most practices unless the credit terms are established to be profitable enough to warrant offering them. No, for most pet owners, accepting all major credit cards, cash, debit cards, and checks (with verification) is as accommodating as most other retail outlets. Additional payment plans, such as through CareCredit or similar agency, gives creditworthy clients the opportunity to pay for unforeseen emergencies.

Remember also that convenience is important in matters of communication. People are busy, and when they telephone the practice or visit the web site, they want their concerns addressed immediately, if not sooner. It is not always possible to get the doctor on the telephone when a client calls, and it is probably not even advisable to be that accessible, but there needs to be a mechanism in place to address issues quickly. Having client liaison personnel (typically technicians assigned to specific clients or doctors) is often the best alternative, and after a while, it is not unusual for clients to call and request the liaison rather than the doctor. That's a good thing. Whatever else you do, do not tie a client up in a telephone message service; give them an option to speak to a live human being quickly and most will be happy.

Competence

It might surprise some veterinarians that competence is so far down the list of what clients want. It's not that they don't want a competent practitioner, but rather that they have very limited ways of discerning that information. That's one of the reasons that we need to concentrate so heavily on the 95% of information that is relayed unconsciously to clients. Clients understand that it is hard to get into veterinary school, and that graduates of veterinary school have earned the title "doctor", but most do not understand much more than that unless we take the time to educate them.

Promotional materials for the practice should concentrate on the accomplishments of all practice personnel. This is important for the paraprofessional staff as well, since most clients don't really understand the accomplishments of technicians, and many don't even appreciate that there are schools of training in this discipline. Dental hygienists went through the same sort of "identity crisis", but they emerged much stronger from the process.

Clients have so little information on which to judge competence that they are excited whenever clues are available to them. Whether it is writing a column in the local newspaper, a speaking engagement (even at a local breed club), or even attending a continuing education forum, if clients don't have this kind of information, they will make up criteria on which to judge competence. We all know of veterinarians who are marginally competent but have a loyal following because of their bedside manner. The surprising thing is that we expect clients to discern that the medicine being practiced elsewhere is less than exemplary. How are they to know?

One of the easiest ways of improving the perceived image of competence is to wholeheartedly endorse the continuing education of your…clients! Handouts are not enough, though, and you should either have sufficient web content for the purpose, or be able to direct clients to web sites that provide accurate and reliable information on the subject. For clients that are very keen, share with them information from veterinary texts, journals, and veterinary web sites. Even if the information is controversial (e.g., vaccination schedules), it is worthwhile if the client understands that the matter is not black and white and is subject to interpretation. When clients feel that are valued partners in your health care team, there is no end to their loyalty.

The interesting thing about competence is that it doesn't mean that you need to be an expert in everything. Telling a client that their pet has a problem that warrants them seeking the opinion of a specialist is not a signal of weakness, but rather a signal that you care deeply about the pet, that you are a team player, and that you value a successful outcome for the client and patient above all else. That sends an impressive message not only to the client, but to staff as well.

Cost

Nobody likes to pay too much for a product or service, and therefore veterinarians do need to be concerned with charges to clients. However, for the most part, veterinarians worry too much about "markups" and not enough about "value".

This is covered in more detail in the chapter on practicing profitably, but I'd like to mention here that there is much more opportunity to be profitable and have clients happy to pay the bill when value services are involved. Clients don't want to pay more for commodities that they can get elsewhere and veterinarians should stock these kinds of items for convenience rather than profit. Giving clients options and alternatives is what customer service is all about.

For example, many veterinary shampoos are expensive and the typical doubling or tripling of costs done by veterinary practices makes them even more expensive to clients. When a client asks if there are over-the-counter (OTC) alternatives, don't be protective of these retail sales by saying no. You are being compensated for your professional knowledge, so your duty is to advocate on behalf of your patients. Get clients used to paying for your professional knowledge, not items sitting on a shelf. Sometimes the best product is a medicated brand that is only available through veterinarians. In other cases, suitable OTC products are available and every bit as effective. Similarly, if a product is available to your clients cheaper at a pharmacy, write a prescription. Save money on your inventory while giving clients more treatment options by utilizing a veterinary Internet pharmacy, such as Vetcentric. The fact is that retail sales will eventually evaporate as a profit center for veterinarians, so protect your real profit potential–client loyalty.

Recommended Reading

Ackerman, L: Business Basics for Veterinarians. ASJA Press, 2002

American Veterinary Medical Association: Results of the AVMA survey on companion animal ownership in US pet-owning households. J Am Vet Med Assoc., 2002; 221(11): 1572-1573.

Giniat, EJ; Libert, BD: Value Rx for Healthcare. HarperBusiness, 2001, 243 pp.

Wise, JK; Heathcott, BL: Results of the 2002 AVMA survey of US pet-owning households regarding use of veterinary services and expenditures. J Am Vet Med Assoc, 2003; 222(11): 1524-1525.

Zaltman, G: How Customers Think: Essential Insights into the Mind of the Market. Harvard Business School Press, 2003, 323pp.

Outstanding Customer Service

Thomas A. Lynch, MA

Thomas A. Lynch, MA is the founder of Veterinary Healthcare Consultants, LLC—a national consulting firm dedicated to providing innovative and resourceful business solutions for veterinary professionals and humane organizations. Earlier in his career, Tom served as Hospital Administrator for a large, 24-hour, full-service, veterinary hospital. Additionally, he served as a member of the adjunct faculty at a private New England college where he taught business courses including Principles of Management, Principles of Marketing, and Small Business Management. Tom holds undergraduate degrees in business management and marketing, and a master's degree with a specialization in management and a concentration in veterinary practice administration. He has been published in the Journal of the American Veterinary Medical Association, Journal of the Veterinary Emergency and Critical Care Society, Veterinary Product News, Veterinary Economics, Veterinary Practice Staff, and DVM Newsmagazine.

An Investment that Pays Off

> *"…Any enterprise which wishes to endure over a long period of time and to remain in a healthy and growing state would certainly want a non-manipulative, trusting relationship with its customers rather than the relationship of the quick fleecing, never to see them again."*

> ~ Dr. Abraham Maslow

It was 1965 when Dr. Abraham Maslow—one of the world's most esteemed experts on human behavior and motivation—first shared his forward-thinking views on business and management with the world. He spoke of building, nurturing and preserving relationships with customers over the long-term. He used words like candor, honesty, truth and efficiency in customer relations at a time when the business world was still decades away from embracing such principles. The same year marked the death of a visionary by the name of Walt Disney, who–a decade earlier–had begun an odyssey of customer service superiority that would become his legacy. Little did Maslow and Disney know that all these years later their ideals would serve as a blueprint for attaining customer service excellence. Such reverence for those who seem to have mastered the art of customer service is not surprising given a business climate more consumed than ever with developing a loyal clientele of satisfied and repeat customers.

Indeed, what drives Disney and others to greatness in customer service is the belief that people ARE the business. They then act on that belief every day–regardless. Those at Disney have made a virtual science out of pleasing the customer, and ANYONE in business would be wise to pay close attention. In veterinary medicine, where numerous products and services are fast becoming commodity-like, differentiating your practice is crucial. Whether you're a veterinarian or practice manager, few people would argue that in today's competitive market, outstanding customer service is not only key to affecting your bottom line, it's absolutely essential for achieving and maintaining a competitive edge. Without it, your customers will simply look elsewhere.

While customers today are well informed and may have high expectations, they still appreciate personalized attention and service. Customers are likely to remain loyal if you expend a little extra effort on their behalf. They are also likely to spread the word of their positive experiences with your practice. Other reasons for running a customer-driven practice include: customers will pay a premium for products and services because you focus on their needs; losing customers means losing money; customers remember poor service; customers are a critical information source; and employees will be happier.

Create an atmosphere of caring, individualized attention to all of the things your customer deems important and you'll create a lifelong professional attachment. After all, customer service is really about intimacy. Learn what it is your customers really want or need. The only way to do this is to ask them. Spending time getting to know your customers is an investment that pays off.

Who is a Customer?

Often when we think of customers, we think of people external to the veterinary practice that interact with the practice and provide money either directly or indirectly. In actuality, a customer is *anyone* who interacts in or with the practice. This includes employees, vendors, suppliers, distributors, contractors, and referring veterinarians, as well as the pet owners who use your services. It is important to treat your employees and your medical equipment suppliers well, as it is your paying customers, because a veterinary practice cannot function without these individuals.

The service that a practice provides to external customers will be a direct reflection on how well various professionals within a practice interact with each other. In essence, the way that employees treat each other and the way they treat customers is directly associated with the way in which they are treated by practice owners, veterinarians, managers and others.

What Today's Customers Expect

There is a new breed of customer in today's business market. They are intelligent and well-educated individuals who expect to be treated as such, with quality products and services at the fairest prices. Today's customers are players in the information technology world, where product and pricing information is as accessible as a keystroke. In addition to being armed with relevant information, they are also—more so than ever—pressed for time. Reliability, convenience, and speedy delivery of normal services are therefore essential.

In a veterinary practice, the following essential elements must be delivered to customers:

Quality

Customers' expectations of a product or service must be met and exceeded. A practice must ensure attractiveness, lack of defects, reliability, and dependability in everything the practice delivers.

Cost

Goods and services must be valuable and at prices the customer is willing to pay. To accomplish this goal, practices must keep costs under control to allow the practice to set fair prices that cover costs and achieve profit.

Innovation

Veterinary practices should constantly strive to quickly create new competitive goods and services that customers value. This is necessary to stay ahead of the competitors.

Speed

Practices must respond to the changing marketplace by being aware of new products and services, and by responding promptly to customers' needs and wants.

In order to satisfy customers, you must know what they want. Don't assume you know without asking. Not surprisingly, customers themselves are the best resource for learning how to achieve customer satisfaction! Employees are also an excellent source of information about customer requirements; they have daily contact with them and take their complaints and compliments.

In order to learn what your customers want, ask them:

- Why are you a client of ours?
- What do you like and dislike about our practice?
- What would you like to change about our practice?
- How do we compare with our competitors?

Often, customers see things from a different perspective than the veterinary practice staff. For example, a practice may have three veterinarians on duty, one seeing patients and the others working behind the scenes at different, equally important jobs. All three are engaged in necessary, productive work, but if a customer has to wait five minutes to see a doctor, he thinks the wait is too long. If all three doctors are seeing patients, the customer perceives that the wait is "justified." He leaves the practice happy and will likely return in the future. Perhaps it's worth scheduling that "behind the scenes" work at times when it won't be perceived as interfering with office visits.

Keep in mind that what today's customers expect is what any one of us would want for ourselves. We want our issue/problem addressed and resolved as quickly as possible; we want fair prices; we want to be heard; we want to feel the veterinarian or other professional is connecting with us and our pet emotionally; we want to develop a trusting relationship; and—most importantly—we want respect.

Respect is the foundation on which many a successful business is built. Len Riggio is a great example of this. Riggio purchased a floundering Manhattan bookshop called Barnes & Noble in 1971 at the age of 30. Today, Barnes & Noble is one of the nation's largest booksellers, with respect for the customer still a top priority. When customers told of wanting bigger selections of books, more convenient locations, and less intimidating environments, Riggio listened. Their input led to the creation of stores with spacious and comfortable interiors, easy chairs for relaxing, and Starbucks coffee bars. Riggio's idea to install public restrooms in his stores he considers one of his best. Of the decision, he says, "You work so hard and invest so much to get people to visit your store, why would you want them to leave?"[1]

Excellence Starts at the Top

"The best interest of the patient is the only interest to be considered."

~ *Credo of William Mayo, co-founder of The Mayo Clinic*

An exceptional customer-driven practice begins with exceptional leadership; there is no denying this. If you are unhappy or frustrated at work, so too will be your staff members, and your outside customers will soon begin to defect. Keep in mind that staff members take their cues from you. You must exude a positive attitude and enthusiasm for your work and maintain professionalism at all costs; be aware that your staff will scrutinize how you handle every situation. Treat your staff with the same respect and courtesy offered to your other customers and the outcome will be a positive one inviting open communication.

The Mayo Clinic is a shining example of excellence in leadership. Indisputably considered top-notch among health care organizations, its stellar reputation is proudly upheld by management and staffers passionate about making a difference.

---

1 The Old Pillars of New Retailing by Leonard L. Berry/Harvard Business Review on Customer Relationship Management, 2001.

But such drive does not happen by accident. At Mayo, there is no room for egos; doctors routinely make follow-up calls to patients at home; care is organized around a patient's needs, not a doctor's schedule; all physicians are salaried, so they do not lose income by referring patients to colleagues; and the organization downplays individual accomplishments in favor of organizational achievements. Says one surgeon quoted by Harvard Business Review, "The kind of people who are attracted to work for Mayo Clinic have a value system that places the care of those in need over personal issues such as salary, prestige, and power. There is little room for turf battles."[2]

It is imperative that leadership implement such a value system in order to lead by example. At Mayo, patients receive an integrated, coordinated response to their medical needs based on the clinic's focus of putting patients' needs above all else. Other outstanding examples of excellence in action can be witnessed at any Ritz-Carlton hotel. Every day, hotel employees receive a memo from the property's director of guest services offering one key service idea for that day. One day it may be "Remember each guest's name and use it often." The next day, "Smile at every guest and make each feel special." After reading and practicing one mantra a day for day after day, the Ritz-Carlton mantras become practices and those practices soon become habits. Eventually those habits become part of the employee's way of thinking and working. The employees perform better, and then become better—more helpful and caring toward their guests.[3]

Horst Schulze, the president of the Ritz-Carlton company, is a man who practices what he preaches. When the chain was opening a new facility in Philadelphia, Schulze personally led the customer service training for the hotel's 460 employees. He brought with him the managers of 83 of their other locations, along with 27 other top executives. He has personally led the training at 36 of their hotels since becoming president in 1988. As a result, the Ritz-Carlton is the only service industry organization to have been awarded the prestigious Malcolm Baldridge National Quality Award—an honor they've received twice since Schulze's tenure as president.[4]

---

2 "Clueing in Customers" by Leonard L. Berry and Neeli Bendapudi/Harvard Business Review, Feb. 2003).

3 Beckwith, H: What Clients Love: A Field Guide to Growing Your Business. Warner Books, 2003, pp. 239-40

4 USA Today, June 29, 2000.

Review Fortune Magazine's annual "America's Most Admired Companies" list and you will see that the names that appear regularly are run by those not afraid of getting their hands dirty. Fred Smith, the founder and chairman of FedEx, begins many of his visits to FedEx facilities in far-flung cities by hopping on a delivery van and going out on the road with a FedEx courier. Bill Marriott, Jr., chairman and CEO of Marriott International, often takes a turn at the hotel registration desk checking in guests; he also empties ashtrays in the lobby and picks up trash in the parking lot.[5]

In your veterinary practice, achieving your goals involves using the same hands-on approach and setting the same outstanding example of team spirit as those running major corporations. Occasionally wielding a mop or cleaning out a cage won't cost you esteem. Talk about your own clinical or ethical dilemmas, when the situation is appropriate, and tell your staff how you overcame moments of doubt (but don't pontificate). Go to professional conferences with your staff to reinforce the notion that learning is a lifelong process. Above all, listen to those around you, regardless of rank or experience. From the least likely quarters, surprising insights emerge. Of all the things you can do on a daily basis, listening well is the best way to build up the kind of rapport that makes others accept your leadership. It also stimulates the team spirit that can save the day in a pinch.

I once had the honor of speaking to a Korean War veteran who described crossing a river under enemy fire while his battalion commander was downstream, out of harm's way. As the commander was posing for a photograph at the prow of an assault boat as if leading the attack, the real assault failed, the unit retreated, and the commander publicly blamed his troops for cowardice. In another instance, the veteran remembers how, during the dispiriting winter of 1950-51, the new Eighth Army commander Matthew Ridgeway sent the troops warm gloves, stationery for writing home, and a message explaining in plain terms why they were in Korea and what they were fighting for. Those acts, he says, did more to turn the tide of battle than any military strategy.

---

5 Performance Research Associates: Delivering Knock Your Socks Off Service Third Edition, p. 103

From these two stories, a key aspect of leadership can be observed. *Leadership creates a contract that binds those who make decisions and those who carry them out.* Under this implied contract, people will endure difficulties, and even perform extraordinary feats, as long as their leaders show genuine concern for their lives and well being. However, it can be very difficult at times for leaders to stick to that contract, especially when tough decisions have to be made and accounted for and when the outcome is uncertain.

An actual clinical situation shows how dilemmas of personal feelings versus critical judgment, and lack of information versus the need to act can play themselves out in a veterinary emergency room. A three-year old intact male pit bull terrier was presented with weakness, depression, and severe cardiovascular shock. His initial physical exam revealed very pale mucous membranes, a heart rate of 210 with extremely weak pulses, and multiple bite wounds along the face, neck and forelimbs. Furthermore, old bite wound scars were found all over the patient. It was apparent to the doctor and her staff that this patient was probably a "fighting dog." After initiating treatment for cardiovascular shock, the technical staff began to comment about the client's lack of care for the patient and expressed to the doctor their unanimous view that the patient should be put to sleep to prevent further fighting and suffering. Shortly afterwards, the veterinarian called the client into the exam room and explained the severe nature of the injury and the risk of death despite aggressive treatment. Denying any history of purposeful fighting, the client claimed that his dog was attacked by a neighbor's dog, insisted on treatment, and handed the receptionist a stack of $20 bills to cover the $600 deposit for treatment.

When the doctor returned to the patient and ordered further treatment for shock, aggressive surgical wound care, bloodwork, and appropriate antibiotics and pain medications, the technicians became upset at the prospect of the dog surviving only to be released to the owner. The doctor, however, was adamant and overrode their objections. Later, once the patient was stabilized, she called her staff together to explain her decision. She reminded them that their legal and moral obligation was to treat the animal, not to pass judgment on the owner. She cautioned them against leaping to conclusions: for all they knew, the dog might have been a fighting dog at an earlier time (hence the old scars), but was adopted as a pet by the presenting client and was truly attacked by the neighbor's dog. Furthermore, she advised, while the animal remained an in-patient, the practice could—in fact was obligated to—convey its suspicions to local authorities, the humane society, and other bodies equipped to investigate the clients.

As it turned out, the staff's suspicions were correct; the ensuing inquiry revealed that the client was fighting his dogs. However, as the doctor realized in the heat of the moment, euthanasia was not the only alternative to further abuse. The dog was held at the clinic and adopted out at a later date. At a critical moment, the doctor showed leadership in looking beyond her staff's initial emotional reactions in order to gain the fullest possible perspective on the situation. She compounded the good effects of her decision by analyzing the case in front of her staff, making it a learning experience for them and showing them that she took their wishes seriously but had good reasons for not following their advice.

Moments of crisis certainly test the mettle of leaders and throw their individual qualities into sharp relief, yet these are not the only times when leadership makes a difference. The daily tasks of running a veterinary practice, dealing with clients, and handling staff issues offer their own tests of and opportunities for leadership. It is more difficult to talk about leadership in this setting, though, because the boundaries between leadership and mere good management are less distinct. Is there a difference at all?

Without doubt, a good leader must also possess good management skills. For instance, any effective manager will keep daily operations running predictably and on schedule to the highest degree practicable; will prioritize tasks, separating the important from the merely timely; will look after the morale and professional development of others in the team; will keep internal and external communications cordial and businesslike; and will make sure no staff member is overtaxed and all are pulling their weight.

There are some specific attributes common to most effective leaders. One of these is the ability to think critically—that is to habitually ask probing questions before committing to a course of action. Are the facts as represented? Whose interests are being served? How widely are the benefits shared? Another attribute is good communications skills—the art of expressing a contested point of view firmly but in a way that invites further dialogue and negotiation. This openness does not necessarily imply compromise; however, for a principled objection often gets a positive response once you make clear that your aim is to protect the organization from immediate or long-term harm.

A third, especially important, attribute is *compassion*—a quality that etymologically (Latin "to feel with [someone]") and in practice is closely related to empathy. Far from a "soft" quality, compassion coexists well with honesty and toughness, especially in the area of personnel decisions. For instance, telling subordinates both frankly and tactfully why you did not promote them is one of the hardest challenges of everyday leadership but, in terms of employee morale, is one of the most important non-clinical actions you will have to take. Real leadership takes the basic integrity that lies at the heart of good management up to the next level where your actions touch the hearts and minds of your staff.

In veterinary medicine, the compassion factor is complicated by love of the animals as well as feelings for people, as the pit bull anecdote reveals. Seeing mistreated animals and having to put unwanted animals to sleep can sour you on people, and the experience of severe injury and death on a regular basis can produce a certain numbing. When that happens, recognizing the signs and reconnecting with the compassion that led you into the profession exemplifies another leadership attribute—self-scrutiny. All these qualities are all important because they are what the staff looks for in you to help them get through difficult times.

Understand that things *will* go wrong under pressure, and when they do you must recover from your mistakes and help the staff recover from theirs. A veterinarian I know once asked his head technician to add potassium chloride to the intravenous fluids of a patient in the intensive care unit—a six-year-old domestic short hair diabetic/keto-acidotic cat that needed intravenous fluid and insulin therapy. The head technician, in turn, directed a recently hired technician to administer the potassium chloride. The new technician, an eager but inexperienced pre-vet college student, administered the potassium chloride to the patient as an intravenous bolus instead of adding it to the fluids. Consequently, the patient went into cardiac arrest and expired.

When the doctor came upon the scene, he saw the head technician severely berating the student. Immediately, he separated the two and asked each individually what had happened. Both told essentially the same story, and the doctor spoke to the head technician in private, reprimanding him for not supervising the student more attentively. Then the doctor conferred with both technicians and asked them what they intended to do about the situation they jointly created. The technicians initially wanted to contact the clients in person and together take responsibility for the mishap. However, the doctor, realizing that neither had had experience with the kind of emotional situation that might ensue, vetoed that plan, dealt with the owners himself *but* allowed the two technicians to write and send personal letters of regret on hospital letterhead.

The doctor's leadership was demonstrated in multiple ways: his immediate distinction between the immediate cause of the catastrophe (the misadministration of the drug) and the underlying cause (the head technician's inattention); his tact-fulness in not disciplining the head technician in front of the subordinate; his respect in allowing both to work out their own response; and his prudence in declining to let the shaken and inexperienced technicians handle a volatile inter-personal encounter while allowing them to write their letters. In his leadership, he found the right balance between intolerance of sloppiness and understanding of human fallibility, command of the situation and willingness to let the staff learn and grow.

Scenarios are illuminating, but to some degree the precise nature of leadership must remain an enigma or paradox. Leadership shows itself in gestures, yet it is not an action; it is deeply involved in ethics, yet it is not a philosophy; it is chan-neled through an individual's personality, yet it is not an inborn trait; it can be cultivated, yet it is not a method. It does not lend itself to definition, yet, like art, we know it when we see it. And like art, we can learn it, practice it and appreciate it. Despite the paradoxes, leadership is what allows us, as decision-makers, to gain the respect, confidence and cooperation of those around us—to the benefit of ourselves, our peers, our staff, *and*–most importantly—our customers. Strong and effective leadership is indeed a crucial element in achieving world-class cus-tomer service.

Having a Plan

"Positive attitudes result from a well-organized, comprehensive human rela-tions plan at the company level, and humanistic, rational, Disney-style lead-ership from all levels of management. People tend to respond 'in kind.' They do as they are 'done unto.'"

~ Disney University Seminar

In order to create a truly customer-driven veterinary practice, one must first have a mission, a plan consisting of broad goals that defines a practice's purpose. A plan must be clearly understood by all employees and must contain only one objective: to please the customer. At Disney, the mission was and is to create an atmosphere of happiness. In order to attain and maintain this plan, Disney encourages employees to be "aggressively friendly" and to focus on four priorities for guest entertainment—safety, courtesy, show and efficiency. Those at Disney take two points to heart when it comes to pleasing customers: first, "the front line is the bottom line," and second, "it's 10 percent product and 90 percent service."

The company consistently strives to pay great attention to detail and exceed guest expectations.[6]

Similar sentiments are echoed at Southwest Airlines, a company that has consistently placed quality customer service at the core of its value system and as such has regularly appeared in Fortune's Top 10 Most Admired Companies. The company's mission statement says it all: "The mission of Southwest Airlines is dedication to the highest quality of customer service deliverable with a sense of warmth, friendliness, individual pride, and company spirit." According to the vice president of customer relations, "We tell our employees we are in the customer service business—we just happen to provide airline transportation."

Having a plan helps shape your veterinary practice through education and understanding. A plan shares with the rest of the staff your mission or vision for the present and future. It teaches staff about the practice, its customers, and each other. Like Disney and Southwest Airlines, you want to create a business culture that truly values people, thus instilling pride in your workforce. Some basics to remember when drafting your plan are: begin by hiring quality people and investing in them by teaching them the skills necessary to perform their job well; arm staff with the knowledge needed to be successful; set standards for customer service; develop accountability; monitor customer service functions; recognize and reward quality service; and finally, and maybe most importantly, treat staff members and co-workers with the same respect, understanding and consideration you want them to offer outside customers.

Because many of the services veterinarians provide are intangible, establishing customer service goals, requirements, and performance measures can be a challenge. While you must strive to be reliable, responsive, reassuring and empathetic (always respecting a customer's point of view, even if you don't agree), the following are some additional guidelines:

---

6 "Disney University: No Mickey Mouse customer service."

- Strive for 100% satisfaction in customer relationships by creating a practice that truly values people—internally and externally.

- Offer superior service quality with a goal of retaining customers.

- Establish requirements to determine customers' needs and wants

- Define quality, and do things right the first time.

- If you don't know something, find out.

- Motivate and empower employees (see next section).

- Keep communication open at all times.

- Measure performance by soliciting and evaluating customer feedback.

- Identify strengths and weaknesses within the practice, as well as opportunities and threats.

- Always go the extra mile for customers, don't promise what you can't deliver, and offer alternatives if you cannot deliver what is requested.

- Maintain positive attitude and body language at all times (call a customer by name, make eye contact, smile, etc.).

- Offer personal touches, respect customers' invaluable time, show genuine compassion/concern for sick pets, and handle with care.

- Follow-up with customers.

In addition to services provided, the tangibles–or visual clues—of a veterinary practice (the appearance and cleanliness of a practice, and the appearance of the personnel, for example) make up the second half of what's important in developing a plan for success. Success depends on delivering quality products and services. And, practically speaking, the person who determines the quality of your practice's products and services is your customer. Total Quality Management (TQM), a method of management in which everyone in the practice is encouraged to strive for continuous improvement, can help you deliver high quality goods every time.

Customers also use the following criteria to measure quality in a practice: innovation; cost competitiveness; consistency of medical, surgical, and other services performed; dependability of the staff; willingness and ability of the staff to provide prompt service; explanation of services performed in easily understood language; perceived trustworthiness of customer-staff relationship; the way staff interacts with their pet; knowledge and skills of doctors and staff; and efforts made by the staff to understand a customer's specific requirements.

Benefits of a well-managed customer service plan include:

- Less time handling complaints
- More revenue
- Less time spent doing work over
- Retaining customers
- Improved employee morale
- Decreased employee turnover
- Good word of mouth
- More repeat business
- Better competitive edge
- Better reputation
- Less stress
- Better communications
- Better retention of market share
- Satisfied customers

Empowering Your Staff

Even the best-laid plans will fail if not executed appropriately by those in a position to make decisions. In a famous study entitled, "Consumer Complaint Handling in America: An Update Study," the U.S. Office of Consumer Affairs found that 96% of unhappy customers don't complain to the company–but they do tell at least ten other people about their problem. Those few who do complain will remain customers if their problem is resolved.

The Ritz Carlton, for example, effectively communicates outstanding personal service by expecting employees at all levels to take note of customer preferences. Employees are then empowered to solve problems on the spot. Empowerment *means giving people the authority, resources, and training to make on-the-spot decisions to resolve customers' complaints and to solve and prevent problems.*

Think about this…if your veterinary practice had only one complaint per day, by the end of one year, over 3,600 people would have heard about a bad experience at your practice. Through a process of empowerment, you can identify customer-service problems and resolve them quickly. Allow all of your employees to take initiative in responding to complaints *immediately*. Encourage them to act as representatives of your practice and to communicate with customers to learn what they want and whether the practice is providing it.

Mistakes cost money: by learning to anticipate and avoid them, or to redress them quickly and graciously, you can prevent customer dissatisfaction and defection, improve your practice's image and reputation, and dramatically increase profits.

Keep in mind, however, that it is important to reward employees for outstanding customer service. Employees can be rewarded with modest prizes or with more elaborate gifts. Establish different levels of rewards to recognize different levels of achievers and present the reward in a ceremony if possible.

The empowered employee—and one who feels rewarded for his or her efforts—has a deep personal commitment to the organization he or she is a part of—an "internal commitment," as one theorist has described it.[7] The alienated employee is concerned only with fulfilling the obligations imposed by his or her managers (or the doctors in charge of a practice)—that is, by doing the minimum work necessary to "get by." This lesser commitment may be described as "external."[8] Most employees are externally committed, achieving no more nor less than what is expected of them; they are unwilling to take the responsibility they assume belongs to their superiors. This virtually guarantees that the organization they belong to will not maximize its potential.

Let us relate this situation to the veterinary profession. Intensified competition in veterinary healthcare has created an environment in which outstanding customer service is necessary for financial success—indeed, for mere survival. It is therefore

---

7 See Chris Argyris, Empowerment: The Emperor's New Clothes. Harvard Business Review, May-June 1998, pp. 98-105.
8 Ibid

crucial that employees be ready and equipped to respond to client problems or complaints, and requests from other professionals. For example, a referring veterinarian calls your receptionist to request, for a second time, a medical record she needs to review. If the receptionist is empowered, he will immediately send the record by overnight express or courier, preventing further inconvenience and annoyance to the other party. This demonstrates a commitment to doing serious, responsible business and maintaining a professional relationship. If the receptionist has to wait for a doctor to emerge from surgery or treatment to ask permission to act, he will impose a longer delay on the referring veterinarian. This would convey to her that her needs are not important enough to warrant immediate action.

Empowerment does not work by management dictate. "It comes from well-designed systems which give employees pertinent information, the skills and knowledge to analyze that information, and efficient communications systems…"[9] In other words, it takes some effort. Doctors, practice owners, and/or managers need to talk with their employees, to educate them about every relevant area of the practice, to inform them fully of the practice philosophy. They need to *prepare* employees for undertaking their jobs as fully as possible. This might start with group training sessions, followed by periodic meetings to discuss expectations and performances, to air concerns and pleasures and grievances. It might involve encouraging staff to develop their own performance criteria and goals, and inviting them to participate in hiring processes.[10]

Talking about empowerment, freely and frankly, is the best way to create it. Once an empowered workplace has been established, remember that employees need to practice having and using authority. Veterinary staff need to use their skills and take responsibility for their decisions. Given responsibility in a controlled setting and provided feedback so they can learn and improve, they'll quickly feel comfortable in emergency situations.

Remember that every member of a veterinary practice should feel a part of its success. Conveying to staffers that they count, that their contributions to the practice

9 Bovino Consulting Group <www.bovino-consulting.com/pyr4.htm>
10 These measures are borrowed and adapted from Bovino Consulting Group's web page.

are valued and respected, means that they will probably take more initiative. And its initiative that makes for successful business. It is important to allow them—to *expect* them—to regularly do what they are trained to do; otherwise their initiative is moot. Eventually, they will feel more like partners in the practice than employees of it—and this distinction can mean the difference between an efficient and professional business and a dysfunctional one.

Tracking Your Success

So, how well are you doing with your customer service program? If you are not regularly monitoring your progress, you probably don't really know. Just as it is important to offer outstanding customer service, it is equally vital to continually capture your customers' attitudes and opinions in order to identify issues and problems before they become catastrophic. Satisfaction measurement provides a roadmap for improving customer retention, and a 10% increase in retention typically increases profits by 30%![11]

There are many ways to keep a finger on the pulse of your customer base. The easiest way—other than verbal communication with your customers—is to have them fill out a quick survey as their bill is being prepared. Focus groups can also provide qualitative data from a varied group of customers brought together for the sole purpose of evaluating your customer service program (sharing their feelings, attitudes, thoughts and ideas about the level of customer service being offered by your practice). Other veterinary professionals track the number and types of customer service issues being handled by the reception staff. This data is critical for identifying trends early on and taking immediate corrective actions.

For indirect measurements, you can track the number of new clients per month, taking special note of those brought in by referrals. Statistics indicate that for businesses doing an average job of customer service, client referrals average 50-60% of new business; for those offering exceptional customer service, that number jumps to over 90%! It is also valuable to track the number of customers that

---

11 satisfactionexpress.com

request their pet's medical records and why. Multiple-year retention rates are an important indicator of how well your customer service program is working.

The results of a research study published in 1999 by Brakke Consulting confirm the importance of measuring your success or failure when it comes to customer service. The study examined how many veterinary practices regularly practiced each of 19 traits identified with successful businesses. Those who adopted many of the business practices exhibited significantly better financial performance compared to those who did not. Among the 19 business traits being utilized by successful practices and specifically relating to customer service include: monitoring client loyalty; using client retention programs; analyzing client loss; conducting client focus groups; measuring employee satisfaction (happy employees=happy customers); encouraging referrals (perhaps using a "graduated referral program," in which customers who refer others will be rewarded for up to 10 referrals–10 being the largest reward); measuring client satisfaction; and soliciting client feedback.

Exceeding Expectations

"Exceed Your Customers' Expectations. If you do, they'll come back over and over. Give them what they want, and a little more."

~ *Sam Walton*
Founder of Wal-Mart

A Mayo Clinic emergency room physician tells the story of how a patient walked into the emergency room with shortness of breath. When the woman was told she had a bacterial infection requiring immediate surgery, she expressed concern about her sick dog, which was in her illegally parked truck. The attending nurse assured her that he would move the truck and take care of the dog, but when he walked outside, what he saw was not a pickup truck but a semi, which he wasn't licensed to drive.

He was about to have it towed for $700 when he stopped to consider ways he might save the patient the expense. In the end, the nurse took it upon himself to obtain permission to park the truck at a nearby shopping center for a few days and find a fellow nurse–a former trucker–to drive the truck there. He took the dog to a veterinarian and then cared for it in his home while the patient recovered. When asked what prompted all this extra effort, the nurse replied, "At Mayo Clinic, the patients' needs come first."

While this story is not extraordinary for Mayo Clinic, it would most likely qualify as exceptional for other businesses. Such outstanding examples of going above and beyond the call of duty are precisely why The Mayo Clinic maintains a level of customer service excellence unsurpassed in the healthcare industry.

Other companies are equally impressive in their commitment to customers. Southwest Airlines has built a multi-billion-dollar industry by exceeding customer expectations over and over again. (The airline's agents have been known to drive passengers to their destinations several hours away in rare cases of delays or schedule mix-ups.) Land's End maintains its promise of reliability no matter what the situation (even during a UPS strike, when the company kept its policy of quick delivery by creating its own mini post office)—making it the nation's leading apparel catalog.

Starbucks Corporation exceeds customers' expectations through continuous innovation in tasty beverages, products, and services—including high-speed internet access. FedEx shattered its image as simply an air express carrier for business to become a one-stop shop for any shipping need. Acquisitions like RPS and American Freightways rounded out its offerings to include ground *and* freight, making a world of difference to so many of its customers. And Wal-Mart's "People Greeter" program is one example of the company's commitment to "aggressive hospitality." The *people greeter* welcomes you as you enter any Wal-Mart store, cheerfully handing out shopping carts and answering questions. "The Sundown Rule" states that associates should respond to any inquiry–from customers, suppliers, and other associates–by sundown on the day it is received. Associates are also encouraged to exceed customer expectations by leading customers to a product they cannot find, rather than simply telling them where to find it.

The strategies of successful companies vary, but their principles remain steadfast: they anticipate consumer needs and find every way to meet those needs, forever challenging themselves to improve their service and demonstrate their respect for customers as individuals. So, how can you as a veterinary professional exceed your customers' expectations? First, recognize what your customers' needs and wants are. Pay attention to their concerns and what they are telling you. Teach customers to become educated consumers. An educated consumer appreciates good service and recognizes when difficulties are unavoidable. Also, maintain an *emotional bond* with your customers. All customers want to feel known, liked, and respected. Finally, show compassion and competence when treating their pets. Taking these measures, on top of respecting customers' time, giving them good value for their money, treating them fairly, and honoring their desire for convenience, will do wonders for your practice.

Creating "value-added" is another phrase you hear often in business. In veterinary practice, it is of the utmost importance to create "value-added" in order to exceed customers' expectations. While some of these ideas may have already been mentioned earlier in this chapter, they bear repeating. Examples of "value-added" include:

- Call the pet and owner by name
- Provide accurate and timely information
- Dress professionally
- Don't rush the client
- Stay current with medical procedures and technology
- Explain things clearly
- Return phone calls promptly
- Perform follow-up calls
- Offer convenient office hours
- Use and refer to Specialists
- Send cards (new client, thank you, sympathy, etc.)
- Offer drop-off services
- Offer counseling services (nutrition, grief, etc.)
- Offer tours of the hospital (Scouts, schools, etc.)
- Offer transportation services

Keeping Customers for Life

"For years and years we've told our customers they can trust us. It's up to each one of us every day to earn our customers' trust and respect."

~ Senior Vice President, Wal-Mart Stores

As Dr. Abraham Maslow maintained in the beginning of this chapter, a non-manipulative, trusting relationship with your customers is one that will endure. Quite simply, retaining customers is easy and costs less than losing them. Numerous studies have shown that high levels of customer satisfaction and high levels of customer retention are strongly connected. Think about this, it costs five times as much time, money, and resources to obtain a new customer as it does to keep an existing one.[12] Even a 10% defection rate, which sounds nominal, will cost you a significant amount in potential revenues. For example, if over a 10-year span your practice loses 10 customers and gains 10 every year (90% retention rate), your growth over that period will be 0%. However, if your practice gains 10 customers a year and loses only five (95% retention rate), you will see a 63% growth! What seems like an insignificant difference is actually enormous.

Retaining customers for life through 100% satisfaction can only be achieved through personal relationships–not only with your paying customers but with your staff as well. Communication is key: find out what they like and dislike about your practice, and try, within reason, to accommodate their preferences. If customers approve of the way you do business, everyone wins. They feel good about the service and you drive costs down (by retaining customers) and earnings up (by attracting more customers).

Always target "100% right, 100% of the time"[13] as your goal. If 99% seems acceptable, consider this: the difference in DNA (genetic code) between human beings and chimpanzees is only 1%[14]. And 99% becomes 90% after ten steps (.99 x .99 x .99…). Would it be acceptable for a veterinary technician to over-medicate 10% of the animals in the ICU? Would it be appropriate for a receptionist to give the wrong change or a veterinarian to amputate the wrong limb 10% of the time? Of course not. Veterinary practices are already achieving "100% right" in certain areas. Why should they achieve less in customer service?

Customers' trust is mandatory in creating life-long relationships. Trust is something that builds over time, yet is rooted in fairness. What is fair to one customer may not be considered fair to the next. So, how do you identify and

---

12 Naumann and Giel, K: Customer Satisfaction Measurement and Management: Using the Voice of the Customer, ASQ Quality Press, 1995, 457 pp.

13 Cannie, Joan Koob and Donale Caplin, *Keeping Customers for Life* (AMACOM, 1994) p. 23.

14 Crosby, Philip B., *Qualtiy without Tears* (New York: McGraw-Hill, 1984) p. 74.

avoid treating customers unfairly and jeopardize making them customers for life? There are a few simple rules to abide by:

- Be clear on what the customer wants in order to ensure–to the best of your ability–a positive outcome for all involved.

- Make the process as painless as possible by keeping customers informed at all times.

- Keep your promises (follow-up with a phone call, etc.).

- Shoot from the hip, with communication that's straightforward and understandable.

- Maintain professionalism at all costs.

- Personalize service, paying special attention to any unique requests.

- Always place the customers' needs ahead of what's convenient for the practice.

See How Truly Profitable a Veterinary Practice Can Be

There are many views of customer service, ranging from all encompassing philosophies to specific actions. In essence, customer service is giving customers what they want or need, the way they want it, the first time. Remember that a customer is *anyone* who interacts with a practice, internally or externally. This includes employees, vendors, suppliers, distributors, contractors and referring veterinarians, as well as the pet owners who use your services.

In order to become a truly customer-driven practice, one must develop a comprehensive multi-faceted plan consisting of many goals. These goals must then be clearly understood by all staffers and achieved as consistently as possible.

Remember the key elements of success in achieving world-class customer service: begin with excellent leadership; establish a plan or "mission" that truly values people, in which customer satisfaction is a primary goal; empower your staff to make critical on-the-spot decisions, redressing problems quickly and graciously; monitor success through communication with customers, customer surveys, focus groups, and indirect measurement (i.e. tracking the number of new customers brought in by referrals); exceed customer expectations by going above and beyond the call of duty; and approach customer service with the intent of keeping customers for life.

Also keep the following in mind:

- Treat internal/external customers with respect at all times.

- Show compassion for your pet patients and be empathetic toward their owners (respecting their point of view, even if you don't agree).

- Establish guidelines to determine customers' needs and wants.

- Provide customers with what they want, when they want it, how they want it, and always at a fair price.

- Strive for 100% satisfaction–meeting or exceeding customers' expectations.

- Act in terms of retaining customers for life, sacrificing short-term profit for long-term customer loyalty.

- Handle complaints/problems promptly.

- Provide consistent, *quality* products and services.

- Keep it personal–call pets and owners by name, follow-up by phone or by sending a personalized note.

- Explain information clearly and in understandable terms.

- Respect customers' time–it is invaluable.

- Mind the "tangibles," or visual clues of your practice–making certain employees are well groomed and dressed appropriately, that the practice is clean and free of any unpleasant odors, etc.

- Maintain professionalism at all costs.

Once established, a well-managed customer service program will serve as a powerful, competitive, value-added tool for your veterinary practice. An effective customer service plan builds goodwill, which is key for future business. Last year's customers will soon become next year's customers–and when you add their referrals to your clientele, you'll see how truly profitable a veterinary practice can be.

HUMAN RESOURCES

Kurt Oster MS SPHR

Kurt A. Oster, MS, SPHR is a practice management consultant with Veterinary Healthcare Consultants, LLC–a national consulting firm dedicated to providing innovative and resourceful business solutions for veterinary professionals and humane organizations. Kurt is certified as a Senior Professional in Human Resources (SPHR), the highest level of certification offered by the Society for Human Resource Management. Prior to consulting, Kurt served as Hospital Administrator for a 16-doctor, 24-hour, full-service, veterinary hospital for six years. Additionally, he worked as an educator for a veterinary software firm for nine years. During this time he educated the staffs of over 325 veterinary practices on all disciplines of practice management. Kurt is the finance instructor for the American Animal Hospital Association's (AAHA) Veterinary Management Development School (VMDS) Level One and Advanced. He is a frequent lecturer and he has been published in the Veterinary Practice News and is regularly featured in AAHA's Trends Magazine. He may be reached via e-mail at kurt@vhc.biz

The management of human resources is arguably the most important and most challenging function you will perform as a practice owner or practice manager. Regardless of all the time you spent developing a marketing plan or a customer service plan, it is your staff that makes these plans come alive (or die) within your practice. Mission statements, policies and procedures will only be as effective as your staff training and motivation program.

In pure financial terms, staffing and its related costs will be your organization's greatest expense. Whether you convert this expense into an asset or a liability is your true test as a practice leader.

On a basic level, we know that there is very little difference between the veterinary services delivered by Practice A and the veterinary services delivered by Practice B. A rabies vaccine is a rabies vaccine and in many cases, Practice A and

38

Practice B may even be using the same brand. As for more sophisticated medical and surgical services, we know the average client does not have enough medical knowledge to make a valid comparison. Think of yourself as a consumer. How do you evaluate a flight experience on an airline? Do you know the maintenance record of the individual plane you are boarding? Do you know how many hours the captain has logged flying that model of aircraft or the last time he or she was tested in a flight simulator? The odds are pretty good that you don't know the answers to these key points that industry savvy people would use to define quality. Instead, you evaluate your flight based on customer service criteria. How long was the line at check-in, was the plane clean, was the flight attendant polite and was your baggage lost or damaged are the basis for your comparisons. Study after study tells us that clients evaluate their experience based on customer service issues and customer service comes from leadership and staff training.

Most practice leaders will agree that poor customer service costs them clients, but few make the connection between poor customer service and staff retention. For many practices, the challenge is not in recruiting new team members, but in the training, motivation and retention of team members. Team members enjoy working with happy and satisfied clients. Morale and productivity plummet however, when a staff has to continuously stamp out fires and interact with unsatisfied clients.

Turnover

In strict financial terms, turnover of a single employee in the service industry is estimated to cost the employer real dollars ranging from 50% to 150% of the employee's annual rate of pay. With turnover costs running that high, it is easy to see how a high rate of turnover could drive a practice that should be profitable into a deficit. Furthermore, the impact of multiple turnovers at a practice does not have a linear effect on the hospital's bottom line. The numerous effects on the remaining staff and their ability to complete daily operations cause multiple staff turnovers to have a downward exponential effect on the practice's bottom line, not to mention the negative perception that can develop in the veterinary community that your practice is not a desirable place to work. This type of erosion of your practice goodwill requires years to rebuild.

The Impact of Management Practices and Business Behaviors on Small Animal Veterinarians' Incomes (known in the industry as "The Brakke Study") helps to further quantify the impact of a sound human resources program. The Brakke

Study was initiated in 1998 and completed in 1999, by Brakke Consulting in conjunction with Cox School of Business at Southern Methodist University. Together, they surveyed thousands of veterinarians and published some rather amazing results. In one portion of the study they examined the application of 19 standard business practices associated with well-managed companies. Veterinarians were surveyed as to whether or not their practice utilized each of the 19 business practices. As an indicator of success, the study compared the average salaries of the associate veterinarians utilizing or not utilizing each of the 19 business practices. Veterinarians working in a practice that used each of the 19 standard business practices reported higher average incomes over those working at practices that did not use each of the standard business practices. The business practices demonstrating the largest average income differential between users and non-users were human resource oriented! The three practices were: 1) does the practice actively pursue strategies to promote employee longevity; 2) is employee satisfaction measured; and, 3) are employee reward programs tied to client satisfaction or client loyalty?

If you would like to read a copy of The Executive Summary of the Brakke Management and Behavior Study you can download it from the National Commission on Veterinary Economic Issues website at: www.ncvei.org.

How much turnover is too much? A general rule of thumb is that a veterinary practice should have 1/3 of its staff members with less than one year of service, 1/3 with one to five years of service and the final 1/3 with greater than five years of service. Caution should always be used when applying rules of thumb. For example, practices experiencing tremendous growth and expansion will likely have results skewed towards shorter length of service.

In analyzing staff turnover in veterinary practices through techniques such as exit interviews, we learn that the majority of staff members leave a practice for "soft" reasons instead of "hard" reasons. Hard reasons are traditional compensation issues such as wages and benefits. Soft issues includes those less tangible forms of compensation including recognition, feeling as though they are part of a team and understanding how their role fits into the practice's larger strategic goals and objectives. Obviously, hard benefits extrapolated beyond the realm of reason can motivate an employee to stay at a practice longer than they would have wanted to, but these "golden handcuffs" can become expensive. Golden handcuffs can also cause great destruction if other team members learn about compensation that they feel is not comparable to contribution. If your wage and benefit package is within the market range for your community, you should pay extra attention to the less tangible components of your staff compensation program.

If you are concerned about staff turnover, the following recommendations can help you regain control. To help decrease the turnover rate of new hires, it is recommended that the hiring function become more decentralized to allow line managers and staff members to play a greater role in the selection process. This will help to ensure that new hires have a more accurate perception of their new position and it will help to identify employees who are a better "fit" in their work teams. The line managers will be better able to address candidate questions, such as the strengths and weaknesses of the practice. Taking a team hiring approach to the selection process will result in team members with a vested interest in seeing the new hire(s) succeed. Yes, you will have to share the credit each time a great new employee is discovered, but you also get to share the blame when a new team member does not live up to their potential.

Staff Retention

Once a new employee is recruited, the focus of the team must shift from selection to retention. The initial emphasis must be placed on training a new staff member. A phase training program is proven to be an extremely effective method for training new team members. A phase training program is a systematic approach to staff training that is methodically outlined in detail to ensure thorough training in an efficient manner. Phase training programs delineate detailed learning objectives for each day of the training period (including weekly examinations for accuracy) and evaluate an employee's retention of these objectives on a regular basis.

Phase training programs introduce employees to material in the most logical order, ensuring that all prerequisite information has been mastered before moving on to the next step in their development. For example, a new receptionist cannot be trained on entering clients and patients into the computer until they understand the practice's vaccination and preventive healthcare policies.

As you consider your training program, there are three key elements that you should keep in mind. First, a mentor has to be assigned to the new team member for the duration of their training program. They must have someone who they can go to when they are confused and someone who can inspire them in a positive manner about the practice. This mentor is responsible for making sure that the new team member receives instruction on everything that is important for them to perform their job to the best of their potential. This does not however mean that the mentor is responsible for all of the training. In many case, the mentor will only do a small portion of the instruction. However, the mentor is responsible for helping identify the best instructor for each part of the phase training. One staff member may be able to teach great computer skills, while another can teach great telephone skills. The mentor is also required to elicit feedback about the new employee's development often, so the training program can be fine tuned to meet specific strengths and weaknesses of the trainee.

The second key element is to designate an individual that will be in charge of evaluating the progress of the trainee. The mentor should never evaluate the trainee. The conflict of interest in this scenario is enormous. A mentor may be too optimistic, or pessimistic about the trainee's progress. The mentor may also feel guilty if they have not lived up to their responsibility and be tempted to report proficiency beyond what the trainee is capable of. Keeping these two important roles separated produces objective evaluations and feedback that can be used to fine tune training needs or help determine if a trainee is not going to be successful and should be terminated. Veterinary practices routinely retain new staff members that they should have terminated for failure to achieve performance standards. In comparison, service industry giants such as the Disney Corporation routinely terminate 6 employees during their introductory training period for each employee they retain. Each employee in training should complete a minimum of one oral and one written examination each week during their entire training period in order to properly evaluate and monitor progress.

The final key element in the training process is to make the employee responsible for his or her own training! We all want self-motivated employees, so why not begin testing this trait immediately upon hiring them? Too many practices believe that employee training is a one-way street with the employer bearing all of the responsibility for success or failure. Feelings of guilt for falling short of this lofty goal are why so many poor performers are retained far too long by practices. The new hire should understand the weekly objectives of their training program and they need to communicate to their mentor, or their mentor's supervisor that they are not getting the training they were promised, or the training required to meet their goals. If they feel their training is falling short of what they anticipated, they need to let someone know. Otherwise, you are sending them a message that their success is unimportant to the practice and that poor performance by others is acceptable.

In order for phase training programs to be developed successfully, routine tasks within the practice must be standardized. The practice leadership must approve the steps submitted for the standard approach to each task so this information can be documented in a Procedure Manual. Procedure Manuals set the minimum performance expectation for all processes within the practice. Once the protocols and procedures in the practice have been documented, the phase training guidelines can be developed.

If your practice has not yet evolved to a fully developed phase training program, yet you have an immediate training need there is an alternative method you can use. The trainee should still be assigned a mentor and an evaluator. The mentor can meet with the trainee at the beginning of each week to develop learning objectives for the week. At the end of the week, the evaluator can sit down with the trainee and learn which of the learning objectives the trainee has met and what additional items they may have had an opportunity to learn. The evaluator can record these findings and help develop a new set of objectives for the next week.

Each week the trainee and the evaluator can meet to repeat the above process. The evaluator can also quiz the trainee on those items they claim to have learned during prior weeks. This allows the evaluator to test the trainee's retention of these learning objectives. While this method is by no means an optimal training method, it does allow for the monitoring of an employee's development and it gives them a pre-determined time each week when they know they will receive one-on-one attention.

Most of the above discussion on training has focused on training the new hire during their introductory period. However, training should be a regular part of every employee's activity throughout his or her length of employment. The rate at which new information on products, services and new technologies appears in our profession is awe-inspiring. The old business adage that "you can be on the right track and still be run over by a faster train" rings truer today, than at any other time in history.

Unfortunately, the way many veterinary practices approach continuing education for existing staff members is almost the exact opposite of the rest of the business world. When educational opportunities arise in veterinary medicine, most practice owners and practice managers select their best performing and most highly skilled long-term employee. They believe that "they have earned it" through all of their hard work and productivity. Veterinarians are frugal by nature, so they do not want to pay for education for an employee that has not proven that they are going to become a long-term asset to the practice. The end result of this logic is that the educational program disappoints most of these employees because they probably already have more experience than the instructor and they probably were already doing everything the course recommended. This feedback goes to the practice owner or manager who then concludes "there just isn't any good veterinary CE out there." The end result is that the gap between the best performing employees and the worse performing employees just gets wider.

The rest of the business world views continuing education opportunities from the perspective of "no chain is stronger than its weakest link." Instead of improving the performance of the top employees, they seek to raise the performance of the poorest performing employees. These are the staff members that cause the greatest numbers of errors and omissions in their work, reducing the productivity of the other team members that must constantly monitor their actions and audit their work product. Taken to the extreme, some practices are held hostage by a few key employees whose only function is damage control. Veterinarians would benefit greatly by providing more educational opportunities for their entry level and mid level workers. If you view your staff as an investment, you will get out much more than you put in. Unfortunately, sometimes practices choose the opposite philosophy. I have had numerous veterinarians explain to me during consultations that "they do not waste any time training employees because they will only quit in a few months anyway." I call this a textbook example of a self-fulfilling prophecy!

Earlier in this chapter we mentioned the enormous cost associated with employee turnover. It is generally impossible and undesirable to completely eliminate employee turnover. If an employee goes to college or gets married and moves to be with their spouse, these are examples of turnover that do not reflect poorly on the practice. It is also important to discharge employees that perform poorly. Removing these staff members actually improves the performance of the practice. However, it is those staff members that we desire to retain, but choose to leave despite our best efforts that create a turnover challenge.

If you are unsuccessful at retaining a staff member, there should always be some type of follow up exit interview. Some managers prefer it at the moment of separation; others prefer 30 or 60 days later. Individual mangers will also have format preferences as well. The three primary formats for an exit interview include; in person, via telephone, or via questionnaire. Whatever your personal preference is, never let a valued team member leave your employ without finding out why.

Employees do leave for purely economic reasons, but more often it is a philosophical, emotional, or combination of issues. Among the most frequently cited reasons for turnover is a lack of regular performance feedback from management. While this may not be the sole reason or the most prominent reason, it is typically cited as the number one or two most frequent contributors to employee turnover. The sad thing is, this is among the easiest issue to fix.

Performance Appraisal

My experience has been that most veterinary practices do not conduct performance appraisals with the consistency and regularity that they should. Furthermore, the least effective type of performance appraisal is the most common one in use in veterinary hospitals; the supervisor's narrative. The supervisor's narrative consists of an employee's supervisor sitting down and writing out how they feel the employee is performing. The first problem with this style of appraisal is the Hawthorne Effect. The Hawthorne Effect recognizes the fact that most employees are on the best behavior when their supervisor is present. Once the supervisor leaves the work area, the employee could behave in a totally different manner. Thus, the supervisor does not have an accurate perception of how well the employee performs overall. In addition, there are numerous other biases that can influence how objectively one person evaluates the performance of another. The more people that participate in the appraisal process, the more the effects of these biases are diluted and the true picture of ones performance emerges.

The second most popular appraisal method that most veterinary practices utilize is historical performance reviews. Historical reviews work well for employees for the first couple of years they are employed in a specific position. However, after this time, historical reviews tend to fall into a repetitive pattern that offers little new information about an employee's capabilities. They also do very little to motivate an employee and quite often have the opposite effect, particularly if reviews are performed once a year. It is difficult to summarize an entire year's performance all at once. Positive performance should be acknowledged and rewarded as it occurs (behavior rewarded is behavior repeated). Poor performance should also be addressed immediately. Dragging up a negative event on a performance evaluation six months after it occurred is demoralizing to an employee and makes them feel that they will always be judged by that event. Poor performance should be addressed as it occurs; then an employee should be encouraged to move forward in a positive manner. Line managers should understand the importance of providing regular feedback to staff members on a timely basis.

Whichever style of performance appraisal is chosen, the completed appraisal should always be signed by the employee and retained in their personnel record for future reference.

For employees who remain at the practice for longer periods of time, proactive goal setting is a more valuable management tool than historical reviews. Proactive goal setting moves management from performance appraisal to performance planning. Proactive performance planning is a strong motivational tool that leads to improved morale, increased employee productivity, and employee retention. This is an important and necessary transition because many employees express frustration with employee training and development that essentially stops after their initial 90-day introductory period.

Many staff members report that without regular feedback form their supervisors, they lose perspective of how their job, or their performance, fit into the big picture of their department, or the mission of the practice as a whole.

Proactive performance planning helps managers keep staff focused on their contributions towards the practice mission. Through the use of such techniques as goal setting, job enlargement, job enrichment, and career-pathing managers can retain and continue to develop existing staff.

Proactive goal setting requires a meeting with an employee at the beginning of each quarter. The employee is then coached on setting three goals to be achieved during the upcoming 90-day period. The goals can be designed to meet specific objectives such as personal development, improving customer service, improving patient care, and increasing the efficiency or effectiveness of practice operations. Examples of acceptable goals could range from learning how to perform fecal examinations for parasites to developing a client education and marketing program for pet dental month.

The employee's choice of goals also may provide management with additional input regarding that specific employee. A receptionist who sets goals of learning to read fecal exams, reorganizing the treatment room for greater efficiency, and starting a client education program for pre-anesthetic blood work is probably telling management that she would rather be a technician instead of a receptionist.

Deadlines should be set at specific intervals to monitor the progress of the employee's work. For example, at 30-days the employee could be required to present an outline of how they plan to achieve each goal. At 60-days, they could give an interim progress report and seek guidance on such issues as how to encourage other staff members to better support their efforts. The final review at 90-days would be to evaluate the success of the goal or to determine if the period to achieve the complete goal needs to be extended into the next quarter. Decisions to raise an employee's compensation should be made at the end of the year by evaluating the difficulty and importance of the goals that were set, as well as the number of goals that were successfully achieved. This type of performance system maintains a positive dialogue and maintains a focus on continual growth and improvement, instead of rehashing prior negative experiences.

This system creates additional work for the supervising manager; however, it also results in significant improvements in the staffs' abilities as well as the overall success of the practice. Regular meetings at 30-day intervals also improve communication and feedback between staff members and management. Lack of feedback, lack of support, poor opportunities for personal growth, and dwelling on the negative are all commonly cited reasons for staff turnover in the veterinary profession. Utilizing proactive goal setting is one tool that can address these issues, while helping to develop staff members to their maximum potential.

Quarterly proactive goal setting for longer-term staff members is essentially a one-on-one process, where the manager becomes a mentor. It can be a time consuming investment in the staff, but one that yields great dividends. If one of the managers "gets stuck" while trying to mentor another staff member, they should be able to the practice manager or practice owner as resources to help them move forward. This system creates an efficient way to utilize the scarce resource of the practice leadership's time by actually mentoring two staff members simultaneously (the manager and the employee).

Historical performance reviews conducted for employees who have been with the practice for less than two years are quite different. The function of these reviews is to evaluate whether an employee has learned the basic skills required for the position, evaluate basic work habits (such as punctuality), and evaluate how well an employee fits in with the practice team. These reviews are most meaningful when many people are involved in the process. Managers should distribute two or three review forms to coworkers within the same department as the employee being reviewed. One or more forms should be distributed to at least one member of each of the other departments in the practice. For example, if a receptionist is being evaluated, the office manager should complete a form, two or three other receptionists should each complete a form, and a technician and a veterinarian should also complete a form on the employee as well. This pattern of distribution is important to help maintain a practice culture of teamwork. A receptionist must respond to their manager, work well with others within their department when their manager is not present (the other receptionists), and "work and play well with others" (the technician and the veterinarian). A receptionist who works well with the reception staff, but does not get along with technicians ultimately undermines patient care, client service, and practice profitability.

Once the individual reviews are completed, they should be collected by the manager and be anonymously combined on a summary sheet. The summary sheet indicates the average score received for each question and the range of scores received for each question. Written comments are encouraged from each participant for each question to provide clarification and/or specific examples of behavior. The comments can range from positive behaviors to be rewarded, to undesirable behaviors that need to be corrected. To help eliminate possible personal bias or the reporting of a single incident, comments should only be carried forward to the summary sheets if a similar comment appears on two or more individual forms. The completed summary is then reviewed with the specific employee, signed, and placed in their personnel file.

Reviews for associate veterinarians are handled in a similar manner to that described previously for support staff. Veterinary reviews are comprised of multiple components. The first component is the "people-skills" component that helps evaluate how well the veterinarian interacts with staff members and clients. The second component is a review of the associate's medical and surgical skills as perceived by practice owner, Medical Director, or other similar title. The final component is the financial performance of the veterinarian, which should be summarized on a spreadsheet or in a table format. This data should include specific healthcare procedure ratios including the Diagnostic/Pharmacy Ratio. This type of comprehensive review process for veterinarians is best handled by the practice manger (except for the evaluation of medical and surgical skills) because many veterinarians find it difficult to discuss non-medical performance and behaviors with other doctors.

All of these performance appraisal procedures emphasize the need for regular performance evaluation, feedback and communication. Contrary to popular belief, most employees would prefer negative feedback to no feedback at all. Your staff wants to know how well they are performing and it is your obligation to tell them.

OFFICE POLITICS

Mark Davis

Mark Davis has been a veterinary practice manager and a practice management consultant for the last eight years in general, specialty and emergency settings. He is a graduate of the AAHA Veterinary Management Institute and has worked in California, Hawaii, Maryland, the District of Columbia and Virginia. He currently resides in Southern California

We work within a social structure, and this social structure is important to our personal and professional well-being, as well as to the well-being of the practice where we work. Every day that we go to work, we interact with clients, patients, other staff members and practice owners. These interactions help ensure that the office is staffed, cages are cleaned, treatments are performed, and everything else is done that is necessary for running a veterinary practice. Our interactions provide the framework for the practice, they set the mood, and they dictate the way in which work will be done. These interactions are also known as Office Politics, and our level of participation in them dictates our position in the work hierarchy.

It is hard to imagine a world without office politics. From the first moment that a group of people came together in a cooperative work environment, office politics have had a major role in guiding our behavior at work. Office politics can have positive consequences, and they can have negative consequences. You may think that you do not play office politics or that you are immune to their effects. In reality, everyone who interacts with other people while at work is an office politician. When we work, office politics are just there, always there. It is important to realize that how well we play office politics determines our success at work.

Positive Politicking

Dr. Smith was an intern at a large specialty practice. He was a good clinician, but his motivation level was low, especially at the beginning of his internship. He enjoyed veterinary medicine, but he wasn't sure what the future would hold for him. Up to that point Dr. Smith had been seen as a rather unproductive, unimpressive intern.

One day, Dr. Smith made a mistake while anesthetizing an animal. With the help of a technician who came walking by, Dr. Smith was able to rectify the situation. Dr. Smith glossed over the situation, telling the technician that the situation was blown out of proportion. The incident was brought to the attention of the practice owner, who had already heard several negative stores about Dr. Smith, his abilities as a clinician, and his bedside manner.

Dr. Smith realized that he was at a crossroads, and that his job and his future would be dictated by what he did in the upcoming weeks. He did several things that made him a good politicker. First, he thanked the technician that helped him get through the anesthesia incident. Next, he approached the practice owner, *before the practice owner had a chance to approach him*, explained what had happened, took full blame and outlined a series of steps that he intended to take to make sure that he didn't allot a similar situation to occur in the future. Then he approached each of the practice's specialists, and solicited advice from them on how they would deal with a similar situation. Finally, he followed through with a memo to the practice owner, describing what steps he had take to ensure that the situation was not repeated. He even suggested some improvements to the practices current anesthesia protocols that would ensure patient safety to a higher degree.

What did Dr. Smith get out of all this? For starters, he was able to complete his internship. His image as a mediocre intern changed. He was now perceived by the doctors and staff as a bright, young veterinarian with a promising future. Did Dr.

Smith really change significantly? No, not really. What he did do was to learn to make a fast recovery from a potentially critical situation, by working the political system inside the practice. Dr. Smith eventually received strong recommendations from two of the specialists that he had worked under. Those recommendations allowed him entry into a very competitive residency program.

Negative Politicking

Dr. Jones was an associate veterinarian at a large general practice. She had many years of experience, and was comfortable in diagnosing a treating a multitude of conditions. She loved her job, she loved her patients, and she took great pride in her medical ability.

Unfortunately, Dr. Jones never learned to be a successful office politician. She spent a good deal of each day complaining. She complained about her clients to her fellow doctors and staff, she complained about the staff to her clients and fellow doctors, and she complained about her fellow doctors to just about anyone who would listen. She frequently expressed comments such as "I'm not treating that dog; those people don't have any money," or "These receptionists are a bunch of idiots." Typically these sentiments were overheard by a group of people, and frequently the individuals that she was criticizing overheard her comments.

Time went on, and Dr. Jones continued her diatribes. It soon became apparent that Dr. Jones was unhappy, and, to make matters worse, she took out her unhappiness on the people that she worked with. The technicians that Dr. Jones worked with began coming to work late, leaving early, or calling in sick and not coming in at all. The reception staff did not want to be the recipients of Dr. Jones' ire, so they stopped scheduling appointments for Dr. Jones, telling the client that she was busy. As Dr. Jones caseload and revenue decreased, and that of her associates increased, two things began to happen: Doctor Jones became the object of (negative) attention from her associate veterinarians because of her inactivity and her negativity; and Doctor

Jones became a liability for the practice owner. Not only had years of experience had increased her salary, placing her at the top of the salary matrix, but her impact on staff morale increased turnover at the practice and caused some significant recruiting costs that were unplanned and avoidable. Through her own efforts, Dr. Smith had become a bitter, unhappy, disliked employee. The practice owner carried Dr. Jones for another year, and then she was finally let go for her inability to cooperate with the staff and her dramatic decrease in productivity.

Dr. Jones played the negative side of office politics, and she ended up paying the price for it with her job.

The following tips will help you to be successful at Office Politics. Most of the tips just involve using good common sense and treating people and issues appropriately.

Tips for succeeding at office politics

Tip #1-Take the high road

A very wise woman, named Susan Myers Taylor, once counseled me to "take the high road" when I was dealing with a particularly contentious co-worker. Have you ever heard the expression about lying down with dogs and getting up with fleas? Taking the high road keeps you in the flea-free zone and ensures that your reputation at work is enhanced rather than harmed.

From time to time, you will encounter individuals who wish you to be harmed professionally. The common term for them is "back stabbers." These are people who will gladly point out your mistakes to anyone willing to listen, and if they cannot uncover any "dirt" on you, they may invent it instead. Whenever we are the target of the back stabber's attention, we may feel inclined to seek revenge on that person for their attempts to impugn our reputation.

What is the best way to deal with a back stabber? Ignore him and his attacks. That is it; it is just that easy. You may say, "But, but, but…it's not fair!" You are right, it is not fair to be maligned in public, but your best defense is to just let it go. This tactic flies in the face of our basic urge to seek out revenge, but the best revenge that you can have is to do your job well. In the end the back stabber will look stupid or petty or jealous, while that halo on your head will have a bit more shine to it.

Tip #2-Work with the good and the bad

Take a piece of paper and write down some words that describe the practice where you work, listing the "good" things about the practice on one side of the paper, and the "bad" things on the other side. Does the "good" side outweigh the "bad" side, or vice versa? If you're like most people, your "bad" list covers a full half page (or more), and your "good" list resembles a short shopping list.

Every veterinary clinic and hospital, large or small, general practice or referral, has its own unique culture. As employees we base our opinion of that culture on our own set of values, and in our minds certain aspects of that culture will be good and other aspects will be bad. The bad things usually make themselves known quickly; the good things aren't always easy to recognize. Is that because the good things do not exist? Or is it because we don't want to see them?

As a veterinarian one of your primary roles is to diagnose and treat problem conditions. Unfortunately, this training in seeking out problems and treating them surfaces in other areas of the job. Before long, you may be spending a good part of your day looking for trouble outside of the exam room. You become critical of the facility, the owner, the support staff or the clients. While you're busy finding fault with things, the good things about your job become hidden by all those things you are busy criticizing. Instead of spending all your time looking for the bad, take some time to recognize the positive aspects of your job. They are there, you may have just forgotten how to recognize them.

How do you work with the good and the bad? It is easy, really. Accept and appreciate the good for what it is. Acknowledge the bad, and work on making it better. Instead of complaining about the situation, try to improve it.

David Johnson was an associate veterinarian working for a small animal practice in Mobile, Alabama. Morale at the practice was very low, and David deduced that it was due to the low wages that the staff was earning. Rather than just join the staff in their weekly complaint sessions, he approached the practice owner with a proposal to evaluate the staff, increase wages and to compensate for the raises with an overdue price increase. It became a win-win situation, where the staff got more money, the owner got more money, and morale and profits improved. David became the practice hero because he chose to seek a constructive solution to the problem.

The first key to being successful at work is to acknowledge the bad things about your job, dig a little deeper until you find the good things, and then utilize the good things to improve the bad. Offer solutions to problems, not complaints; be the problem solver instead of the instigator.

Tip #3–Avoid Gossiping

Exchanging work-related information is an essential part of work. Contrary to popular opinion, exchanging malicious gossip about your co-workers is not. For many people, the difficulty lies in determining what is a positive exchange of information, and what is gossip. That little bit of nasty information that we over-heard seems to burn in our brain until we can share it with someone else. Having that information, and sharing it with others, makes us feel powerful, in control, and knowledgeable.

Sometimes it is hard to tell what is gossip and what is not. A bona fide work-related conversation can quickly degenerate into gossip without prior warning. The best way to assess the level of gossip is to ask yourself if the person to whom you are speaking has a need to know the information that you are sharing. If the answer is, "no," then you are most likely gossiping.

And what about gossip that includes you as the main character? As hard as it may be to do so, just try to ignore it. Gossip and rumors are hard to squelch, and paying too much attention to them just seems to validate their existence. Gossip and rumors frequently die a slow, painful death, but you should not breathe life back into them by attempting to refute them. Just let them go, the sooner that everyone realizes that you place no value on them, the sooner that you will stop being the main by-product of the gossip mill.

Gossiping does have a place at work, however. It can be an excellent way of gathering information pertaining to the operation of your workplace. The challenge is to determine the right thing to do with the information that you have just acquired. Information that can help you get along with a difficult co-worker or information that gives you notification of impending events can be very useful. The key to handling this information lies in how you deal with it. If you use gossip to improve your situation, you are using it to your advantage. If all you do is spread the gossip on to someone else, you have opened yourself up to criticism for being a "troublemaker." The other point to remember is the most of the gossip that works its way through the grapevine is about the people who do the gossiping. If you do not want to be grist for the gossip mill, do not participate in the gossip

Tip #4-Choose your battles

Some people are seen as trouble makers. Others are seen as strategic components of a clinic's effort to improve. What is the difference? For the most part the difference is that the strategic players know how to choose their battles. They acknowledge problems that exist within the practice, but they decide what battles are worth fighting for, what battles are winnable, and what battles aren't really that important.

> Dave Thompson worked at a mixed practice in Boulder, Colorado. The affluent clientele called upon the practice to treat a wide range of animals, everything from dogs and cats to pythons and llamas. Dave was a great clinician; no one in the practice could diagnose and treat an ailment better than Dave. Dave's downfall was that he chose to communicate through arguments and criticism. He'd argue with the office manager about the way their invoices looked, he'd argue with the owner about the color of the walls in the exam rooms, and he'd criticize anything to anyone who he was able to corner. He did not understand the concept of choosing his battles.

> After Dave had worked at the practice for a couple of years, the owner and staff grew tired of Dave's constant arguing and his need to always express his viewpoint on everything. It was not long before Dave was viewed as a troublemaker, someone who would never let anything go. Everyone began to ignore his arguing and criticism, and David began to view everyone as apathetic, since they chose not to participate in his tirades. The situation continued until David left. At his exit interview he told the owner that he was going elsewhere because no one at that clinic cared. The owner was relieved to get this albatross off his neck, and neither David nor the owner realized that the clinic was losing a valuable employee, whose constructive criticism had taken a wrong turn somewhere.

Learn what is important and worth fighting for, and learn to recognize the things that you should just let go. No one wins every battle, and very often the battles we choose are the losing ones. Choose your battles carefully!

Tip #5-Establish and maintain yourself as an authority figure to staff

This tip may unnerve you, but it is one that is often ignored by new associates, and some senior associates as well. You, as the doctor, are an authority figure. You may not feel like an authority figure, but you are one. That difficult case that you are working on is your responsibility, and your license is at stake if mistakes are made. The technician with whom you are working may be very well-qualified, but he or she is your assistant, not your supervisor. Makes sure that you are the one calling the shots. That does not mean that you cannot ask for assistance, but it does mean that the way in which a case is handled must be based on your decisions.

Once you are recognized as an authority figure by the staff, you need to act like an authority figure. This means that you are publicly supportive of your boss, regardless of your personal view of how he is doing his job. You do not maliciously gossip about the rest of the staff, and you voice your criticisms to the appropriate people, not to everyone who will listen.

> Dr. Michaels accepted a position as the co-director of a small animal clinic in Milwaukee. He had been in practice for several years and was an accomplished clinician. As the months passed, Dr. Michaels became disenchanted with his co-director and, in an attempt to become more friendly with the staff, began making derogatory comments about the co-director to the staff. He would talk about her while she was out of the room, or whisper to the staff about her when she was within earshot. Dr. Michaels' co-director spoke to him several times about his negative comments, but Dr. Michaels seemed to feel that it was more important to speak poorly of his co-director. He wanted the staff to like him and saw this as his opportunity to "get in good" with the staff. Dr. Michaels quickly undermined his own authority, and the staff lost respect for him and his ability as a doctor. His comments were also extremely demoralizing to the

staff, and the number of new faces at the practice began to grow as he chased away employees.

After this went on for a couple of months, no one at the practice was happy. Morale was lower than it had ever been, and no one enjoyed coming to work anymore. Dr. Michaels was finally asked to leave. He left and soon found a position with another practice in the area, where he again began criticizing the owner in front of the staff. Dr. Michaels' tenure at that clinic lasted about three months, and he was again out looking for a job. Dr. Michaels still has not learned that attempting to be liked by the staff by creating an environment of negativity is not a recipe for success. Hopefully some day he will understand.

Tip #6-Don't burn any bridges

The world of veterinary medicine is a very small, tight-knit, one. It seems that everyone has worked together, or gone to school together, or fought each other over the years. One of the worse things that you can do is to intentionally burn bridges. There are many ways to burn bridges, and relatively few ways to mend those bridges once they have been burned.

You may burn bridges through intentional or unintentional acts. While you may not be able to repair the situation, knowing that a relationship has been harmed is still useful information to have. It may be difficult to know beforehand what causes a bridge burning, and it may be a totally innocent act on your part. You may be burning bridges if you: extend your office hours beyond what the competition provides; testify as an expert witness in a case where the defendant is a colleague of yours; quit a job on bad terms, or quit a job without giving notice; earn the reputation as a troublemaker; or make derogatory statements about your colleagues, both those in the clinic where you work and those who work in other clinics.

It is important to remember that "off the record" statements seldom remain off the record. Any confidence that you share with a colleague has a good chance to be disseminated fairly quickly, in spite of any reassurances that you may have been given. The best advice is to avoid saying anything that you would not say out loud at your local VMA meeting.

Tip #7-Balancing Your Loyalties

All too often we are put into a situation where we are forced to choose between our loyalties to two different groups that have opposing opinions. We may be asked to side with the doctors over the technicians, the technicians over the receptionists, the clients over the doctors, etc. The best way to handle these situations is to claim neutrality, if possible. Sometimes you cannot claim neutrality, however. If you have **two** practice owners to whom you report, and those two owners have differing opinions about a particular issue, hope that they don't ask whether or not you agree with one of them.

If they do ask your opinion, you do have several options. You can tell them that both are correct, listing X, Y and Z reasons why they are correct. You can tell them that you see the merits of both arguments, but you agree with one opinion over the other, you can tell them that you do not want to get caught in the middle of their disagreement, or you can tell them that they are both wrong. Just remember that when you express your opinion, you should be as objective as possible. Allowing your emotions to sway your judgment can quickly put you into a no-win situation

Exhibiting favoritism toward employees is a bad idea, exhibiting it toward one owner over the other is a terrible idea. At some point during your career you may have the distinct displeasure of observing an all-out shouting match between two owners. Your best option is to stay out of it. Owners are in some ways bonded together permanently; you, on the other hand, can probably be "let go" with little or no notice. Do not allow yourself to be put into that situation. Stay out of owners' arguments, your career will be much healthier if you do.

Tip #8-Solicit help and advice from co-workers and supervisors

Many of us feel that asking for help is a sign of weakness or inability. We feel that it is a signal to everyone that we do not know what we are doing, or that we are not qualified for the job that we hold. In reality, asking for help accomplishes several positive things. It enables us to get our job done better by providing us with information that we did not have previously, it ensures that we are communicating with our peers, and, if done correctly, it ingratiates us to the people that we're working with.

If you are unsure about the procedure involved for performing a particular task, ask someone. Not knowing how to perform a procedure, especially one that you are not familiar with, is preferable to performing a procedure incorrectly. Not knowing how to use the CBC machine is a situation that is easily rectified; using the CBC machine and breaking it is something that creates much more trouble.

If you are working up a case and do not feel comfortable with the treatment plan that you have outlined, consult a colleague. Consulting a colleague is a great way to validate your plan, and it also provides you an opportunity to establish dialogue with that colleague. People really do want to help, and a consult is a great way of getting help, while at the same time breaking down some of the barriers that we put up around ourselves. Your colleague will probably be flattered that you asked for help.

In the realm of office politics, asking for help or advice can benefit your career significantly. Asking for help shows that you care, that you acknowledge that there are others in the workplace who know things that you do not, and that you are willing to learn from the experience of others. Sometimes asking for help or advice, even when you already know the answer, is a means to ingratiate yourself to others. Used sparingly, this tactic can make you look great.

Tip #9-Take donuts to work every now and then

Employees love food. Donuts, a pizza, or bagels are all big favorites with the staff. If you can, take a treat that everyone will enjoy. Think of it as a reward to them for having put up with you while you figure your way around the clinic. Sometimes this may feel like you are bribing the staff to get along with you. Call it what you will, food is a big winner.

Most employees appreciate being thanked, and bringing in food is one way to show them that you appreciate them. If you want to get along with everyone, show them that you care. You can also make yourself more popular with the staff just by saying "please" and "thank you." These common words are not spoken as frequently as they should be, and go a long ways toward making your work environment a positive one.

Tip #10-Take a breath before you speak (Otherwise know as avoiding "Foot in Mouth Disease")

We have all let loose with comments that we immediately regret making. Once the comment is made, it cannot be taken back. To avoid making "unfortunate" comments, take a breath before you speak. Think about what you are going to say before you say it. This may be hard to do, if you are accustomed to blurting out the first thing that comes into your head, but your brain can process a good response very quickly. Just give it a chance.

Some people are so good at responding tactfully to anything thrown at them that you may wonder if they ever make a misstatement. They probably have, but they have taken the time to learn to filter their response process. You can also avoid putting your foot in your mouth by responding to a question with another question or by asking the person to explain himself more clearly. This tactic will provide you with more information, while at the same time giving you a chance to think about your response, instead of just blurting it out.

Tip #11-When to go over your boss' head

When should you go over your boss' head? A good rule of thumb is "Never!" Your boss got his job for some good reason, it maybe because he is the owner, it may be because he is the owner's son-in-law, it may be because he is good at office politics. Whatever the reason, he is your boss, and, if you want to succeed, you need to get along with him. Going over his head is a potentially disastrous way of attempting to get things accomplished. Why not try working with your boss, instead of trying to work around him? If you have a problem with the way that management works, suggest ways to improve the situation. If you have a problem with the way your boss gets things done, find a way to discuss your concerns tactfully. Be sure to acknowledge to yourself that there are some things that you do not have control over and some things that your boss does not have control over. If your boss is that much of a loser, or acts so offensively that you cannot tolerate it, you have a couple of options. You can "tough it out," and hope that he retires or quits or gets fired, or you can seek opportunities elsewhere. If you think that your work life is miserable because of your boss, imagine what it would be if it were ten times worse. That is what you would have to contend with if you try to go over your boss and he finds out what you are up to.

Of course, you may have the option of attempting to depose your boss. Again, this is a very risky premise that can lead to career suicide (your career suicide, that is.) Instead of looking for ways to get rid of the boss, try walking a few steps in your boss' shoes. Would the situation be any better for anyone if you were the boss? Or would you turn into that person that you're trying to getting rid of?

Tip #12-Play golf with the boss (or tennis, or bowling or whatever)

Some tactics that we use in playing successful office politics benefit our co-workers, some tactics are mutually beneficial, and other are done just so that we, as individuals, can get ahead. The most self-serving of these tactics are the "brown-nosing" ones. They are the things that we do so that we will "get in good" with the boss. Playing golf with your boss is one of these tactics.

Hundreds of deals are struck on the golf course every week. Why not take advantage of the opportunity to get your agenda heard? Hitting the course for a round of 18 holes may seem perfectly respectable, even admirable. Spending a Saturday with the boss can makes us look like a team player, someone who is willing to sacrifice his time off to round out the boss' foursome. We have an opportunity to spend more time with the boss, complimenting him on his ability to drive that ball off the green, to putt like a professional, or even his ability to maneuver that golf cart. At the same time we can discuss the hottest topics at work, share our own ingenious ideas, and make him feel like we're putting his interests ahead of ours.

The only participant in this game of golf who is scoring an eagle on every hole is you, the employee who has the boss' ear, at least for the next four hours. Now is the time to make a pitch for that new ultrasound machine that you been drooling over, or that endoscope that you have been dreaming about, or that raise that you have been hoping to get. Things that seem totally unreasonable when you are running around a frenetic treatment area can seem totally reasonable in the calm of the 12th green.

Should you play golf, or tennis or whatever, with your boss? Certainly, and enjoy yourself. But go with an agenda. Take your most burning issues and be prepared to discuss them in a calm, easygoing, unobtrusive manner. Do not think that just because you have the boss' ear, that you can blurt things out and expect him to respond positively:

> *Hey, Sam, when am I going to get that raise you promised me six months ago? I've got two kids in orthodontia, and I need that money.*

Here is a news flash, it'll be another six months before Sam even thinks about your raise. How about approaching it this way:

Nice shot, Sam. Hey, Sam, do you remember a while back we talked about renewing my employment agreement. Things are going so well for me at the clinic that I'd like to go ahead and renew. Do you think we could sit down and talk about it in the next week or two?

If I know Sam, he will probably end up discussing the renewal and the raise with you while you are finishing your golf game. The low-key nature of your request, as well as the relaxed environment on the golf course, makes him much more willing to discuss the deal, without feeling like he is backed into a corner.

How do you cope with office politics? You must first acknowledge that they exist in all work environments, and that everyone (including you) is an active participate. If you avoid interaction with your co-workers because you do not want to deal with the politics, then you may be seen as aloof or uncaring. If you participate too intensely in the political scene, you may be seen a brown-noser or a troublemaker. If you can find a pleasant medium, participating in office politics without enabling them to overtake your life or impair your ability to do your job, you will probably be seen as a friendly, concerned team member. Good office politicians play the game just enough, bad ones don't play it enough, or they play it too much.

The names and locations of the individuals mentioned in this chapter are fictitious; the examples themselves are true.

COMPENSATION AND BENEFITS

Tracy Dowdy, CVPM

Tracy Dowdy is a career consultant who is dedicated to helping veterinarians and all those who work with them reach new levels of success in all aspects of their business. She gained experience in the personnel industry working with Fortune 500 companies before entering the veterinary field. Since Tracy's father is a veterinarian, she has had years of opportunities to gain knowledge about the profession throughout her life. In 1995, Tracy joined Advanced Animal Care Centre located in Bedford, Texas. Within three years of leading the practice in a new, client and service oriented direction, the practice tripled in gross revenues and received a Hospital Design Merit Award (June 1998) and the Practice of Excellence Award (June 2000) from Veterinary Healthcare Communications, the publishers of Veterinary Economics magazine.

In March of 1998, Ms. Dowdy started Veterinary Management Solutions to help veterinarians and practice owners achieve the same success she was able to provide to Advanced Animal Care Centre. Ms. Dowdy has consulted with over 100 practices nationwide in the areas of financial growth, staff retention, client service and many other aspects of practice management.

Ms. Dowdy has built on her management and training experiences to create her own, unique hands-on approach. By working alongside veterinary teams and their leaders, she helps them develop a practice that is service and client centered by setting and training to standards of service, empowering the healthcare team, building effective and efficient workflow systems, improving communications, conduct, and appearances, creating a culture of emotional wealth sharing, and ultimately moving the entire practice to higher levels of personal and collective enjoyment as well as improved financial success.

Tracy has been published in local and national veterinary journals and has spoken at local, regional and national veterinary meetings. She is available to speak on topics such as leadership, client service and staff training at national and regional conferences. Ms.

Dowdy is a Certified Veterinary Practice Manager and a Charter Member of the Association of Veterinary Practice Management Consultants and Advisors.

What Is Important To Employees?

Traditionally, employers tend to think that the main thing on employees' minds is a paycheck, accompanied by regular and (hopefully) generous raises.

In actual practice, employers frequently don't <u>know</u> what employees want. Kenneth Blanchard (author of The One-Minute Manager) surveyed 10,000 employees about job satisfaction. He also surveyed managers and supervisors as to what they thought made employees satisfied with their jobs. Interestingly enough, the answers were very different.

Employees listed the top five components of job satisfaction as being: appreciation of work done, feeling of being "in on things", help with personal problems, job security and high salary or wages.

Employers, by contrast, thought the things that made employees satisfied were high salary or wages, job security, promotion in the company, good working conditions and interesting work.

The truly remarkable finding from this study is that the top item on the employers' list was the last item on the employees' list.

This is not to say that great working conditions will make up for poor salary—salary does matter. But the point is that some other things matter as well. In recent years, finding and keeping good employees has been the most difficult task facing the veterinary profession. Without good employees, veterinarians cannot offer high levels of medical and surgical care, nor provide the kind of service that keeps clients returning to a practice, allowing the business to prosper financially. Thus it is essential that the compensation program be designed with the hospital staff's goals in mind, as well as the practice owners.

A veterinary practice is an ideal environment for attracting people who are highly motivated by personal goals of service to others. By empowering employees, a culture is created that fosters employee growth, satisfaction, appreciation and motivation. Creating a client-centered vision motivates them to focus on achieving attainable goals and creates a culture of intense employee satisfaction. The hospital team members grow because the veterinarians share knowledge, and train them to more actively participate in the practice.

Developing A Compensation System

Employee compensation is a two-part program: salaries/wages and benefits. The objectives of the program are to:

- Attract, retain, and motivate high performers
- Maintain internal consistency and external competitiveness
- Recognize and reward performance

Salary/wages and benefits work together and must be planned together. In one practice, team members may opt for higher benefits and a lower pay scale; in another practice, benefits may take a back seat to higher pay. To ensure employee satisfaction, it is important to know the employees when planning the compensation program.

Salaries And Wages

The first step in creating an equitable and effective wage and compensation system is to develop a consistent protocol for setting pay levels for each position.

1. List all of the jobs in the practice.
2. Group the jobs by major function—management, client relations/administrative, technical and so on.
3. Rank the jobs according to their relationship to the practice's mission.

This job ranking is <u>not</u> a rating of individuals. It shows the relative importance of each job with respect to the hospital's mission and strategic goals.

For a new practice in the planning stages that has yet to hire its first employee, this is an ideal method because it is easy to ensure that the most valuable positions have the highest compensation.

In an existing practice, however, this is seldom the case—pay is frequently a real hodge-podge. The head receptionist is making more than the best veterinary assistant because the receptionist was just hired, and receptionists are at a premium these days, whereas the vet assistant was originally hired as a kennel staff person, in high school, five years ago, and the pay never really caught up as the job changed.

Pay as it currently exists

The next step is to chart what employees are actually being paid.

NAME	POSITION	FT/PT	$/HR	LENGTH	PERFORM APPR RATING	COMMENT
Brandy	Reception	FT	7.25	6 mos	7	Learning fast, enthusiastic, young
Susan	Reception	FT	10.25	5 years	7	Dr. M's wife
Linda	Reception	PT	7.25	1 year	6	Wants FT
Matt	Tech	FT	7	2 years	4	good person, slow learner, average worker
Jennifer	Tech	FT	8.6	1 year	5	intelligent, good skill, not team player,
Andria	Tech	PT	7.25	4 years	6	1-2 days/month, 2 small children
Johnny	Tech	FT	8.5	6 mos	7	Very responsible, much potential, pleasant
Angela	Tech	PT	10	2 years	7	Susan's sister
Heather	Tech	FT	8.5	3 years	7	very loyal, pleasant
Joel	Kennel	FT	6	1 month	5	very intelligent, lazy, has potential
Sara	Kennel	FT	6.25	1 month	6	much potential, introvert, young
Chad	Kennel	PT	6	6 months	7	18 yrs old; has potential to become DVM

The end result of this analysis will be a compensation table that shows minimum, maximum and average ranges for each position, plus a strategy to reconcile the inequities discovered in the two exercises above. The next step is an examination of the factors that influence actual salary decisions.

Local Market Rates

It is essential to know not only the pay ranges for veterinary practices in the area but also the going rates for positions in other businesses where current staff members or job candidates might apply. If veterinary receptionists are making $8, but receptionists in general are paid $10, then $8 probably won't attract top candidates. Getting accurate salary information is not easy but there are some sources: newspaper want ads; internet sources of local wage information; staff members who know what counterparts are earning in other practices; job candidates with recent experience, etc.

Given this information, the general recommendation is that all salaries in the hospital, new and old, should be in the upper 75th percentile of these local ranges. To find and keep better-than-average people, it is necessary to pay better-than-average salaries.

Education, Job Skills, and Experience

There is a good correlation between the productivity of employees and their education levels, skill sets and work experiences, although more experience and more education don't always translate into better work. In salary determination, the key is to make sure that the education, skills and experience being rewarded are specific requirements of the position.

Top quality staff members are important not only for client care, but so they can assume many of the routine functions of the doctors, freeing doctors for high-level and more income-producing activities.

While technical skills can be learned, it is much harder to change or improve interpersonal skills. Veterinarians tend to make hiring and compensation decisions based on technical skills because it is something they understand well. In small businesses such as veterinary practices, strong people skills, and a good attitude are essential and should be rewarded. One whiner and one chronic gossip can destroy the work environment. Ability to train other staff members, personal initiative, and dedication to the practice are all factors that should be considered in determining compensation.

Pay for Performance

It would seem logical to pay more to employees who produce more. The key is to know how to measure job performance and how to tie it with the practice's mission and goals. This is where defined job descriptions and a well-designed performance appraisal system come into play. Employees need to know exactly what tasks and duties their job requires and the level of competence at which these are to be performed. Then salary ranges and increases can be set based on specific job performance standards.

When new employees join the hospital team, it is essential that they know exactly what is expected, by means of a thorough job description and a phased training program. They also should be given the date of the first performance appraisal and a copy of the performance appraisal form.

An effective performance appraisal system enables matching pay to performance. For some it may be an "annual adjustment"—those who are doing their jobs adequately but not exceptionally. Some veterinarians feel that salary should have ceilings, for example, a receptionist should never receive more than $10.00 an hour. The problem with this thinking is that it is unrealistic. The economy never stands still, and neither should the salaries of employees. More competent employees should receive more than an annual adjustment. If an employee has increased the level of responsibility, moved into a new position, acquired new skills that make him/her more valuable, he or she should be rewarded with a "merit raise," in addition to the regular annual raise. This merit raise might match or exceed the annual adjustment.

Seniority is a widespread workforce sacred cow. If seniority means a top employee who can work in several areas when needed, who volunteers to help out in difficult situations, who is knowledgeable and has great people skills—then seniority in this sense is a factor in compensation: years spent on the job, per se, should not be.

Develop the hospital's salary table

With the job ranking protocol and the table of actual salaries at hand, the final step is to develop a salary table for the hospital, considering all various factors discussed above.

The chart below, as adapted from AAHA's *Compensation & Benefits*, Second Edition is a model, and provides comparisons to national averages. It is essential to keep in mind that local compensation will never match the national averages, and that this is a model, only.

The salary structure should be reviewed annually; once the initial development is completed, updating is relatively easy.

Annual Salary: Full-Time Positions

Position	Total		
	Mean	Median	Cases
Veterinarian Owner	$95,268	$80,000	1,062
Non-veterinarian Owner	$67,827	$61,100	159
Associate Veterinarian	$59,357	$55,000	665
Practice Administrator	$42,458	$40,000	67
Hospital Manager	$33,388	$32,500	171
Office Manager	$27,414	$27,000	226
Head Technician/ Technician Manager	$27,944	$27,040	349
Registered/ Certified Technician	$25,453	$24,960	414
Non-registered Technician	$21,715	$20,800	622
Veterinary Assistant	$19,923	$18,200	536
Head Receptionist/Reception Manager	$23,658	$23,000	293
Receptionist	$19,827	$19,680	156
Kennel Manager	$20,421	$19,273	136
Kennel Assistant	$16,437	$15,898	240
Groomer	$27,942	$25,000	57

Note: Full-time is defined as 40 or more hours worked per week.

Associate Veterinarian Salaries

Associate veterinarians may be compensated by:

- Straight salary,
- Percentage of production
- Some combination of the two

There is no universal answer—each practice must determine what works best. It is also important that hospital owners understand the kind of a message the compensation structure is sending to the associates about performance expectations.

According to AAHA's *Compensation & Benefits*, Second Edition, 54% of full-time associate veterinarians are compensated by salary-only, 12% by percent of production only, and 35% by base salary plus a percent of personal production.

Straight salary

An advantage of straight salary is that the doctor is compensated for all of his/her work, not just medical/surgical production. All doctors will spend some of their work time on management and administrative functions—assisting with strategic planning, preparing and tracking budgets, training and supervising employees, meeting with vendors, working on marketing and so on. Salary ensures that they are paid for these duties without complicated formulas. Disadvantages are that is does not encourage the doctor to focus on the business side of the practice, nor does it encourage the doctor to find ways to increase production.

Percent of production

One advantage of production-based pay is that earnings are determined objectively and understood by all—they are not based on decisions made by the owners or practice manager. It is usually attractive to doctors because they see a ready way to increase income. Disadvantages are that the doctor loses the incentive to do anything but production work, may sacrifice time with client for volume of clients, and may use inappropriate sales tactics. Further, it leaves the owners with no clear-cut way to reward for excellence in non-production functions.

It can also result in some unfortunate staff-infighting. For example, a practice recently switched its doctors to a production-based compensation scheme and, in the case of one of the associates, it created a monster. One veterinarian ran amok. He routinely took the charts of all the drop-off patients and hid them on his desk until he had time to see them. He monopolized the walk-ins. He rechecked other doctors' patients. Clients and staff complained about the number and cost of procedures and medications prescribed for their pets. Income of the other associates dropped. Everyone seethed. What used to be a happy, helpful, cooperative work environment became a nightmare. The newly-put-on-production veterinarian ultimately backed off but only after several "frank" conversations with his colleagues and a threat from the owners to put him back on straight salary.

Combination of salary and production

The best compensation structure is one that rewards efforts in <u>all</u> areas. Combinations seem to be effective. There are several options:

- Percent of production for medical/surgical with flat salary for other activities

- Salary with automatic bonus
- Salary with production-based bonus: salary is initially calculated on approximate production and then modified for other activities; the bonus is based on production; benefits are given in addition to salary.
- Salary with bonus at owner's discretion: salary is initially calculated on approximate production; bonus based on whatever owner considers exemplary; benefits are given in addition to salary.

Issues in Calculating percent of production

- Whether percent includes or does not include benefits—benefits probably represent 2-3% of personal production.
- With a 100% production system, the production percent is usually higher than with a base salary plus production (example 22% vs. 20%).
- Period in which production is calculated——monthly or quarterly.
- How shortfalls are treated with a base system.
- What is included in production? If included, how does doctor get credit for refills and OTC products; prescription diets, heartworm medications, and flea/tick products.
- How to deal with services done by different doctors on same patient.

Owner Veterinarian Salaries

The compensation systems for owner veterinarians are different from that for associates in that they are more likely to be compensated explicitly for management duties, and they also benefit from the practice's profits.

Veterinarian owners typically have anywhere from three to five tiers of compensation, depending on the system used. Here is one example of a three-tiered system showing the resulting compensation.

- Tier I. Personal Production—a percentage of their medical and surgical services (the same issues apply for calculating the percent as for associates, above. (18-22% of production is standard)

- Tier II. Management—a percentage of gross revenues times the percent of total time spent in management activities such as strategic planning, financial planning and tracking, training and supervising employees, meeting with vendors, marketing and so on (generally 2-4% of gross divided amongst owners based on split of duties)

- Tier III. Return on Investment (ROI)—remaining profits.

The following chart shows how these three tiers would apply to a practice with two owner veterinarians:

Assumptions:

1. Gross revenues for practice = $500,000
2. Personal production for Dr. A = $250,000
3. Personal production for Dr. B = $200,000
4. Management duties split 50/50 based on 2% of gross revenues
5. Remaining profits after medicine/surgery earnings & management pay = $40,000
6. Profit is split 50/50

Component	Factor	Dr. A	Dr. B
Individual production	20%	$50,000	$40,000
Management	50% of 2%	$10,000	$10,000
Remaining profit	50%	$20,000	$20,000
Total		$80,000	$70,000

Support staff salaries and wages

In planning for support staff salaries, it is essential to consider the total compensation package including benefits, to ensure that this total comes within the limits of compensation money available in the practice.

Registered and certified veterinary technicians (RVTs and CVTs). Because these employees are specific to the veterinary profession, it is important that they are paid the local market rates in veterinary practices, remembering the recommendation that the pay should be in the upper 75th percentile of these local ranges in order to attract top quality.

Veterinary assistants and other technical workers. Although some of these staff members choose to work only in veterinary practices, others can work in a variety of different businesses, so it is harder here to determine an appropriate rate of pay. If workers are leaving/not accepting a position because the pay is too low, or if their quality is insufficient, then the pay scale is probably wrong.

Receptionists. These employees clearly have many work opportunities, and it is important to determine general area pay scales for receptionists.

Kennel staff. These workers also have other opportunities; it is probably most useful to determine what has historically been successful in the practice, and also what other veterinarians are paying.

Practice Manager Salary

The actual title for this position and the job responsibilities can vary greatly depending on the size of the hospital, and the philosophy of the owners. It can be called *practice administrator, hospital manager, office manager*, and so on. In the same way, it can be a heavy-duty management position that "runs" the practice, or it can be a clerical position, or something in between.

At its highest level of responsibility, a veterinary practice manager manages virtually all of the business activities of the hospital. This is highly beneficial because it frees the doctors for income-producing activities.

A Practice Manager's primary responsibilities frequently include:
- Staffing
    - Hiring and retaining employees capable of fulfilling assignments and achieving set objectives
    - Staff scheduling and organizing

- Developing and maintaining an employee handbook and employee files
- Mediating staff problems
- Oversee building, equipment, maintenance activities
- Ensuring high standards for client/staff relationships
- Preparing/supervising or contracting for preparation and maintenance of all financial records and activities
- Purchasing or supervising purchase of all supplies and equipment

Top-level Practice Managers are not easy to find, and their compensation should be carefully considered so that it encourages job satisfaction and retention. Because they can work in other types of businesses, it can be difficult to determine the right pay scale. Pay research should be a combination of what other practices of comparable size are paying, and what office managers and administrators with a similar scope of duties are paid.

Benefits

It is useful to plan for salary and benefits at the same time because they are both a part of the same program—employee compensation. The benefits program can be simple or complex, and will be influenced by the overall profitability of the practice, as well as the types of benefits that other comparable practices in the area offer. Looking at the total compensation package (salary and benefits), hospital owners will sometimes lower salaries overall in order to increase benefits, or vice versa.

Examples of benefits are:

- Annual vacation
- Sick leave/personal leave
- Paid legal holidays
- Medical/hospitalization insurance
- Liability insurance
- Continuing education
- Dues, registration and licenses

- Retirement plan

Less frequently offered are:
- Dental insurance
- Life insurance
- Disability insurance
- Pet health insurance
- "Cafeteria plan" benefits where employees have a certain amount of money to use for benefit and choose the benefits they want, within the plan offering.

Annual vacation

Basic issues to be determined are: the total vacation days per year; the increments in which vacation can be taken; employee eligibility; how the daily vacation pay rate is calculated; how vacation days are accrued; how vacation is scheduled and what happens to unused vacation upon termination.

According to AAHA's *Compensation & Benefits,* Second Edition, the average number of paid vacation days offered to full-time employees increases with length of employment. Staff members start with about seven paid vacation days and get a maximum of about fifteen. Associates start with an additional two days and max out at sixteen.

Sick leave/personal leave

Basic issues to be determined are: whether to track separately or together; total days per year; increments in which it can be taken; employee eligibility; how the daily sick leave/personal leave pay rate is calculated; how days are accrued; how days are scheduled; the notification process when an employee want to use days; and termination and unused days.

AAHA's *Compensation & Benefits,* Second Edition notes that approximately 55% of full-time and 10-15% of part-time veterinary practice employees receive paid sick days.

Paid Legal Holidays

Basic issues to be determined are: which holidays will be observed; employee eligibility; how the daily holiday pay rate is calculated; how emergency coverage is handled; how hospital coverage is handled, and; the policy for religious holidays.

Almost all practices close their practices and pay employees for six major holidays per year, according to AAHA's *Compensation & Benefits,* Second Edition.

Medical/Hospitalization Insurance

It goes without saying that health insurance is complex, and a good agent is an absolute necessity. It is valuable to talk with other veterinarians in the area to determine their satisfaction with both their agent and their plan. Basic issues to be determined are: types of plans available; selecting the most appropriate plan for the practice; determining who pays the employee premium; specific tax deductions for employers and savings for employees; and employee eligibility.

According to AAHA's *Compensation & Benefits,* Second Edition, 74% of full-time associates, 67% of full-time managers and 70% of full-time staff are offered health insurance. The mean percentage of the insurance premium paid by the practice for those same groups is 89%, 82% and 80%.

Liability Insurance

As with all insurance, this is complex and should be purchased with some care. Basic issues to be determined are: size of coverage needed; scope and coverage of the insurance purchased (independent contractors, coverage in off-hours, what is not covered); who pays the premium; how the claim is settled.

It is noted in AAHA's *Compensation & Benefits,* Second Edition, that 81% of the practices pay this insurance for associates.,

Continuing Education

A strong Continuing Education (CE) program is essential to a successful practice, and must be planned with care to ensure that the right people get the right CE. A wide variety of activities and programs can be classified as Continuing Education: publications, in-house seminars, local seminars, seminars requiring travel and lodging, internet-based courses, certification training, and so on. Basic issues to be determined are the categories of CE allowable; the CE allowance; the number of CE days allowed per year (taking state and national requirements into account); employee eligibility; the process for scheduling/approval; written contract for the coverage and reimbursement policy; travel and tuition expense allowances.

AAHA's *Compensation & Benefits,* Second Edition provides data on Continuing Education, noting that for full-time employees, 81% of associates, 63% of managers, 72% of technicians and 56% of staff are offered CE allowances. 25% or fewer part-time employees receive an allowance. In regard to paying employees for CE days, over half of the practices surveyed reported paying full-time associates, managers and technicians for CE days taken.

Dues, Registration And Licenses

Basic issues to be determined are the items to include; employee eligibility and how much of the license or registration should be paid by the practice.

As a useful benchmark, AAHA's *Compensation & Benefits,* Second Edition notes that practices pay license fees for full-time employees as follows: 65% for associates, 18% for managers and 40% for technicians. Only about a third of the practices pay these fees for part-time employees.

For professional association dues, 68% of the practices pay them for full-time associates, 23% for full-time managers, and 38% for full-time technicians. 71% of the practices do not pay them for part-time employees.

Retirement Plans

Retirement plans are increasingly offered in veterinary practices and are often an important factor in the employment decision. They are extremely complex and require the services of an agent. As with health insurance, it is wise to check with other veterinarians to determine their satisfaction with both plans and agents. Basic issues to be determined are: types of plans available; the most appropriate plan for the practice; employer/employee portion of the premium; vesting; and employee eligibility.

AAHA's *Compensation & Benefits,* Second Edition reports that two-thirds of the practices responding to its survey offer a retirement plan to their employees. Of these, over one-third offered the SIMPLE IRA, which was the plan offered most frequently. 25% offered SEP (Simplified Employee Pension), 14% offered profit sharing, and 13% the 401(k).

The Importance of Communicating Benefits to Employees

It is essential that employees know the value of their benefits. Frequently they don't realize the monetary value of what they are receiving—many employees do not understand that vacation, sick leave and holiday are "benefits" that have a specific (and large) cost to the owners of the practice. Every employee should receive an itemized annual statement, as is the example below:

Wage and Benefit Summary				
Your wage based on hours worked: $17,050/yr or $10.75 /hour				
Company benefits provided the following:				
Bonuses (if same as last year) will add:	$524	/yr or	$0.33	/ hour worked
Health insurance adds:	$2,810	/yr or	$1.77	/ hour worked
Uniform Allowance adds:	$80	/yr or	$0.05	/ hour worked
Paid Time Off adds:	$1,397	/yr or	$0.88	/ hour worked
Pet Care Benefits adds:	$367	/yr or	$0.23	/ hour worked
Annual Pet Preventative Care adds:	$350	/yr or	$0.22	/ hour worked
Continuing Education & Dues adds:	$114	/yr or	$0.07	/ hour worked
Total Company Benefits add:	**$5,117**	**/yr or**	**$3.56**	**/ hour worked**
Cost of your Salary and Company Benefits: $22,168 /yr or $14.31 /hour				
Mandated benefits cost the following:				
Social Security Contribution adds:	$1,144	/yr or	$0.72	/ hour worked
Medicare Contribution adds:	$267	/yr or	$0.17	/ hour worked
Worker's Compensation adds:	$443	/yr or	$0.28	/ hour worked
Unemployment adds:	$240	/yr or	$0.15	/ hour worked
Total Mandated Benefits add:	**$2,094**	**/yr or**	**$1.32**	**/ hour worked**
Cost of Salary + Practice and Mandated Benefits: $24,261 /yr or $15.63 /hour				
Company and Mandated Benefits increased your base wage cost by: 45.4%				

Literature Cited

American Animal Hospital Association: *Compensation & Benefits*, Second Edition. AAHA Press, Lakewood, Colorado, 2002.

[Editor's Note: This chapter reflects the current state of compensation and benefits in the industry. A major challenge facing the profession is the adoption of new models of compensation that more fairly reward associates, staff, and owners for their relative contributions towards the success of practices. As veterinarians face competitive pressures for retail sales, pharmaceutical dispensing, and even laboratory testing, these new models will need to provide incentives on the basis of value-added contributions to the practice. This is a wonderful opportunity for the profession to grow beyond its current limitations, and to embrace alternatives to the current economic paradigm.]—Lowell Ackerman DVM DACVD MBA MPA

GETTING PAID FOR SERVICES RENDERED

Lowell Ackerman DVM DACVD MBA MPA

Dr. Lowell Ackerman is a Diplomate of the American College of Veterinary Dermatology and in addition holds an MBA from the University of Phoenix and an MPA from Harvard University. He is involved in clinical practice as a clinical assistant professor at Tufts University School of Veterinary Medicine as well as helping to develop the business skills curriculum there. In addition, Dr. Ackerman is affiliated with Veterinary Healthcare Consultants LLC–a national consulting firm dedicated to providing innovative and resourceful business solutions for veterinary professionals and humane organizations. His primary business interests include leadership, team building, customer relationship management, strategic planning, Total Quality Management, profit center development, veterinary fee issues, marketing, promotion, action planning, and performance measurement. Dr. Ackerman developed the BARK^{sm} system for performance evaluation of veterinary practices.

Dr. Ackerman is the author/co-author of 75 books to date (including Business Basics for Veterinarians) and numerous book chapters and articles. He lectures extensively, on an international basis. Dr. Ackerman is a member of the American Animal Hospital Association, the American Veterinary Medical Association, the Association of Veterinary Practice Management Consultants & Advisors, the American Society of Journalists and Authors, and the Association of Veterinary Communicators.

Veterinary medicine is also veterinary business and it is not enough just to provide excellent service, but to also receive prompt payment for this exemplary service. In fact, even the very best customer service and excellent medical care will lead to practice failure if they don't result in commensurate revenues. It is expensive to practice high-quality veterinary medicine, to hire and keep the best employees, to keep up with new developments and receive continuing education, to constantly improve the tools used in the practice, and to heighten the skills employed by doctors and staff in that practice. Accordingly, getting paid for the services you offer is every bit as important as the quality of customer service and medical care that you provide.

There are many strategies for assuring revenues and some of the most effective are those most underutilized by practices. All have the same underlying premise–practice excellent medicine, keep the client informed at all times about medical and cost issues, and EXPECT payment for services rendered. This may seem straightforward, but too many practices invest heavily in staff and equipment, deliver excellent service, and then seem to find any excuse possible not to have the client pay for it. Sometimes there is a mental block about large bills, about crossing an imaginary boundary between reasonable and unreasonable amounts. Then there is the argument about a doctor's perceived inadequacies, about charging for tests that more experienced veterinarians might not need to run, that costs for veterinary care must be discounted to the public (after all, it's only an animal...right?) or running tests for the veterinarian's benefit so not charging the client (because that would be inappropriate, or so the argument goes).

It is a fact of life that providing excellent medical care is a costly enterprise. Not being able to collect on that provision of excellent medical care is a costly mistake that few veterinarians can afford.

Establishing policies for prompt payment and not being apologetic for veterinary charges is a good place to start. If fees have been established with value pricing or cost-plus pricing in mind, there are no apologies to be made. Things are costly today. Medicine is expensive; cars are expensive; a good cup of coffee is expensive. Nobody but veterinarians seems to be apologizing, or taking global responsibility for holding down charges. Imagine going into a Starbucks, or a Mercedes dealership, and saying you want the product but not the price. Also, although a car dealership may, in fact, offer financing, be assured that you are paying for it, and that you won't even get it unless you qualify for it.

What about veterinary medicine? Say you are a pet owner and just bought a new pup from a pet store. It's not even a purebred and you paid $800 for it because that is the price that you were quoted, the sales clerk was not prepared to lower the price, and so you believe that is the value of the animal. You take that pup to your neighborhood veterinary hospital and they are prepared to perform an ovariohysterectomy for $200–including the time and expertise of a veterinary doctor, her staff, full general anesthesia, use of the operating room, monitoring equipment, and a night of hospitalization. Is that really possible?

The result of such an experience is that the ridiculously low price of the spay has set a benchmark for the cost of veterinary surgery in the mind of the customer and reinforced in the client's mind that the veterinarian believes it is his/her job to subsidize the health care of animals. This is not a lecture on fees, though, but rather a primer on how to get paid for services rendered. The approach to be explored is thus how to provide "value" to clients for the services provided, and a variety of techniques to ensure that clients do pay for the value that they receive.

Guide to Getting Paid

Don't "pre-decide" for clients

Many veterinarians are not comfortable with the notion of charging what might be considered large sums of money for the care that is provided and this may interfere with the process of getting paid by "pre-deciding" what a client can afford. Not only is this "profiling" discriminatory, but also it is an injustice to the client and how they would choose to care for their pet.

If the argument of discrimination is not powerful enough, many states are now toying with laws that consider pets more than chattel, and permit legal awards for more than just replacement value. In this instance, not offering the best care to clients could end up costing you in court. Be honest in your appraisal, offer the service that is in the best interest of the client and patient, and then let the owner decide what they can afford. No veterinarian ever got in trouble for offering the best health care possible. The same cannot be said for those who decided to take it upon themselves to decide what the client could or could not afford. Don't worry. If a client cannot afford your recommendations, they will let you know.

Will clients really pay for veterinary services? According to the 2002 AAHA National Pet Owner Survey, 47% say there's no limit on what they would spend for veterinary care. In fact, 41% of clients had spent over $500 on veterinary care during the previous year, 23% having spent over $1,000. Veterinarians should clearly and honestly explain all aspects and risks of the case, and then stand back and let clients make up their own minds.

Expect Payment

It sounds obvious that veterinary practice is a cash business, but many clients are left with the impression that veterinary medicine comes with easy payment terms. They must have gotten that notion from somewhere. The easiest way to deal with the issue is to make payment terms obvious from the very first visit and stick with established policies. If you take your car in for needed repairs, nobody offers discounts, payment plans, or is apologetic for the costs involved. It's just a fact of doing business. Why should veterinary medicine be any different? If you are embarrassed about talking about money issues with clients–get over it! While you can always foist the responsibility on receptionists or technicians, if you have trouble talking about fees, then both clients and staff will get the impression that you don't feel they are justified. Chances are that if you are embarrassed about the fees that you don't have a good enough idea about the costs of running a veterinary practice. Read the other chapters of this book, and the ones in "Business Basics for Veterinarians" and you will get a new appreciation of just what a bargain veterinary medicine is to clients, and how extremely reasonable the fees actually are.

To make things convenient, practices should accept cash, checks (with verification) and credit/debit cards. That puts them in the same class as any other retail service. Go even farther with credit plans such as CareCredit that will provide financing for clients in need. If a client is turned down for financing by such an agency, accept the fact that the client is not creditworthy. Too many veterinarians resort to making payment terms for clients that are denied credit, reinforcing the misconception that veterinarians are in the business of financing those that are poor credit risks. In most cases, veterinarians don't even take down a credit report for the client, or charge extra for financing. While all clients should be treated with respect and all animals deserve humane treatment, veterinarians should not dabble in financing the needs of clients.

It is also important to be able to provide services for truly indigent clients. In some communities, medical care will be available from a non-profit agency, but if enough clients in your area need financial help with their veterinary costs, there are methods that allow this without requiring veterinarians to subsidize that care themselves. For large hospitals, either creating a non-profit foundation, or affiliating with an existing non-profit agency to create one, may be an answer. However, veterinarians involved with such a foundation will learn what non-profit animal hospitals have known for years–that there is a big difference between that client that is unable to pay, and the ones that actually have the resources but choose not to pay for veterinary services. In any case, having a charitable foundation offers more than just care for the needy. It provides an avenue for veterinarians to direct clients that say that they can't afford veterinary care (even if they can). Most non-profits perform fairly rigorous means testing to determine who should receive funding, and this removes the veterinarian from the role of feeling they need to give a break to every client that pleads poverty.

Provide value

Elsewhere in this book you will read about giving clients what they want most and, if you do, you'll find that clients are not hesitant to pay for it. Most consumers are value shoppers, not price shoppers. They may not have a lot of brand loyalty to products that they believe are commodities, but they are often fiercely protective of brands they perceive as having value–and this includes veterinary services. The other good thing about value is that it is independent of cost. The price of a Rolex has little to do with the costs associated with making a watch, and the price of veterinary service has little to do with the commodities used in the service. Once you realize this fundamental truth, getting paid is not nearly as much of a challenge.

When we provide valued service, clients want to pay for it because they perceive the value delivered. There is a very strong human need for reciprocity, or *quid pro quo*. When we do a favor for someone, we anticipate that they will reciprocate. If they fail to do so when we believe it would be appropriate, we feel slighted. While we cannot control what other individuals do, relationships are strengthened in the vast majority of instances simply by doing favors for others. It is even more effective when these favors are not done in anticipation of immediate payback, because that need to reciprocate is often strong in individuals, and spans time as well as space.

What sorts of things convey value to clients? Read the chapter on "giving clients what they want most", but sometimes clients just need to know that the people caring for their pets are compassionate. The doctor who takes the time to call after surgery, just to say that everything went well. The technician, who trims the toenails of a pet while it is anesthetized and doesn't even mention or charge for the service. The assistant who spends a little extra time with a hospitalized patient, and realizes that this animal is somebody's beloved family member. The receptionist who recognizes a client (and their pet) by sight, and seems honestly glad to see them. In this kind of practice, isn't it obvious why value is independent of cost?

Avoid Surprises

Nobody likes surprises where they end up owing more money than they expected. This is a problem regardless of the industry. Keeping the lines of communication open, and setting payment points that correspond to milestones in the treatment-to-discharge pathway are the best ways to minimize these kinds of surprises.

For all procedures performed, there should be standard estimates, and the practice should have established standards of care so that patients are recommended equivalent services with equivalent fees, and an equivalent payment policy. It is also important to have appropriate waivers that apprise clients of possible adverse consequences of procedures so that clients may provide informed consent. Taking the time to get informed consent goes a long way to minimizing the trauma when things go wrong, and also being able to collect for additional procedures that might be necessary when things go wrong.

Similarly, it is important that clients appreciate the total costs involved in the process, so that they can plan accordingly. In some cases, pre-charging the client may actually make the process more palatable, and easier to budget. For instance, if you are going to start immunotherapy (allergy shots) for a patient, pre-charge for the entire series of injections to be given. Then the client can just schedule a technician appointment, come in for the injections, and not be held up having to pay something at each visit. If a patient is having a surgical procedure and a recheck appointment is mandatory, build that into the estimate and the amount collected upon discharge, so that the client does not need to pay again at the re-examination visit. This not only makes it easier for the client to budget, but greatly increases compliance as well. This is one instance in which "bundling" is actually good for the client and the practice.

Spread the Charges

There are ways to provide excellent service without charging for everything all at once. Sometimes, it is possible to do some preliminary work first, and then have the client back for follow-up work. This allows clients the opportunity to better budget for these services. For example, if a client needs a dental "prophy" but doesn't have the money to have everything done the same day, consider collecting blood for a pre-anesthetic profile and scheduling the procedure for some time in the near future. This alone may be sufficient to allow the client to say "yes" today, and without having to ask for a payment plan.

Another big charge that needn't appear on a bill that already seems challenging is that for pharmaceuticals. With many of the medications used today, there is considerable expense, and this is sometimes difficult to justify to clients who may believe that you are charging too much for these medications. There are alternatives. One of the best is to use an online service like VetCentric where clients can purchase the product according to your specified fee schedule and the product is shipped to them directly. This not only saves on inventory costs, but the bill from the veterinary practice is actually lighter because drug charges have been unbundled. Another alternative is to write a prescription and allow clients to get their medications from a pharmacy. If the thought of losing pharmaceutical revenue is disturbing, charge a one-time prescription registration charge for each new prescription. Once again, the end result is that the client pays for medical services at the veterinary hospital and the medications elsewhere. The result is that the veterinary bill will be less and the client more able to pay it.

Insurance

Pet insurance has been around for over 20 years, and it is embarrassing that only about one-half of one percent of pets in the United States are protected by it. Of course, not all forms of insurance are worthwhile, and many are not really even insurance policies at all; some are discount plans and others are buying clubs. However, true indemnity insurance is alive and well and available for pet owners across the country. Somehow a myth has been perpetuated in the industry that insurance is bad and will end up dictating what veterinarians can charge. This hasn't happened, and with true indemnity insurance, there is no reason why this needs to happen.

Indemnity insurance compensates individuals for loss or damage. Veterinarians are not agents for the company, do not receive commissions, and do not typically collect directly from the insurance company. The process is third-party payment in its purest form–the client pays the veterinary bill and submits documentation to the insurance company for reimbursement.

In pet insurance, a client pays a premium to purchase an insurance policy on their pet that compensates them for health care costs. The actuarially fair premium is the portion of the premium that the insurance company expects to pay out. If the insurance company didn't charge more than this, it would not be able to cover its administrative costs and would go out of business (as many pet insurance companies have done). The policy must also carry a risk premium, which is the insurance company's reward for bearing a client's risk for them. Why is this important to veterinarians?

In most cases, we buy insurance to cover us in case losses are more than we can comfortably cover. Most people are risk-averse and prefer certainty of protection against risk rather than gambling on outcomes. Owners need pet insurance because a single hospitalization, a visit to a specialist, or an emergency can end up costing thousands of dollars. The average American cannot cover this unexpected expense with what they have in their checking accounts, or the credit available on their credit cards.

It is interesting that there often seems to be a disconnect between veterinary impressions and those of clients. Pet health insurance, especially true indemnity insurance, is woefully underutilized, not because clients don't see the utility of it, but because veterinarians often don't. If clients appreciated that a trip to an emergency clinic, a referral to a specialist, or treatment for a serious condition could cost them thousands of dollars, they'd be clamoring for a way to manage their risk. It is typically at this juncture, faced with a large, unanticipated expense that clients ask why their veterinarians never told them about pet insurance. When clients perceive that their annual veterinary bills will typically always be less than $200, it is hard to justify the insurance premium. If clients were aware that the prices that veterinarians charge for a spay (ovariohysterectomy) are not representative of typical surgeries, and that animals often require some very expensive intervention at some occasions during their lives, then insurance would be a more common way of clients to afford proper veterinary care. The bonus for veterinarians would be that when clients have insurance, they are much less resistant to having a problem appropriately managed, and can afford to do so.

Documentation & Education

Veterinary medicine, like all forms of health care, is an expensive undertaking. Most consumers are hesitant to spend money on things that they don't understand, so client education is critical if we expect clients to eagerly pay for the services we offer. In addition, there are also family members at home that may not have been present when the explanation was given in the office, so documentation is important if we want clients to be able to explain the needs for health care to other interested parties at home, especially if those individuals are important to giving consent for procedures to be done and bills to be paid.

For example, video endoscopic units have been extremely valuable in providing photographic images that can be shared with clients. Imagine the advantages of explaining the management of sarcoptic mange to clients and sending them home with a picture of the mites that you just took through your microscope. It's not only great at getting consent, but works wonders for compliance as well. The imaging technology can also be used to take clinical photographs, reproduce features on radiographs for owners to take home, and be used to take endoscopic images in areas that clients might not otherwise be able to see (ear canal and tympanum, oral cavity, rectum, nares, etc.). Anything that we can share with clients that help them to understand the medical process and the costs involved makes them better prepared to advocate for proper medical care in their discussions at home. In the same vein, taking "before" and "after" pictures help assure owners that their money was well spent.

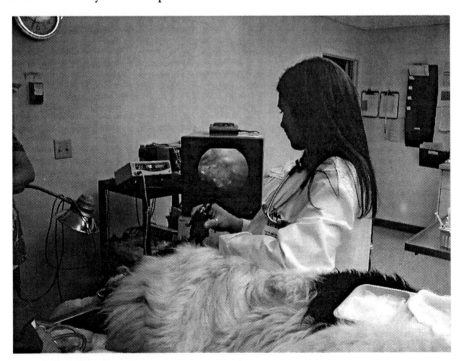

Avoid Discounts and Coupons

Unless you are also selling pizza in your practice, there is no need for discounts and coupons. While everyone likes to save money, most businesses that have introduced discounts and coupons have found it very difficult to get customers to then spend at the non-discounted rates again. When giants such as McDonald's and Burger King are battling each other to see who loses more money on "value" meals, where is the incentive for veterinarians to start?

Offering discounts does not make it more likely for clients to pay their bills. However, it does make it more likely that they won't want to pay non-discounted bills in the future, and that's a bad thing for veterinary practices.

Discounting may seem like a way of getting new clients in the door, but what it really does is create an expectation that services will always be provided at bargain basement rates. All across the country, businesses are trying to deal with the new world order that customers have come to expect that they rarely need to pay retail for products; they prefer to wait for a sale. Veterinary medicine is not a commodity, and therefore there is no need for a sale. If you concentrate on delivering value, you are already giving your clients what they want most, so why would you even consider discounting?

To keep the mathematics simple, let's investigate what happens when a practice that performs 10,000 client transactions a year and has an average transaction of $100, decides to offer a 20% discount that applies to 25% of the client base. Assuming that expenses are 80% of undiscounted revenues (i.e., 20% profit), the practice brings in $1 million in revenues and has $800,000 in expenses. The net profit is $200,000 on revenues of $1,000,000, a profit margin of 20%. If the practice enacts a 20% discount policy on 2,500 client transactions (25% of 10,000), revenues are now $950,000 with the same overhead of $800,000 (the laboratory, drug distributors, and pet food suppliers did not extend you the same discount that you gave to your clients), giving a net profit of $150,000 rather than $200,000 and a profit margin of 15% rather than 20%. In fact, you managed to cut your net profit by 25% (from $200,000 to $150,000) with that 20% discount!

Since most veterinary practices are already charging less than they should for services, discounting rarely has the effect that is envisioned—that of increasing profits. On the contrary, for many practices, increasing fees by 20% will have a much more positive effect on net profit, even if some clients leave the practice because of them.

Let's say that we raised fees by 20% and by such action we actually scared away 15% of our clients. Surely that would be catastrophic to our bottom line. Let's see. Now, instead of seeing 10,000 client transactions, the price increase has caused the practice to only see 8,500 transactions, with an average transaction charge of $120 ($100+20%). Revenues are now $1,020,000 and expenses are still $800,000 (although it is probably less than that because there are fewer clients to serve), providing $220,000 net profit. Why would we possibly consider discounting?

Provide Unique Services

The key to value pricing is to avoid commoditization. Commoditization is a big word, but it means the difference between breakthrough profits and me-too sustenance. Products that are commodities are pretty much the same as those sold everywhere and therefore it is hard to charge more than anyone else for the same product. If you decided to buy a specific brand and model of television, you'd buy it from the store that offered the best price and terms. Because the product is a commodity and virtually identical no matter which store you select, the stores are forced to compete with one another on the basis of price and terms. Add Internet venues and this competition forces the price down to a level that is barely profitable for any of the stores. The customer gets a good deal, but no loyalty was built in the process. The next time they want something, the search resumes for the outlet that will offer the best price and terms.

While veterinary medicine has some "shoppable" services that might be considered commodities (e.g., neutering, vaccination, product sales, etc.), practices should endeavor to minimize their reliance on commodities and instead build their practices on the basis of unique services and experiences. Excellent customer service is the best cure for commoditization, and the only thing necessary to make commodity pricing irrelevant. If you think that it's hard to beat commodity pricing in veterinary medicine, you should truly appreciate the hurdles that Starbucks had to overcome to charge premium prices for a very real commodity–coffee. If you offer even a commodity with a novel consumer-friendly approach, you will build a loyal following. If clients feel that they can get veterinary services elsewhere, but not with the same quality or experience that they have come to expect with you, they will show brand loyalty and pay the going rate for that experience.

The best way to ensure getting paid is to have clients feel that they could not get what you offer by going elsewhere.

Make clients active partners in their pets' health care

The one great thing about medicine is that there are always options and alternatives for getting things done. To be hardnosed and definitive is not being the best advocate for clients and their pets. Being adversarial also means that clients are less likely to willingly pay for your expertise and service, and value it less. The interesting aspect of this is that some options, that might at first seem to be less profitable, might end up being more profitable. For example, it wasn't that long ago that if a client suggested skipping a year between vaccines that most veterinarians would have lectured them that annual vaccines are the mainstay of infectious disease prevention and that evidence clearly demonstrates that they must be given yearly. What evidence? The fact is that veterinary medicine needs more evidence-based studies to support common practices. Should a Chihuahua receive the same dose of vaccine as a Great Dane?

Having these kinds of discussions with owners builds loyalty and creates a framework in which owners are considered part of the health care team rather than just the entity (and sometimes an annoying entity at that) that pays the bills. Of course, as the health care professional in the partnership, it is important to use factual information where needed. The client that suggests that using an antibiotic at half the effective dose for twice the typical duration (because the full dose causes digestive upset, for example) poses an interesting question, but one that can be countered with available evidence. In any case, creating a team approach to a pet's health care issues is one of the best ways to ensure that the client will willingly pay for those services. After all, they helped plan them!

Recommended Reading

Ackerman, L: Business Basics for Veterinarians. ASJA Press, 2002

Consumer Reports Investigations: Veterinary Care Without the Bite. Consumer Reports, 2003; 68(7): 12-17.

Heinke, ML; McCarthy, JB: Practice made Perfect. A Guide to Veterinary Practice Management. AAHA Press, Lakewood Colorado, 2001, 459pp.

Opperman, M: The Art of Veterinary Practice Management. Veterinary Medicine Publishing Group, Lenexa Kansa, 1999, 248pp.

Stowe, JD: Effective Veterinary Practice. Lifelearn, Guelph, Ontario, 2001, 412pp.

PRACTICING PROFITABLY

Lowell Ackerman DVM DACVD MBA MPA

Dr. Lowell Ackerman is a Diplomate of the American College of Veterinary Dermatology and in addition holds an MBA from the University of Phoenix and an MPA from Harvard University. He is involved in clinical practice as a clinical assistant professor at Tufts University School of Veterinary Medicine as well as helping to develop the business skills curriculum there. In addition, Dr. Ackerman is affiliated with Veterinary Healthcare Consultants, LLC–a national consulting firm dedicated to providing innovative and resourceful business solutions for veterinary professionals and humane organizations. His primary business interests include leadership, team building, customer relationship management, strategic planning, Total Quality Management, profit center development, veterinary fee issues, marketing, promotion, action planning, and performance measurement. Dr. Ackerman developed the BARK^{sm} system for performance evaluation of veterinary practices.

Dr. Ackerman is the author/co-author of 75 books to date (including Business Basics for Veterinarians) and numerous book chapters and articles. He lectures extensively, on an international basis. Dr. Ackerman is a member of the American Animal Hospital Association, the American Veterinary Medical Association, the Association of Veterinary Practice Management Consultants & Advisors, the American Society of Journalists and Authors, and the Association of Veterinary Communicators.

Operating a veterinary practice is an expensive proposition. Because of this fact, charges to clients must be enough not only to cover expenses, but to provide a return on money invested as well.

Here's a scenario that illustrates the point well. Suppose you had a million dollars, and were deciding whether to buy an existing veterinary practice or invest in the stock market. Here are our assumptions.

- The stock market has historically returned about 10% annually

- Your earning power as a veterinarian should be about $100,000 annually.

- If you buy the practice, after paying everyone else and all other practice bills, there is $100,000 left for you.

So, which is a better investment—investing $1 million in a stock market index fund for an average return of $100,000 a year, or buying a veterinary clinic for $1 million and drawing $100,000 a year for your salary after all expenses have been paid. If you think that the choice is about even, and many veterinary students and new graduates do, then let's take a minute or two to explore why the choices aren't even close, and why it's a good thing that you are reading this chapter.

The truth is that if you invest in a practice and it pays you as much as you could make elsewhere, then your effective return on investment is…zero! Look at it this way. If you invested in the stock market index and your return was $100,000, you could still be practicing elsewhere as an associate and making $100,000. Your revenues would amount to $200,000 a year. The way to judge return on investment for the practice is to judge how much profit is left if you had to hire someone else to perform your functions at the hospital (both clinical and management). In this case, if you invested a million dollars in the practice and had to pay an associate $100,000 to work in it, then given our previous assumptions, there wouldn't be any profit left over for you at the end of the year. Unfortunately, too many veterinarians *invest* in veterinary practices, only to provide themselves with a place to work.

Some veterinarians might make the argument that they will recoup their investment when they sell their practices, and this might be a legitimate argument except that practice sales rarely offer much of a payback these days. Even corporate consolidators have cut way back on buying practices, because they just haven't been able to make the acquisitions profitable. How about if the practice also owns the land on which it is located? This was a good investment, but in most instances, the land can be more profitably used by businesses other than veterinary hospitals so, once again, the value of the practice must be heavily discounted to make the sale to somebody who wants to continue running the veterinary hospital. You would have been as far ahead buying the land and not building a veterinary hospital on it. The lesson to be learned—don't expect a big payout on the sale of the practice. It is only worth the present value of the profitable fraction of anticipated future cash flows. If the practice growth has been slow-paced, stagnant, or decreasing, then the value as an investment is very low indeed.

How much profit is profit enough?

The answer to this question is not as difficult as you might think. In any investment, your best choice is always the one that provides the best returns, accounting for the risk involved. This is often referred to as the opportunity cost. The opportunity cost of an investment is the next best option that you would be forsaking. In the example provided, the opportunity cost of investing in the practice and earning a salary only ($100,000) and no effective return on investment is working as an associate for $100,000 AND earning $100,000 on average in a stock market index fund. Clearly, working as an associate and investing the money would be a better choice. If you believed that the risk in the stock market was about the same as the risk in owning a veterinary practice, the practice would need to pay you a salary for your clinical/management duties of $100,000 AS WELL AS a return on your million-dollar investment of 10% ($100,000) for the two to be even remotely equivalent. Even given this scenario, most would argue that you are better to invest in the stock market index fund than invest in the veterinary practice in which you plan to work. While working in your own practice, you have all your investment eggs in one basket, and this is poor diversification indeed. No, if the practice is to be your main investment, then it must return significantly higher than the passive investment in the stock market. After all, if you become incapacitated and can't work in the practice, the stock market keeps ticking along without you. If the stock market rises or falls, for the most part it does so independently of your earnings in the practice.

Each person must determine their own opportunity cost of investing in a practice, but if it is to be an investment as well as a workplace for a veterinarian, then the return on investment must be significantly higher than the 10% anticipated return of the stock market. Also, do not factor in a potential re-sale windfall for when you decide to sell the practice. If it comes, consider it a bonus. Given the inherent risks of such an investment, expecting a return on investment of 20-40% or more is not being greedy–it is just reflecting the risk-adjusted return on investment.

How do I practice to make that kind of profit?

Veterinary medicine will be experiencing many changes in the coming years, and so profitable practices are adjusting to those changes now.

Many practices have seriously limited their profit potential by having veterinarians playing too many roles within the hospital. When veterinarians collect their own blood samples, hold animals for radiographs, or do any other technical duties, they provide expensive services for which there can be no adequate compensation. After all, would you pay more for your gasoline if a medical professional pumped it? Every time veterinarians perform duties that could be more cost effectively done by paraprofessionals, they are eating into practice profits.

Another practice that is very limiting in a profit perspective for veterinarians is the notion of seeing only one client at a time and taking care of their needs completely before moving on the to next appointment. This evolved from the old agrarian model of dealing with livestock, but small animal medicine should actually have much more in common with human medicine or dentistry. In these professions, a doctor's time is leveraged by staff to be able to see many more clients in a day than the typical veterinarian. To accomplish this in the veterinary profession, it will be necessary to convince veterinarians that they really don't need to be involved in every step in the health care process. This is a difficult mindset to overcome for some veterinarians, even though they rationally understand that this is the model on which the human primary care health system is based. If they can be convinced to train and to trust their paraprofessional staff, then profits are enhanced just by the efficient and appropriate use of human assets.

For most veterinary practices, the examination rooms are the most profitable part of the hospital. Still, many veterinarians invest in new gadgets and the training to use them in the hopes of increasing practice profits. Unfortunately, this purchase is rarely made on the basis of sound financial analysis and typically does not dramatically increase profits. For example, buying internal fixation equipment might allow you to perform orthopedic surgery, but typically not at the quality level of a board-certified surgeon, not for the fees that a surgeon could charge, not in a time frame that is cost effective, and not with the experience to handle post-operative complications. Chances are that if the primary care veterinarian could see just one more case a day and referred all orthopedic cases, they would be practicing infinitely more profitably.

Another impediment to profitable practice, and one that is a touchy subject for veterinarians is the concept of bundling. Too many practices are "bundling" charges to clients, trying to recoup professional fees in pharmaceutical revenues, laboratory charges, radiology, retail sales and anything else they can find. This is a mistake, since the most profitable aspect of practice is the value-added contributions of veterinary professionals, not markups. Do clients notice? If they didn't before, they will. If you don't believe that, check out the July 2003 issue of Consumer Reports in which the investigative report "Veterinary Care Without the Bite" recommends not buying prescription medications or flea & tick products from veterinarians, getting estimates from 2-3 veterinarians on all procedures, and for clients to question the need for laboratory and imaging studies. The report repeatedly cites inappropriate markups by veterinarians.

The investigative report could be regarded as muckraking, except that there are some truths to the allegations. For example, it is not unusual for veterinarians to double or even triple laboratory costs and pharmaceutical sales to clients, trying to build professional profit into a retail markup. However, even though this is a common practice, it is really a professional conflict of interest, as well as being potentially illegal in some states. Why is it a conflict of interest? Say you are trying to decide whether to dispense a tablet that costs ten cents apiece, versus one that costs a dollar apiece. If you routinely double drug costs and you intend to dispense 100 of such tablets, you would make 10 times a much (2 x $100-$100 cost=$100) dispensing the expensive tablet as the cheap one (2 x $10-$10 cost=$10). If the client paid for your professional judgment in the office visit, then why should there be such an inequity in the dispensing of the drugs? Was there ten times the professional involvement in selecting the more expensive drug, or could inventory costs really account for that type of differential?

The same question applies to laboratory fees. If you use the same doubling calculation, you make more profit on expensive tests than cheap tests, even though the professional time associated with each may be similar. For example, if the laboratory charges $15 for a complete blood count (CBC) and $150 for an erythropoietin assay, the charge would be $30 (2 x $15) to the client for the cheaper test and $300 (2 x $150) for the more expensive one. Once again, did the value added by the veterinarian amount to ten times more ($150 profit) for the expensive test than the cheaper test ($15)? In at least some states, there is a legal requirement to pass along charges provided by outside laboratories without "marking up" the charges for which no real value was provided by the practice. While it might sound like discontinuing this practice will cost you profit, the converse is actually true. For example, instead of marking up laboratory costs from outside laboratories, pass this charge along to clients and instead charge for all the value-added components, such as venipuncture, interpretation, processing, etc. These are actually much more profitable to the practice. Also, without the markups, there is the opportunity to run more tests for the same money and increase the chances of actually making a correct diagnosis.

Value in Veterinary Health Care

Most veterinary practices aren't publicly traded, so it is sometimes difficult to see what the outside world values when looking at practice financial statements. Clearly, however, the assets that appear on the balance sheet do not reveal the true value in a practice. Missing are the intangible assets and relationships that make a practice vital and successful. On the other hand, many practices invest in tangible but relatively unproductive assets that may, in fact, destroy more value that they create. This model worked in a day when profit was determined by marketing a product or service at the lowest possible price. Today, when value determines marketability, it is the intangible assets, including staff (human capital), processes, and relationships with customers and suppliers that determine real value in the marketplace. Giniat and Libert, in Value Rx for Healthcare, propose a new framework that they call Value Dynamics that considers the organization and its relationship to customers, employees and suppliers, finances and physical assets. As true in veterinary medicine as in human medicine, overcapacity and advances in medical and information technologies are making physical assets less valuable, if not obsolete.

Another feature of veterinary medicine, and one that is necessary to remedy, is the notion that seeing the patient is an episodic event. Creating an ongoing relationship with clients through both physical and virtual channels is needed. After all, hospital comes from Medieval Latin for guest dwelling, the same root as hotel. Doctors of all descriptions will need to interface with their clients/patients on a more regular basis than an annual examination to meet the health care needs of clients, and to remain profitable.

The value chain is also an important concept largely ignored by veterinarians. It consists of all participants involved in delivering value to clients and is much more than just the doctor-client relationship. Employees are important, but so are suppliers and partners. While it may go unappreciated by some, a huge amount of retail traffic is driven to veterinary practices by pharmaceutical advertising. Newer flea and tick control products, available only through veterinarians, have especially contributed to retail practice revenues.

A Veterinary Value Chain

The advantage of looking at a value chain is that it is easier to see the points at which one can add value. For example, the veterinary health care delivery system typically involves people coming in for visits during a standard workday. This often causes problems, not just in terms of getting time off work, but potentially lost wages as well. How much might it be worth to a client to find an affordable alternative in delivery of service? Some look at clients' hectic schedules as practice inconveniences. Others see the profitable opportunities in providing solutions for client problems.

Understanding Profit

There is a lot of discussion about veterinary fees today, but the logical conclusion that all must reach is that there are only a few ways of making veterinary practices more profitable. If we can all agree that profit equals revenues minus expenses and that profit increases when the ratio of revenues to expenses increases, then clearly profit can increase with rising revenues or falling expenses, or a combination of the two. Let's take a closer look at these factors.

Increasing revenues can be accomplished by increasing the number of appointments seen or procedures performed, increasing the average client transaction, or a combination of the two. It is important to remember that this increases our *top line*, but expenses also need to be held in check to maintain our profitable *bottom line*.

The most efficient way of increasing revenues is to see more patients and to charge appropriately for those visits. In *Business Basics for Veterinarians*, I introduced the topic of elasticity of demand and its applications are important for running a practice profitably. To review the concept briefly, the price elasticity of demand is the percentage change in quantity demanded divided by the percentage change in price.

Price elasticity of demand = percentage change in quantity demanded
Percentage change in price

If changes in prices don't affect the quantity demanded much (absolute value of elasticity < 1), we say they are price inelastic. For example, if you were treating a diabetic cat with insulin, and you increased the price of insulin by 30%, do you think that there would be a significant decrease in the number of owners prepared to pay for the insulin for their pets? Not likely, and certainly not 30% of clients. If a percentage change in quantity demanded is greater than the percentage change in price, then demand is said to be price elastic.

The elasticity of demand for a particular good or service offers important clues regarding total revenues. If a good is price inelastic, you can increase revenues by raising price! Fortunately, most veterinary prices are relatively price inelastic. That is, if you raise your prices by 10%, you should expect that quantities demanded should drop by something less than 10%. That's why raising prices may scare away some clients, but total revenues tend to increase such that they more than compensate for lost quantity.

Let's illustrate with an example. Say you work in a practice that does 25 dental prophies a week at $150 each. That translates into $3,750 (25 x $150) of revenue weekly from dental prophylaxis in the practice. You've been told that the elasticity of demand for veterinary services is about-0.4, meaning that demand drops by 4% when you raise fees by 10%. Sure enough, you raise your fees be 10% to $165 and demand drops by 4%, so now the practice is only doing 24 prophies a week. Should the practice drop its price to attract back the clients they are no longer servicing? Not for financial reasons. Raising the prices to $165 did scare off 1 client a week, but led to revenues of $3,960 per week instead of $3,750, while doing one less procedure. You decide.

In addition to raising fees, we increase profits by increasing the number of services provided at each visit. For example, for more senior pets, it might be advisable to perform not only a clinical evaluation, but screen the pet with blood profiles, radiographs, and an electrocardiogram as well. Of course, it is important to only perform tests that provide true value for clients and pets, but we still have a long way to go in the profession in providing all of the services that pets really need.

The combination of charges and services provided during a visit result in a transaction charge for the client, and the average client transaction (ACT), sometimes referred to as the average transaction charge (ATC) or average transaction fee (ATF), provides a useful guide to the revenues anticipated per client visit.

As previously discussed, our *top line* can also be increased by seeing more appointments or doing more procedures in a typical work day. While this can be accomplished by hiring more veterinarians, it is an important consideration that the profession actually needs to more efficiently see more appointments by better leveraging paraprofessional staff. While veterinarians typically see one appointment at a time, and finish with that client before starting the next, this is both an inefficient and unprofitable method of health care delivery. Since many things done by veterinarians can be more cost effectively done by paraprofessional staff without sacrificing quality, veterinarians are often their worst enemies in this regard. In any case, veterinarians, like doctors and dentists, should be able to move between multiple rooms at a time providing consultations, greatly increasing the revenues per doctor for every shift worked.

We can improve the *top line* by increasing our average client transactions and increasing the number of clients served per doctor per shift, but profit is also determined by keeping expenses in check so our *bottom line* doesn't suffer. Once again, veterinarians are expensive, so making them work efficiently is one of the best ways of reigning in expenses. Hiring additional support staff so that veterinarians can do more of what they are being paid to do is typically the best and most profitable route to take.

Veterinarians should also be aware that high-priced gadgets may increase revenues, but usually do so at high cost. For example, unless you have a definite plan to utilize the expensive equipment routinely and with appropriate client charges, then don't expect this equipment to deliver nearly the profit potential as changing the way the practice operates. Typically, expensive equipment is more profitable in the hands of specialists, who have the opportunity to use that equipment more routinely and spread the expenses over clients from many different practices.

Products and Services

When all products are considered identical (e.g., a bag of Brand X dog food), these products become commodities and sellers become "price takers". There isn't much that can be done to "differentiate" their product from that offered at another veterinary clinic, or from a pet superstore. Everyone gets paid pretty much the same going rate, and competition has forced that rate lower. In small animal practice, much goes into adding value to services (hospital appearance, expertise of veterinarians, attention by staff, dedication to service, etc.) and so pricing for value-added services can be determined independently by practices and their clients.

For veterinarians and other service providers that are price-setters rather than price-takers, lessons from the retail marketplace are a great place to start. While you can't charge much of a premium on a commodity just because it is sold through a veterinary hospital, veterinarians still continue to try. The real profit to be made is in services, although veterinarians are increasingly banking on revenues from product sales. When was the last time you saw your own primary care physician selling products? In 1992, medical services accounted for 82% of veterinary revenues, with product sales providing 18%. By 1999, revenues from medical services dropped to 75%, while product sales increased to 25%. Unfortunately, product sales can disappear with any real competition (e.g., Internet, pet retail superstores, etc.) and are even very sensitive to competition from other veterinary clinics. Veterinarians had a windfall when manufacturers openly promoted flea/tick control and heartworm products directly to consumers that were only available through veterinarians. What do you think would happen to that revenue stream if those same or similar products started to become available over the Internet or in pet stores at a fraction of the price charged by veterinarians? It's happening today. The services that veterinarians perform allow them to be price-setters. The products that veterinarians sell are commodities, the profits from which could disappear in a heartbeat if the marketplace changed.

Veterinary Fees

Few practices are complete price-setters, immune to the pressures of the marketplace. In general, fees for goods and services do vary with:

- Location and client base
- Fees of competitors
- Actual costs
- Who's performing the service (specialist versus general practitioner)
- Perceived value by clients
- Industry "Standards?"

The subject of veterinary fees was covered in considerable detail in *Business Basics for Veterinarians*, and it is worth reviewing that information for a more complete discussion of the topic. Only an abbreviated synopsis will appear here.

How Fees are Currently Set

Most fees in veterinary hospitals are only very loosely cost-based. Most products on the shelf are priced at 2-3 times cost (a markup of 100-200%). Even at this figure, some products at this markup make lots of money, and some are relative money losers. Other fees are *benchmarked*, and excellent comparisons are available from the National Committee on Veterinary Economic Issues (www.ncvei.org) and in Financial & Productivity Pulsepoints (AAHA Press). Wutchiett & Associates also publishes a Well-Managed Practice Study in which service fees are represented as multiples of the examination fee.

Of course, the main problem with existing benchmarks is that they are based primarily on the same service model, and we have already determined that this model is fairly inefficient and unprofitable.

When setting prices for products or services, it is important to consider everything that should be a component of the final price. The equation should look like this:

Sales price = Overhead + Direct Labor + Materials + Profit +/- Commissions

Operating a veterinary hospital is an expensive undertaking. On the human side, most general practitioners function with only examination rooms and staff, which they leverage to see as many patients as possible with minimal overhead and materials charges. They don't hospitalize, they don't run the majority of their own laboratory work, they don't take radiographs, and often they don't even collect blood samples. Most veterinary hospitals, on the other hand, have surgeries, radiology departments, laboratories, kennels, rooms for special procedures, and lots of expensive gadgets.

When we look at the above list of reasons for charging fees, veterinarians tend to balance out their higher overhead with lower wages and poor return on investment. This isn't a fair exchange. Even when veterinarians are prepared to charge less for services and compensate themselves less than comparably trained professionals, the results of low fees are that technicians, assistants, receptionists and kennel attendants are also forced to accept low wages for the privilege of working in a veterinary hospital. Without fair fees and fair compensation, staff turnover becomes an issue and the quality of medical care suffers.

Profit Centers

The best way of matching hospital revenues to expenses is to develop profit centers within the hospital to which these costs can be allocated. Only by doing this can you actually determine which services within the hospital are truly profitable, and which ones are draining profits from other sectors. To do such a comparison, it is necessary to *allocate* ALL hospital expenses (overhead, labor, materials) to individual profit centers. Whenever possible, it is best to directly attribute expenses to the appropriate center (e.g., attributing all of the x-ray machine rent to the radiology profit center), but in other cases we need to *allocate* expenses in a more indirect fashion (e.g., rent, utilities, etc.). For example, rent and utilities can probably be allocated to different profit centers based on their area representation within the hospital. However, it is important to allocate all of these expenses only across centers that can earn revenue. For example, in a hospital of 2,000 square feet, it is not useful to calculate a per-square-foot charge equally across the hospital. How is the reception area to pay its portion of the overhead? If 400 square feet of space in the hospital is non-revenue generating, then the overhead charge needs to be divided among the 1,600 square feet (2,000 minus 400) that can generate revenue. For example, if in this hospital rent, utilities and other general expenses (including reception, telephones, security, etc.) were $4,800 a month ($57,600 per year) and we wanted to allocate a fair portion of this expense to the radiology profit center, we could do so. If radiology occupied 200 square feet in the hospital, then their fair share of rent and utilities (etc.) would be 200/1,600 or 12.5% of the total ($7,200 for the year). Note that overhead was not allocated to the exact proportion of the radiology department to the entire hospital (200/2000 or 10%), but only to the proportion of the hospital capable of generating revenues. To that would be added the costs of the x-ray machine (e.g., the annual lease payment and other relevant charges directly attributed to radiology).

Just as we divvied up overhead charges to the different profit centers, the same needs to be done for labor and materials. In the end, all expenses will have been allocated across the different profit centers in the hospital in a fair and representative fashion. Only by doing this can we truly see what is profitable and what is not.

Allocating on the basis of square footage is convenient for rent and utilities and such, but there are a variety of *drivers* that might be used for different expenses that might be a fairer representation of expense. For example, allocating technician time to radiology may not be closely linked with the square footage the department represents. Technicians are needed not only to take the radiographs, but also to position and sometimes restrain the patient and potentially also to develop the films. Should we just charge the technician's time based on hourly wage? Unfortunately, this won't capture all of the expense of having staff available since technicians likely have a lot of related jobs that aren't directly billable (e.g., re-taking films, filing films, ordering radiology supplies, etc.). One solution is to estimate the total time that technicians are spending doing radiology-related activities and then allocate that proportion of total technician expenses (including salaries, benefits, continuing education, uniforms, etc.). For example, if a hospital has two technicians with total technician compensation of $60,000 (including all benefits) and the technicians spend 15% of their time in radiology, then radiology should be allocated $9,000 yearly (15% of $60,000) for technician contribution.

While profit center analysis is definitely the proper way to approach activity-based costing, there are times when what is needed is just a time-based formulaic approach to determining charges. After all, how would you calculate the proper charges for placing a catheter, or performing a fecal, or doing a bandage change?

In *Business Basics for Veterinarians*, I proposed a method for calculating charges that factored in overhead, labor, materials and profit. This involved stripping out labor costs not just of veterinarians, but any employee who provides services that can be recovered in the direct labor contribution to services. We can also remove costs that are clearly recovered within specific profit centers, such as lease payments on an x-ray machine, or a laser surgery unit. What we are then left with are the true overhead costs to be shared across all services in the hospital (e.g., rent, utilities, security, telephones, reception, etc.) without including expenses that are covered in other overhead categories (e.g., radiology profit center, surgery profit center, etc.).

We can spread the overhead charges out over the contributions of all of these professionals and paraprofessionals. Since veterinarians, technicians and assistants are paid different wages, it makes sense to consolidate the work time into standardized units, such as veterinary time equivalents (VTE). As an example, in an individual practice it might be the norm for average technician salaries to be one-third of an average veterinary salary. Perhaps assistants receive pay approximately one-quarter of that of the typical practice veterinarian. To calculate the total VTE for a period, just add up the total number of hours worked by doctors (multiplied by one), the hours worked by technicians (multiplied by 0.33) and the hours worked by assistants (multiplied by 0.25). The VTE calculated would be fine if all of those hours were considered billable, but the fact is that there are many hours in the day when the actions of veterinarians, technicians and assistants are not directly billable to any client. By some estimates, this can account for 50% of a veterinarian's time at a hospital. The same is true for technicians and assistants, who may be cleaning cages, doing laundry, or taking longer than anticipated doing a procedure (e.g., venipuncture fee based on 4 minutes to collect sample, but it actually takes 20 minutes and two extra people on a particular animal)—with no individual client being directly billed. To deal with this, we need another factor, a billing factor, to adjust the VTE for the amount of directly billable VTE hours. After all, it doesn't make sense to try to spread the overhead over the total VTE, if only half of those hours are billable. So, if the practice concludes that 20% of its time spent in the hospital is not directly billable to clients, then the *corrected* VTE is the total VTE hours multiplied by the billing factor—in this case 0.8.

Now, you can calculate the overhead per hour by dividing the overhead determined previously by the *corrected* VTE total for the same period. Dividing that number by 60 gives an overhead charge per minute. Note that this formula is not comparing how fast a veterinarian could do a task versus that of a technician or assistant. It reflects the difference in costs between having tasks performed by professionals versus different classes of paraprofessionals.

Overhead per hour= $\dfrac{\text{Corrected overhead}}{\text{Total VTE x billing factor}}$

For example, a hospital might have overhead costs (stripping out all of the expenses cited above) of $12,000 for the month. In that month, there are 200 hours of veterinary time (200 hours VTE), 450 hours of technician time (150 hours VTE) and 200 hours of assistant time (50 hours VTE) amounting to 400 total VTE hours (i.e., 200+150+50). The practice believes that 50% of its available professional/paraprofessional time is "billable", so the *corrected* VTE is 200 hours. The general overhead rate would then be $60/hour ($12,000/200 hours) or $1 per minute. Each practice will be different, depending on their fixed expenses, the number of staff that they employ, and how "billable" their time.

The same can be done for labor. Most veterinary time is currently billed at a rate of $4 to $6 per minute. If a veterinarian's time is billed at $4 per minute ($240 per hour) and a veterinarian is paid 20-25% of revenues generated in production, then compensation to the veterinarian is approximately $50-$60 per productive hour. Unfortunately, only about one-half of a veterinarian's time may be fully billable, with much time spent talking with clients on the telephone, providing technical services for which a technician could be better utilized, or sitting idle with holes in the schedule. This explains why current surveys cite associates as only making about $25 per hour! So, when veterinarians provide service, the direct labor contribution should be at least $4 to $6 per minute; it doesn't translate to as much as you might initially think. Using the previous example, you would bill the time of technicians at roughly 1/3rd that of veterinarians, and assistants at ¼ that of veterinarians. For example, if veterinarians in the practice bill at $6 per minute, then the labor expense associated with placing a catheter utilizing one technician and one assistant (and NO veterinary time) can be easily calculated depending of the time contributions of participants. In this case, you predict that the average time requirement for placing a catheter utilizing one technician and one assistant should average 6 minutes. The labor charge should be $12 for the technician (6 minutes x 1/3 x $6) and $9 for the assistant (6 minutes x ¼ x $6), suggesting a paraprofessional labor cost of $21.

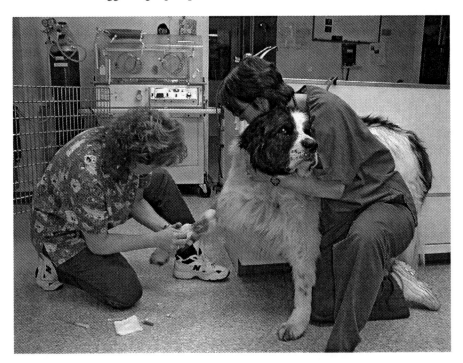

The cost of materials must also be reflected in the final price. This necessarily includes not only the direct cost of the materials, but the indirect costs of ordering and maintaining them. These indirect costs (ordering, holding, shortage, payment costs) typically add about 25-40% to the direct costs.

Profit Margin

Looking at the original formula, after all expenses (overhead, labor, materials) are factored into the charge, it is still necessary to add a profit margin, and potentially also a commission for veterinarians. The profit equation is sometimes a deceptive piece of algebra, but the commission for veterinarians is an extremely complicated part of a compensation scheme that could be the subject of its own chapter. Let's tackle the algebra question first.

Let's say that we have a hospital procedure for which total expenses equal $100 and we would like to make a profit of 25% on the procedure. The gut impulse is that the charge to the client should be $125 and veterinarians are sometimes surprised to learn that charging $125 will not deliver them a 25% profit. Is that so? Yes, when we look at profit, we think of taking that amount "off the top", applying the percentage to the total amount of the bill. However, 25% of $125 is not $25; it is $31.25. In this example, if you charged the client $125, it would only be delivering 20% profit (i.e., 25/125), not 25%.

To claim a fixed percentage of the final charge, C in this example, the equation would need to be set up as:

$C = \$100 + 0.25C$
Solving for C,
$0.75C = \$100$
$C = \$133.33$

Now, to claim 25% profit "off the top" will give $33.33 (i.e., 25% of $133.33), leaving $100 (i.e., $133.33-$33.33) to pay for the costs.

Commissions

We run into a similar dilemma when we need to pay an associate a commission on the sale or procedure. Once again, this amount gets taken "off the top". So, if we need to pay a 25% commission as well as make 25% profit (total 50%) and costs are still $100, then the equation needs to be:

$C = \$100 + 0.5C$
$0.5C = \$100$
$C = \$200$

Now, the final price is $200 of which 25% ($50) goes to pay commission, 25% ($50) is profit and $100 is left to pay the bills. Note also that $33.33 was enough to give us a 25% profit margin before we had to pay commission, but that rose to $50 to give the same 25% profit margin once we figured in commission. In addition, in order to accommodate 25% for profit and 25% for commission, the bill to the client had to be increased by 100%!

Value Pricing

Veterinarians tend to "bundle" fees, and this only complicates matters for the client and the practice. When you don't know how much it costs to take a radiograph, setting a fee based on a benchmark doesn't do much for you. It may even sound like a lot of money, but it still doesn't guarantee you that you are making a reasonable profit. There is no doubt that it is much easier to markup a retail product where the costs are known (e.g., laboratory costs, medications, retail sales), but a veterinary degree allows us to bill much higher for our services than would be reasonable for commissioned sales people.

One of the reasons that veterinarians and veterinary clients are potential targets for retail raiders is that fees to clients don't always represent value-added services. That is, veterinarians tend to mark up prices on things beyond the value that others would consider reasonable for commodities and do so in a relatively protected environment (i.e., prescription item versus non-prescription item). For example, it is not unusual for veterinary hospitals to double or triple the price of a medication to set a retail cost, and then add a dispensing fee. This does help pay the considerable bills of the hospital, but where is the veterinarian really adding "value"? If the professional knowledge of the veterinarian to select a medication is adequately compensated with the office examination fee, and if no compounding is required, then compensation for medication should be based on standard retail markups if veterinarians would like to fend off competition. As an example, if the veterinarian recommends a harness for behavior management, is it reasonable to charge a 100-200% markup on the product when it is available from a pet store at a markup of 65%? If the veterinarian recommends a book on pet health care, can the hospital charge several times what the book would cost at a bookstore or Internet bookseller, just because the veterinary hospital is a professional office? The value is added by the professional consultation, not the commodity itself.

There is another aspect of the current markup strategy that may be considered inherently unfair for consumers. Standard markups most profoundly affect clients whose pets require expensive drugs, tests or products, without providing the client real value for the money. We explored this issue earlier.

The recommendation is not that veterinarians should lower their prices—quite the contrary. The goal is to allocate charges appropriately, earning professional fees for those services in which the veterinarian adds value, and reasonable retail fees for goods for which no intrinsic value is added other than convenience.

Clients will not begrudge spending more at a veterinary office than at a pharmacy for a similar product—within reason. If they perceive that it is more convenient to get the product at the veterinarian's office and it saves them a trip to the pharmacy, they are prepared to spend a small premium for that convenience, time saving, and real or perceived value.

Value pricing sets service fees using information on relevant labor figures, overhead, materials, profit and ultimate value to the consumer; product fees based on direct and indirect product costs and profit, and; laboratory fees based on hard costs, professional collection and submission, professional interpretation, and profit.

Here's one way of looking at pharmaceutical sales that is fair to consumers and profitable to veterinarians. For any pharmaceutical dispensed, charge a per-tablet fee (typically $0.10-$0.30) in addition to the direct and indirect product cost, plus a dispensing fee. This equalizes the playing field since the profit is a fixed per-tablet fee, regardless of the actual price of the medication. In addition, the increased costs of holding inventory of expensive drugs is accounted for by using the indirect costing factor.

This also removes any potential ethical conflict, since the hospital doesn't make bigger returns on more expensive medications (other than the increased costs of holding the inventory). In addition, it is easy to make changes to the per-tablet charge to reflect inflation and price increases.

What about laboratory charges?

Laboratory charges are similar to pharmaceutical charges in that value is added by the veterinarian in selecting and interpreting laboratory tests, not in the costing of the test itself. By using standard markups, the client is penalized for needing expensive tests without the veterinarian providing additional services.

If the laboratory tests are run in-house, one can account for direct labor hours (DLH) of the veterinarian or technician, the direct and indirect materials charges, and an overhead determined for the laboratory profit center. Then, it is simply a matter of deciding the profit margin under which the laboratory is expected to function.

For samples that are sent to an outside laboratory, there is little that the veterinarian does to add value to the testing itself. Therefore, marking up laboratory costs is a non-value-added exercise. Instead, it makes more sense for the practice to concentrate on the veterinary activities that do make a value-added contribution. For example, sample collection is a very legitimate charge. The veterinarian should also factor in an interpretative fee for the laboratory tests, reflecting the likely time required for interpretation. Finally, there should be base charge for laboratory submission, which should reflect the time required for the samples to be centrifuged (if needed), labeled, packaged, requisitions completed and the samples sent off to the laboratory. If samples require special handling, or to be delivered by an overnight service, these are also valid charges.

As with the pharmaceutical example, inexpensive tests become relatively more expensive, while the more expensive tests become less expensive. This is beneficial in several regards. First, it elegantly addresses a real problem in hospitals in which clinicians heavily discount expensive tests (and drugs) because they feel guilty about the final cost to the clients. In this scenario, there is no markup on the test, so no tendency or reason to discount it. Second, it mitigates problems that result when clients know the real cost of the test. Alternatively, clients may show up for an office visit with laboratory results already in hand. With this model, one can still charge an appropriate laboratory interpretation fee. Third, it encourages running multiple tests while only marginally increasing the lab charges. Once you have the collection and processing charges, there is only a moderate increase likely in interpretation fees, and only the laboratory costs themselves for the extra tests. Finally, the charges are completely defensible to staff, associates and clients because they reflect real costs in the hospital setting, not a markup of testing done outside the hospital.

New Services

Profit is much more than just adding up the costs associated with a product or service. If functionality were the only consideration, then nobody would drive a luxury car, shop for brand-name accessories, or drink overpriced cups of coffee. No, this is a marketplace of consumers seeking service, so there is a much better potential for profit in those practices catering to the needs of such clients. In many cases, time is more critical than money, so there is significant profit to be made in leveraging such opportunities. Consumers are used to affinity programs, brand loyalty, and Internet connectivity, while most veterinarians still embrace an almost assembly line approach to health care. News alert! Clients are prepared to pay for customized service and welcome the opportunity. Will veterinarians be there to meet the need, or will they continue to lose market share to better-managed competitors.

Veterinary Compensation And Profit

There is an entire chapter in this book on compensation, but I'd like to just interject here that paying commissions to veterinarians on the basis of their professional services is completely defensible, but across-the-board commissions are much more difficult to justify.

If we use the examples cited here, then veterinary compensation increases dramatically as more patients are serviced and higher average transactions are in place. However, as the profession will need to cope with the compensation inequities for paraprofessionals, it is time to start looking at their real contributions in earnest. Just as nurses and dental hygienists had to fight for improvements in their career opportunities, so will veterinary technicians or they will never become the skilled workforce needed to make veterinary medicine profitable for everybody. As such, going through the exercises outlined here as to labor, overhead, and materials costs helps us determine where compensation changes are required.

Let's look at an example that might make the issue easier to fathom. At XYZ Pet Hospital, dental prophylaxis is routinely performed. During a routine office visit, the veterinarian notices tartar accumulation and recommends a dental prophylaxis, which the client accepts. While under the direction of a veterinarian, anesthesia is induced and maintained by a technician, the technician performs the actual procedure (which takes about 45 minutes) and the veterinarian spends about 5 minutes examining the oral cavity and a few more minutes looking at dental radiographs if they are taken. The total charge to the client is $265. How much of that should go to the veterinarian? How much of that, if any, should go to the technician?

Here's another example. An associate veterinarian sees a client and is paid a commission on the office visit. An antibiotic is recommended and is dispensed in the value-pricing method suggested in this chapter. How much, if any, of the medication revenues is the veterinarian fairly entitled to? If the client brings in a fecal sample, is the veterinarian entitled to a percentage of the laboratory charge, even if s/he is not involved at all in the process? A client comes in to buy prescription dog food. Is anyone entitled to a percentage of that sale?

The point that I am trying to make here is that, because current veterinary models are inherently unprofitable, the profession has attempted to compensate by bundling charges rather than honestly determining where value is provided. Because veterinarians are underpaid in this unprofitable model, they seek compensation in areas in which it is not logically found. This is illegal in most other health care fields. Adding charges to the prescription to compensate for commissions greatly inflates the cost to the consumer without providing additional value. They paid for the expertise of the veterinarian during the examination, which included selection of pharmaceuticals. Their physician would have sent them on their way with a prescription. Paying a commission on the final drug charge would greatly inflate the charge to the client. For example, if the final medication charge is $100 and the veterinarian gets a 25% commission, the charge must be adjusted upward by one-third (to $133.33) to still provide the practice with its needed margin. This is a non-value-added expense to the client, and one that is difficult to justify in most instances. The same holds true for any product or service provided by another.

Once again, for calculation purposes, charges to the client should be as follows. Direct labor hours (DLH) can be calculated on the basis of veterinary time equivalents (VTE). Overhead should be charged at that calculated for the particular profit center. The material costs must reflect the direct costs from the distributor, as well as ordering and holding costs. These indirect costs may add 25-100% to the unit cost. Non-billable time can be compensated for with a billing factor. Finally, profit to the practice can be determined and added to the algebraic equation. If you want to add veterinary commissions to the total, expect a big price jump to the client.

By way of example, GoodPet Veterinary Hospital has a dental operatory overhead expense of $1.50 per minute, based on profit center analysis. In pricing the dental prophylaxis procedure, they estimated that it would require 35 minutes of technician time (at a VTE rate of $2.00/minute), 10 minutes of assistant time (at a VTE rate of $1.50/minute) 5 minutes of veterinary time (at $6 per minute), 30 minutes of anesthesia (at $1 per minute) and $6 of materials (including indirect costs of 35% of unit cost). The base charge should be:

Overhead	$52.50
Veterinary time	$30.00
Technician time	$70.00
Assistant time	$15.00
Anesthesia	$30.00
Materials	$ 6.00
Total	**$203.50**

Remember, this is a very basic pricing system, and hasn't included a variety of charges that should be there, such as catheterization, monitoring during anesthesia, induction, medical waste, etc. It also doesn't include any profit, or revenue sharing for associates. To build in a 20% profit margin would raise the cost to $254.38 (P=203.50+0.20P) and including a 25% commission would raise the tab to $370 (P=203.50+0.45P)! Can you start to appreciate the problems of calculating commissions on the final bill? Imagine the cost if you really want to make 30-40% profit on this procedure. It's hard to do so and pay commissions.

Summary

There is much talk in the industry about the financial woes of the profession and the limited profit potential for those entering the field. However, there are wonderful opportunities within the profession that are not available elsewhere, and the picture looks rosy indeed for the prepared practice. There has never been a better time for veterinarians to profit from the practice of excellent medicine.

Recommended Reading

Ackerman, L: Business Basics for Veterinarians. ASJA Press, 2002

American Animal Hospital Association: Financial & Productivity Pulsepoints, 2nd Edition. AAHAPress, Lakewood, Colorado, 2002, 180pp.

American Veterinary Medical Association: Employment of male and female graduates of US veterinary medical colleges, 2002. J Am Vet Med Assoc, 2003; 222(5): 598-600.

Bower, J; Gripper J; Gripper, P; Gunn, D: Veterinary Practice Management, 3rd Edition. Blackwell Science, Oxford, 2001, 254pp.

Consumer Reports Investigations: Veterinary Care Without the Bite. Consumer Reports, 2003; 68(7): 12-17.

Giniat, EJ; Libert, BD: Value Rx for Healthcare. HarperBusiness, 2001, 243 pp.

Heinke, ML; McCarthy, JB: Practice made Perfect. A Guide to Veterinary Practice Management. AAHA Press, Lakewood Colorado, 2001, 459pp.

Myers, W: Your high-performance practice. Merial, 2002, 126pp.

Nagle, TT; Holden, RK: The Strategy and Tactics of Pricing: A Guide to Profitable Decision Making (3rd Edition). Prentice Hall, 2002, 432pp.

Opperman, M: The Art of Veterinary Practice Management. Veterinary Medicine Publishing Group, Lenexa Kansa, 1999, 248pp.

Stowe, JD: Effective Veterinary Practice. Lifelearn, Guelph, Ontario, 2001, 412pp.

Wise, JK; Gonzalez, ML: Veterinary Income per hour, 1999. J Am Vet Med Assoc, 2002; 220(8): 1157-1158.

ACHIEVING BREAKTHROUGH PERFORMANCE

Lowell Ackerman DVM DACVD MBA MPA

Dr. Lowell Ackerman is a Diplomate of the American College of Veterinary Dermatology and in addition holds an MBA from the University of Phoenix and an MPA from Harvard University. He is involved in clinical practice as a clinical assistant professor at Tufts University School of Veterinary Medicine as well as helping to develop the business skills curriculum there. In addition, Dr. Ackerman is affiliated with Veterinary Healthcare Consultants, LLC–a national consulting firm dedicated to providing innovative and resourceful business solutions for veterinary professionals and humane organizations. His primary business interests include leadership, team building, customer relationship management, strategic planning, Total Quality Management, profit center development, veterinary fee issues, marketing, promotion, action planning, and performance measurement. Dr. Ackerman developed the BARK^{sm} system for performance evaluation of veterinary practices.

Dr. Ackerman is the author/co-author of 75 books to date (including Business Basics for Veterinarians) and numerous book chapters and articles. He lectures extensively, on an international basis. Dr. Ackerman is a member of the American Animal Hospital Association, the American Veterinary Medical Association, the Association of Veterinary Practice Management Consultants & Advisors, the American Society of Journalists and Authors, and the Association of Veterinary Communicators.

How do you judge if a veterinary practice is successful? While traditional measures such as Net Profit, Return on Investment, and Return on Capital Employed are the standards of the industry, they actually fall short of discerning a vibrant from a troubled practice. Publicly traded companies are open to much more scrutiny, and a pharmaceutical company, for example, can't rely only on its latest blockbuster drugs to command top share price. Those in the know look further into the future, to products in the pipeline, products that may have liability issues, potential human resource problems, and a host of other issues. The result of such scrutiny is a grade (share price), of sorts, reflecting the present value of

120

future cash flows. Even if a company is currently doing well, its stock price reflects public opinion as to how well the company will continue to do in the future.

While many veterinary practices may be content with whether there were more vaccination visits this year than last, the successful practices of the future will need to be more proactive, to develop strategic plans for success 2, 3, 5 or either 10 years into the future.

Why? First, strategic planning is the lifeblood of all businesses, although it has largely been neglected in the veterinary profession. Accordingly, veterinarians are often forced to react to industry pressures rather than proactively managing them. Second, the profession will be squeezed when upcoming graduating classes of veterinarians and veterinary paraprofessionals decide they don't like the status quo of student debt and low starting salaries, and small practices won't be able to afford to hire them. The corollary to this is that new graduates will not only have no interest in working for small practices, but even less interest in eventually buying them and continuing the practice as a viable business. Where does that leave the small practice owners of today, that hope one day to sell their practices and retire? Third, unless practices are run more efficiently, there will be insufficient return on investment to warrant building large veterinary hospitals, with costly equipment and even more costly payroll. All too often veterinarians finance a veterinary hospital to provide a place for them to work. The actual return on their financial investment is sometimes a secondary consideration. Finally, there are a lot more hurdles for the profession on the way, including likely challenges on flea/tick control products, pharmaceuticals, laboratory fees and even routine neutering surgeries. If veterinarians can't run their practices as successful and competitive businesses, they might just find themselves challenged by better-managed ventures that can offer comparable products and services for better value to the customer.

There is not a problem with the veterinary profession, or a fundamental problem that makes veterinary practice unprofitable. On the contrary–the opportunities are fantastic. What has been lacking to date is a standardized approach to veterinary practice that is quantifiable and that allows all veterinary staff to participate in the improvement process.

Why not just increase fees across the board and capture profit that way? Strategies that focus on short-term financial results can cause practices to overinvest in short-term fixes and to underinvest in long-term value creation, allowing the practice to do fine in the short run, but decidedly worse in the long run. This has been seen far too often recently, evidenced by so many failures of large companies, such as Enron, Adelphia, and Worldcom. Accounting statements fail to capture value creation or destruction; they are lagging indicators of what is really going on in the organization. There is a better way.

The Philosophy of Performance Measurement

In veterinary school, we judged our progress towards a goal (graduation) by the successful completion of individual steps (classes) and that progress was recorded on a report card. The same kind of process can be used to measure performance in practice. I like to define that process with an acronym–BARK (Business Assessment Report Kard).

BARK is an excellent way to empower practice teams and make practices more profitable, not just in the short term, but in the long term as well. Similar processes include the Balanced Scorecard (www.balancedscorecard.org), and Value Dynamics (as described by Giniat and Libert in Value Rx for Healthcare). The basic premise of such programs is to unite staff to common strategic goals; staff needn't focus specifically on profit–that's management's job. After all, what does it mean to staff that you want to increase revenues? Even with profit sharing, this does not align the efforts of staff with the best interests of the practice.

For example, suppose you create a profit-sharing program for the sale of pet foods because you believe that increased pet food sales will translate into increased practice profits. Expect staff to apply the behavior that will get them the reward–in this case, the sale of the pet food. In some cases, staff may pressure clients to buy the food because the staff has inadvertently been turned into commissioned salespeople. This is not in the best interest of the client or the practice. What we want is to cultivate a corporate culture of wanting to provide exceptional customer service and deal in customer relationship management, not high-pressure sales. Can it be done in the veterinary practice? Absolutely-with BARK, it's not just wishful thinking, but a process to be planned and anticipated.

Running a successful veterinary organization is much more like piloting an aircraft, being captain of a ship or driving a bus, than it is a military chain of command, yet many practices operate on this latter command-and-control philosophy. Being the boss stifles creative solutions by staff and makes dramatic profitability enhancements more difficult to achieve.

BARK is also a form of internal marketing, reaching out to the staff to accomplish the strategic goals of the practice. Many practices fail miserably at this task when the goal is to motivate staff to bring in more revenue. This tactic often falls flat when employees perceive that their relatively low-paying positions are being leveraged to separate more money from clients, solely for the purposes of profit.

The BARK method takes a balanced approach to scoring strategic outcomes. While management usually determines the strategic vision and mission of the organization, all other aspects of BARK are planned and achieved by the involvement of all staff members. In many veterinary organizations, a command-and-control style of management is employed, with orders coming down from the owner(s)/managers, and tasks being carried out by employees, most with little or no opportunity to advance in their positions. In many cases, this top-down approach gives the veterinarian/owner/manager a feeling of power, but little real progress can typically be made with this regimented approach.

Seven Steps to Improved Practice Performance

Like a diagnostic algorithm, BARK works best when all facets of performance measurement are assessed simultaneously. Since the steps are interrelated, the program's balance comes from a perspective that things happen best when they involve small steps to a well-established goal, and that if steps are measured, they can be effectively managed. Just like building a house, we first need to have a vision of the final product, and then do all the little steps necessary to create it. We need to know details (how many floors? Basement? Square footage?) so we can take the next step (working backwards) to determine the materials needed and how framers, electricians, plumbers and others will work together as teams so that the project will be completed on schedule. There are little milestones that occur along the way, including building inspections, where you make sure that your vision and the project as still well aligned. You just don't start building and hope in the end that you get the house you want. A business strategy is no different.

BARK is a top-down process driven by mission and strategy. The process starts by translating the mission into specific strategic objectives. Management aligns the mission with financial goals, such as revenue and market growth, profitability, or cash flow generation. The management team must be explicit about the customer and market segments in which it has decided to compete. Then, teams must consider value delivery and the processes that will allow the delivery to be efficient. The final steps involve grading the process, and continually refining it to improve performance.

There are seven steps to ensuring that a project meets expectations, and we will work through these seven steps individually. However, first, take a look below at all the steps and then we'll start putting the process together.

1. Explore Strategic Opportunities
2. Create Actionable Missions
3. Develop Value Propositions
4. Set Verifiable Goals and Milestones
5. Improve Capabilities
6. Keep Score
7. Continuous Quality Improvement

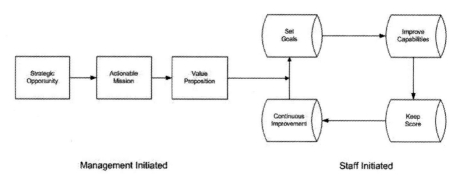

Management Initiated   Staff Initiated

Step 1: Explore Strategic Opportunities

When veterinarians see clients, manage the practice, and try to have a hand in everything going on in the clinic, something has got to give—and that thing is usually profit. This work-and-manage paradigm really doesn't allow for creative and strategic planning, looking at success years into the future. The result is incremental improvement, such as seeing one more case in the day, using a marketing campaign to get in a few more dentals, or raising fees to create periodic revenue boosts. These are all fine, but they won't turn a practice return on investment (ROI) from 5% to 25%. That requires examining opportunities that might take months or years to develop but that have the potential to provide much higher returns in the long term.

To accomplish this, it is critical to mine for strategic opportunities and this takes effort. For most practices, this will also involve a consultant that is capable of evaluating those opportunities, helping with the setup, and BARKing the system to make sure that the goals are being achieved.

Some of the main steps used in evaluating opportunities are to analyze the practice financials and benchmark them with comparable practices, evaluate as complete a demographic analysis as possible, and postulate value-added services that could be added to the practice.

Analyzing financials is much simpler than it used to be, since there are some wonderful resources to provide benchmark data. The National Commission on Veterinary Economic Issues (NCVEI) has information on its web site (www.NCVEI.org) to help compare your practice on the basis of some important criteria, including: fees; income; top producers in the practice; which services are producing the most income; accounts receivable; marketing; management; and others. There were also five working groups created in 2000: Pricing strategies; promoting greater efficiency in the delivery system; increased understanding of customers and their needs; gender issues; and, strategies to increase the skills, knowledge, aptitude and attitude of veterinarians.

It has also become much easier to perform a demographic analysis on the main neighborhoods being serviced by a practice. Within the United States, there are several services that will provide summaries of the demographic information of those living in zip codes relevant to your practice. One of the most useful is ESRI (www.esribis.com), which even provides information on pet expenditures on a neighborhood basis, including how that neighborhood rates against the national average. This information alone is important in strategic targeting of customers and market segments. However, a staff meeting may allow you to segment your existing customer base, and the results may be surprising. For example, your existing market segmentation may look like this:

Market Segments	Proportion	Comments
Obsessive	10% of clients	Will do anything for their pets, regardless of cost
Committed	25% of clients	Value their pets highly and would spend up to $750 yearly on their pets if needed, and if they saw value in the procedure.
Uncommitted	25% of clients	Value their pets and would spend up to $375 yearly on their pets if convinced that it was needed and they saw value in the procedure
Generation X+	20% of clients	Spend money on convenience; don't fully appreciate needs for veterinary services and cannot predict what they will or will not spend
Price shoppers	20% of clients	Aren't loyal to the hospital and are looking for basic care at the most affordable price

When you summarize your market segmentation, you may be surprised, not only where your client base is, but where you are spending the most attention and expense.

Step 2—Create Actionable Missions

While teamwork is critical to fulfilling an action plan, the mission is a job for management. Many veterinarians have mission statements or vision statements, but few are actionable. Many claim to provide the highest-quality veterinary medicine or to provide the utmost in customer service, but these are not visions that can actually guide a practice. Doesn't everyone want to practice the highest-quality veterinary medicine and provide the utmost in customer service? How are staff supposed to embrace and act on such a mission. No, we're talking about a different type of mission here. The management team and consultants need to create specific missions for the practice, concrete actions that, when achieved, should be profitable. Visions that are actionable are the only ones that work. BARK just serves as the method of verifying the assumptions made by the mission.

A practice shouldn't set a financial goal as part of its mission, for the same reason that your mission shouldn't be to be a millionaire. It's fine to want things, but there is no real connection between the goal and how it will be achieved. So a practice may create a goal of increasing revenues a set amount by increasing the number of dental procedures from 2% of gross billings to 5% of gross billings over the course of 12 months.

Step 3: Develop Value Proposition

The value proposition examines how your vision provides value for all stakeholders. It's the "what's in it for me" aspect of the program. The value proposition doesn't just look at the value to the practice, but also to the client, the staff, and even the shareholders or governing board if the practice has them.

Typically, when we create value propositions, we do so individually for each stakeholder. This often points out where the real value is, and often the client is not the main beneficiary (but they better be if the approach is to succeed).

The value proposition is done for the practice first, since if there is no value to the practice, there is no point in going farther in the exercise. The value to the practice is tangible if the mission solves a problem in a cost-effective way.

The value proposition for the client is an objective way of specifying why clients are coming to you, and not to the veterinarian down the block. It is typically because of value that you have created based on service attributes (you give clients appointments at times requested), customer relationships (you have developed loyalty in your client base), or by reputation (clients attribute value to you or to your hospital brand, based on things that they have heard, seen, or read).

When veterinarians provide services or sell goods, they do so at an expense related to materials, labor and overhead. Interestingly enough, however, the value added is actually independent of the costs. Imagine considering a pharmaceutical dispensing machine, such as used in large hospitals and pharmacies. The price tag is $1.5 million, but the machine counts the drugs, puts them in a vial and labels them, with near perfect efficiency. It might even achieve Six Sigma (more about this later)! Based on your current dispensing load, you estimate that this will add approximately $85 to each prescription. While such a gadget is useful, and certainly will save technician time, does it really deliver "value" to clients, and would they be prepared to pay for it? The answer is that while clients might be impressed with this expensive piece of technology, they aren't likely to pay more for it because it really doesn't add to their utility (i.e., they just want the medication and don't really care if the technician counts the pills, the machine does it, or you send them to a pharmacy). By adding functionality, convenience, aesthetics, branding and so forth, value is added that makes the final product or service more valuable to the consumer. The "added value" of a product or service is the value to the client after your intervention less the value before you were involved. Just as the credit card commercials suggest, some activities are "priceless" when compared to others that are a sum of their costs. It is this differential that allows veterinarians to earn a respectable livelihood by delivering true added value to clients–the good health and longevity of their pets.

You can sell a client anything once, but long-term business relationships stem from customer loyalty and delivering value. In any service offering, it is critical to determine the market segment that you want to compete for, and how you are going to deliver services of exceptional value. Value doesn't mean selling things cheaply. On the contrary, products such as Rolex and Mercedes can charge very high prices because of the perceived value, which is independent of the true cost of the products.

It is not enough to state in your mission that you will provide exceptional service to customers. Like every aspect of the process, it is important to be able to measure your results. Core outcome measures of client relationships include statistics related to customer satisfaction, customer retention, new customer acquisition, customer profitability, and market and account share in targeted segments. It is important to translate the mission and strategy into specific market-and customer-based objectives.

After value has been established for the practice and the client, there is one other important component–staff. Why is it so important to keep staff happy with the program? The reason is that unless there is direct staff buy-in to the concept, and they are actively aligned and engaged by the project, making it happen may consume more resources than it saves. For instance, suppose the practice decided that it needed more client contact than just an annual vaccination visit and so offered clients free toenail trims by technicians on a monthly basis. The receptionists aren't happy because clients are constantly calling for their free toenail trim appointments and others show up without appointments. Technicians aren't happy about having to provide the added service, and they eventually, in a passive-aggressive fashion, cause the program to fail to meet its goals.

Buy-in by the staff is critical and, especially in the veterinary profession, the goal for them cannot and should not be financial return. Let's look at a common practice scenario to see how the standard approach differs from BARK. The practice owner feels the practice is only marginally profitable and wants to increase revenues. In the old command-and-control model, the benevolent veterinary dictator gives a decree that prices should be raised across the board and wants the staff to openly support the new policy. The front line staff will follow orders but since they are also the front line for owner complaints about prices, they are not excited about it. There is no teamwork and no buy-in for the policy. It will raise revenues, but what will you do in 2 months when you realize that the practice is still only marginally profitable?

Veterinarians are sometimes hesitant to relinquish control in favor of empowered teams, but this is most often due to a misconception of power and its implications. Power is not domination, supremacy, or control. Ultimately, power arises from many sources and is the ability to get things done and to effectively mobilize and utilize resources needed to meet goals. Interestingly, power is not diminished when it is shared. Empowering others to have control over their actions allows more to get done. The despot with complete control is ineffectual as a true leader. Having power over those who are powerless allows nothing meaningful to be accomplished.

Power is the ability to do and the powerful are those who have access to the tools to get things done. This includes the support of empowered individuals who themselves can make things happen. Leadership is about having willing followers, not domination of those followers. Taking responsibility for the care of your followers is what makes them happy and keeps them motivated. With BARK, staff are a critical component of the strategy, and their ability to function somewhat autonomously and to make decisions, is the foundation of the process. The more independently people can work to complete their tasks, the less "politics" are necessary within that organization. When individuals are dependent on others giving approval for every step in a process, these supervisors can be considered as roadblocks and hindrances rather than worthy teammates.

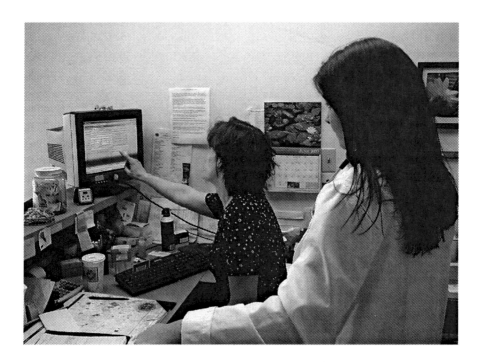

The key with BARK is not to get staff to buy in to your financial needs. After all, they are not working in a veterinary hospital because of its pay scale. They are there because they love and want to work with animals. In fact, it is depressing how few veterinary staff can even afford to have the veterinary work done that practice owners want them to promote to clients.

Suppose, though, that the practice owner had the practice BARKed with a consultant, and determined that among other things, only 30% of the dogs in the practice were on heartworm preventative. Now imagine calling a practice team meeting and reporting the sad fact that the practice was failing its clients and putting them at risk of a terrible and potentially fatal disease, and one that could be entirely prevented. A team was formed of doctors, technicians, receptionists and assistants to prepare a presentation for the hospital staff about heartworm and the different ways that it can be prevented, and what happens when it isn't. Another team was to explore innovative ways of getting this message to practice clients. A goal was set at getting compliance to 50% within 3 months, 65% within 6 months, and 75% within a year. The practice owner didn't tell the staff how to accomplish this, but asked them not only to achieve these numbers but for every promotional or educational method they proposed, to also develop a way to assess how well it was working. For example, one technician recommended using heartworm pamphlets and putting a personal note inside to call for an appointment to get heartworm testing and receive preventative medicine. Only 27% of clients did, in fact, make an appointment within 2 weeks of getting the pamphlet, so that method was abandoned and the process continued. The staff altered their experiment and refined it until their goal was achieved. Throughout the entire process, the entire staff was apprised regularly of progress to date, with little charts on the treatment room walls, a gauge on the computer screen, and updates at hospital meetings. A staff party was held when the goals were met–3 months ahead of schedule.

Notice that practice profit was not part of the mission assigned to the staff! Their challenge was to provide better healthcare for practice patients.

BARK focuses on vision and strategy and keeping an eye on the big picture, while allowing practice teams to come up with creative solutions to achieve desired outcomes. For example, practice owners (preferably with the assistance of a properly-trained consultant) will create strategic goals for a practice, with profit in mind, but with direct actions to be undertaken by staff. This is then converted to an action plan that staff manage and monitor. BARK serves as the monitoring device for determining whether the practice remains on course and whether objectives are being achieved. If the practice owner is considered the pilot of the practice aircraft, then BARK serves as the instrumentation, providing immediate feedback, similar to the gauges in the cockpit.

Some key aspects of maintaining responsive staff are to consider motivation, empowerment, and alignment. In most cases, motivation cannot be bought with increased wages. Motivation comes from making important contributions to the practice and to the lives of pets, and having that contribution appreciated and the effort respected. If financial rewards are deemed important, then it is important to ensure that the rewards are actually aligned with the practice mission. To reward suggestions that lead to desired outcomes, one might track the metric "suggestions implemented per employee". Sometimes, publishing or widely acknowledging successful suggestions is enough of a reward and will increase the visibility and credibility of the process. In any case, like all other aspects of the BARK process, it is important to track metrics of employee alignment, such as satisfaction, retention, and productivity.

Aspect	Metric
Employee satisfaction	Satisfaction survey
Employee retention	Key staff turnover
Employee productivity	Revenue per employee; value-added per employee
Employee Alignment	Awareness survey

Don't keep the vision a secret. A prerequisite for implementing strategy is that all employees understand the strategy and the required progress needed to achieve the strategic objectives. Individuals and teams must translate the strategic objectives into personal and team objectives. If staff don't understand the vision, they can't share or act upon it.

While motivation is not predicated on wages, it is important that the starting point be a livable wage. A survey of year 2002 veterinary graduates conducted by the AVMA revealed that starting salaries were $39,995 for females and $41,172 for males. The same study showed that mean debt among those with debt was $68,131 for males and $74,423 for females. Practice owners should contemplate how difficult it is to remain motivated on that type of salary and servicing that kind of debt.

While salaries of veterinary associates are modest at best, the salaries paid to veterinary technicians, assistants and receptionists are deplorable in many practices. In some practices, the wages paid are little better than might be expected for working in a fast-food restaurant, and may not even provide benefits. Once again, when employees are living paycheck to paycheck, it is difficult for them to sustain a peak level of motivation. Once employees are compensated fairly for their efforts, they can concentrate better on helping the practice to deliver excellent client service.

Step 4-Set Verifiable Goals and Milestones for the Mission

It's fine to create visions and set goals, but unless there is a way to verify results, then the vision is still too fuzzy to be a good target. How will you know when you get there when you set the attainable goal of being the veterinary practice with 28% market share in a zip code that includes 6 veterinary practices? Do you or your consultant have a way of determining market share?

Setting a goal of having an ROI of 30% is laudable, but your mission needs to specifically outline the exact path by which this will be achieved, and it must have milestones along the way that can be verified. That's the information that you will need to keep you on course.

For our dental example, this might involve creating a plan in which, rather than performing 6 "prophys" a month as has been the norm, the practice must do 15/month to meet its goal. To achieve this, the practice sets a policy that the receptionist inquires about dental care at the time of scheduling an appointment for any patient 4 years of age or older, the technician discusses oral care during the initial portion of the examination, and the veterinarian spends a significant portion of the examination on the teeth and makes sure to discuss dental prophylaxis. A scorecard hangs in the treatment area, a constant reminder of whether the process is on target. In the long term, the practice will need to be more aggressive in promoting dental health to all clients, starting with proper puppy counseling. The goal should be to improve the dental health of pets in the practice, not just to do more procedures.

Step 5: Improve Capabilities

The days are past when significant practice efficiencies are technology driven, but some changes in business processes may be needed to achieve strategic missions and it is important for them to be considered in a BARK assessment. It is important to determine the critical internal processes in which the practice must excel to deliver value and to identify entirely new processes to meet customer and financial objectives.

Typically, when we examine our mission targets, there is a gap between our existing capabilities and those required to achieve breakthrough performance. Sometimes a medical or technological breakthrough is required, while in other instances the same result can be achieved by re-skilling employees, enhanced information technology and systems, or changing the way things are done.

To determine which practice capabilities need to be enhanced, it is first important to identify the processes that are most critical for achieving objectives. What changes to business processes and staff need to be accomplished in order to successfully achieve the mission? Is a new computer software module needed to track profit centers? Does staff need to be sent to continuing education venues to gain experience performing dental prophylaxis? Does scheduling need to be changed to better accommodate the mission? The advantage of this type of approach is that this sequential, top-down process may reveal entirely new business processes organization must excel. This is the kind of approach that leads to breakthrough performance for customers and practice owners.

For example, veterinarians have long found it difficult to perform surgical sterilization at profitable prices. An analysis of the financial component suggests that if the current prices for these procedures are to become profitable, then substantial savings must be made in the anesthetic and surgical aspects of the procedure. The customer relationship piece is in place, with clients happy to pay a premium for minimizing risk due to anesthesia and surgery. What was missing was a process that would allow the procedure to be done while minimizing the surgical time and anesthesia costs. It is possible that this problem may have been erased as far as sterilizing male puppies, now that the world's first FDA-approved injectable sterilant is available. It is worth stating once again that value is independent of cost. If this becomes a safe and effective way of neutering male puppies (and as of this writing it is too soon to tell), then it can be offered to the public as a profitable cost-effective way of neutering, without the risk and expense of anesthesia and surgery. Everybody wins!

Step 6: Keep Score

The BARK system turns from qualitative to quantitative by utilizing continuous performance measurement, just as using the odometer and speedometer help keep a journey on track, or measuring heart rate, tissue oxygenation, and blood pressure help assure a successful outcome to a surgical procedure.

BARK relies on a sensible mission to provide a profitable roadmap for the practice, and then using continuous monitoring of critical functions to make sure the practice stays on track. Those critical functions include: financial benchmarks; relationship management; appropriate business processes; and, innovations. Each function on its own is important, but not enough to guide the process successfully. It is the balanced approach that helps ensure that the practice is not making headway by one function at the expense of another.

Where does financial assessment fit into the BARK system? The financial analysis is an important component of BARK, but it serves more like a rear-view mirror than a front-looking gauge of speed, course, and performance. Financial analysis tells us the results of our previous decisions, and is only a very loose predictor of future performance. If we look at our past average transaction charges, this tells us what we have being doing to date, but doesn't tell us how to increase that amount by 20%. For that we need to look forwards, not backwards.

It is important to also note that financial perspectives can change depending on the stage of the business cycle. For example a new clinic in an area may need to commit considerable resources to develop and enhance new services; construct and expand facilities; invest in systems; market services; and, nurture and develop customer relationships. These practices have a high "burn rate", going through cash faster than it is coming in the door. Looking at financial reports, these growth-stage businesses may operate with negative cash flows and low current returns; judging the practice based on these financial indicators fails to account for the long-term value creation in the process. A more appropriate measure is ongoing growth in appointments and sales. On the other hand, most existing practices are in sustain mode, still warranting reinvestment but geared to earning excellent returns on invested capital. At this stage, investment may be aimed at increasing efficiencies and enhancing continuous improvement; money may also be needed for expanding capacity. Here the financial objectives are maximizing profitability, and suitable metrics are return on capital employed (ROCE), Gross Margin, and Economic Value Added (EVA). For veterinarians about to retire, the final stage is harvest in which there is only enough investment to maintain equipment and capabilities, not to expand or build new capabilities. Here the main goal is to maximize cash flow back to the owner, with cash flow being the main metric employed.

To put the concept in medical terms, imagine that the practice is a patient, and the owner is the doctor in charge. The doctor has a variety of assistants and myriad monitoring devices that can be used to assess the patient, and make changes as the situation warrants. The morbidity and mortality data from previous such operations play the role of financial data. They are evidence-based indicators of past such operations but these only relate indirectly to the outcome for the current operation. The assistants are there to perform critical support functions, but if they can't act and react spontaneously to the patient's needs without direct instruction from the doctor, the patient's risk increases. If the individual monitoring anesthesia is not free to respond to the needs of the patient without waiting for the doctor to notice and provide directions, the outcome is likely to be compromised and the ultimate success of the operation impeded. The doctor must concentrate on the big picture (successful outcome for the entire operation) and allow support staff to perform their own autonomous roles in the process.

If financial analysis is the part of BARK that reports on our past performance, what measures are used to direct our future trajectory? The three forward-looking aspects of the balanced BARK are the three main drivers of future profitability:

customer and staff relationships and value; innovation, and supportive business processes.

Once again, knowing these things about your customers is important but improvements are made by making changes that cause a positive effect and that means being able to measure that effect. The metrics that we use in this regard are typically:

Metric	Definition
Market share	Proportion of business in given market
Customer Retention	Rate at which clinic maintains ongoing relationships with client
Customer Acquisition	Rate at which clinics attracts or wins new clients
Customer Satisfaction	Satisfaction level of clients
Customer Profitability	Net profit of a client or segment considering specific expenses of that client or segment

If we make a strategic change in our practice, then we should be able to measure the effect of this change with an appropriate metric, typically more than one. For example, if we lowered our prices, we might acquire more clients, but our client profitability would decrease, canceling out any potential benefit. Whatever strategic changes we are considering, we need to think the process through to a profitable conclusion.

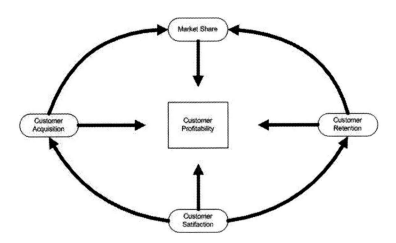

Adapted from Kaplan & Norton (1996), The Balanced Scorecard

How one scores things with BARK is not nearly as important as getting a group consensus on the process. Some people like to see percentages, some grades, some bar charts, but there must be practice-wide agreement as to the rules of scoring. For example, looking at expanding the dental service requires promotion to clients, reskilling staff, acquiring equipment, and making schedule changes, etc. To achieve a satisfactory outcome, all of these individual aspects must be successful, and all require continuous incremental improvements to achieve the end result. The mission might call for having two full-time equivalent (FTE) technicians skilled in dentistry, spread across a staff of 6 technicians. To meet this goal, the practice intends to have 6 CE hours of dental instruction monthly for 6 months, with all technicians in the practice attending at least 3 hours of sessions monthly. Thus, the goal is to have 18 technician-CE hours (6 technicians x 3 hours) each month. This must be achieved or it won't be possible for scheduling to accommodate the anticipated dental caseload, because there won't be enough trained technicians to staff the service. How should the practice grade the process if there were only 16 technician-CE hours in the month, instead of 18? Once again, the grade itself is not as important as achieving consensus. The true strength of the process is that everyone in the practice can instantly see instantaneously how the mission is doing and where improvements need to be made.

BARK for Dental Services

Function	Actual	Target	Grade
Staff Training	16 hours	18 hours	A-
Scheduling	38 staffed spots	46	B+
Equipment	100%	90%	A+
Marketing	600 Mailings	600	A
Procedures	28	32	A-
First Time dental clients	6	11	C
Customer Satisfaction	85%	85%	A
Staff alignment	80%	90%	B+
ROI	12%	16%	B

In the dental example, the Report Kard signifies that the main lapse is in attracting clients to use the dental service for the first time. Our mission predicted that if we bought the equipment, trained the staff and notified clients of the service, that they would use it; that, in turn, should lead to increased revenue and increased return on investment. By BARKing the process, we should now be questioning our assumptions. Have we built enough value into the system? Do clients appreciate the benefits of dental care for their pets? Did we misjudge the value of this service, or was our marketing not convincing enough? By using the BARK system, we have immediate feedback and can make appropriate changes without having to wait for period-end financials.

Keeping clients and staff happy are important goals, but this loses perspective and balance without considering them as they relate to financials. Otherwise, employee empowerment, total quality management and many other strategies may not lead to outcomes that directly deliver future financial performance. For example, while it is important for clients to have an appointment in a timely fashion, leaving blocks of appointments unfilled in case a preferred client calls will likely keep some clients happy, but won't necessarily translate to increased profitability.

BARK creates the visible model of the strategy that allows all employees to see how they contribute to the ultimate success of the program. If the right objectives and measures are identified, successful implementation will likely occur.

Step 7: Continuous Quality Improvement

No matter how well a practice is doing, success depends on continuous quality improvement. There are many different buzzwords and catch phrases to describe the process, and total quality management (TQM) is probably the most well known. The process is about value chain management and team building, and ultimately about customer satisfaction.

The concept is that you create a detailed Action Plan, implement that plan, check the outcomes against your original objectives and make appropriate revisions, and then act on those revisions utilizing the new game plan. But don't stop there. While implementing that plan, you will generate new outcomes to compare against your objectives, make more refinements and start the whole process over again. As your outcomes more closely parallel your goals, you might increase your objectives (even higher client satisfaction, client throughput, surgical efficiency, etc.) to continually refine and improve the process. At the root of it all is a very simple paradigm often referred to as the PDCA cycle–Plan, Do, Check, Act.

In responding to changes in the marketplace, there is still time to respond quickly and utilize the principles of continuous quality improvement. This is accomplished by utilizing the three Ms-Map, Mobilize, and Measure (or monitor). We often do this intuitively, but the aim is to standardize the process and force us to look at outcomes. More and more we are also doing this in the actual practice of medicine, using objective outcomes (evidence-based medicine) to refine medical processes. We are starting to do this with even age-old veterinary practices such as vaccination. Should we be vaccinating on an annual basis? Should a 5-pound Chihuahua be given the same dose of vaccine as a 150-pound Great Dane? Should a Doberman pinscher receive the same dose of parvovirus vaccine as a Labrador retriever? Only by continuing to ask questions do we allow the real evidence to direct our actions.

Whereas TQM is concerned with incremental improvements and minimizing variance, for very important processes, an extraordinary management tool is referred to as Six Sigma. This approach is used when even 99% accuracy is not good enough. For example, with 99% accuracy, there would still be 5,000 incorrect surgical procedures done each week in human hospitals. There would be at least 200,000 wrong drug prescriptions each year. Amazingly, that would also cause 20,000 lost articles of mail each hour! When something reaches six sigma (6 standard deviations from the mean), it has a failure rate of only 3.4 per million, or 99.99966% accuracy. Six Sigma uses an approach called DMAIC (Define,

Measure, Analyze, Improve and Control) to reduce variation, and thereby increase predictability. There have been no veterinary forays into Six Sigma, but preventing foreign animal diseases from entering the country may be a place to start.

Overview of the Entire Process

Step	Premise
Explore Strategic Opportunities	Determine a mission or strategy to gain long-term competitive advantage
Create Actionable Issues	Create specific targets that have the potential of superior financial returns
Develop Value Propositions	Ensure value delivery to practice, clients and staff
Set Verifiable Goals	Break pathway down into stepwise milestones that can be verified
Improve Capabilities	Ensure staff training, equipment, and other resources to successfully achieve mission
Keep Score	Use metrics to measure progress along entire pathway.
Continuous Quality Improvement	Review process continuously, making changes as appropriate

An example of how BARK works

The situation

Drs. Earl Jones and Jennifer James operate XYZ Veterinary Hospital with three other associates and despite continuous attempts at increasing profitability, practice growth has not been encouraging. They seem to be mining their existing clientele well, but new clients are not beating down the door. They advertise aggressively on radio as well as in print, and Dr. James has visited all of the elementary schools in town, distributing pet-related coloring books, and of course a magnet with the clinic telephone number of it. Can BARK help?

Step 1–Explore Strategic Opportunities

The consultant evaluates the clinic statistics, demographics of the area, and the objectives of the owner and staff, and some realities begin to be defined. The clinic is in a fairly prosperous neighborhood with a lot of young families. The demographic study shows that most of the growth has come from Hispanic families and many of these families have pets, especially dogs. In fact, while 18% of the community is Hispanic, only 3% of the client base of the hospital is Hispanic. This seemed to be an attractive market segment because this Hispanic community seemed reasonably affluent, and they don't seem to be frequenting any one veterinary hospital in the area.

There were several options worth considering, and these were posed to the practice owners. One of those options was to actively pursue the Hispanic market segment.

Step 2–Create Actionable Missions

If the decision was a wise one, the practice should expect to see an increased return on investment as the number of Hispanic clients increases. Currently the practice ROI is around 10% and the owners and consultant believe that if this strategy is successful, that number should increase by 2% within 2 years if the Hispanic client base increases to 8% in that time period, without implementing any other strategies. Of course, this is just one mission, and the practice could be operating on several simultaneously. The consultant's goal is to get the ROI over 20% within 2 years, but he estimates that at least 2% of that should come from increasing services to Hispanics in the community. An additional metric selected was segment profitability, the net profit of a market segment considering specific expenses of that segment.

The owners addressed the staff and announced that there would be an active strategy to better serve the entire community, including Hispanic pet owners. Management set forth a goal of how many new Hispanic clients would need to be seen each month to meet the goal. The staff decided that there were a number of strategies that might reach out to the Hispanic pet owner, including:

- Advertising in Hispanic media,
- Producing handout and computer-generated materials in Spanish,
- Getting staff to speak Spanish functionally if not fluently.
- Actively recruiting Spanish-speaking staff

Step 3–Develop Value Propositions

The value proposition for the practice is that being more responsive to the pet care needs of the community should translate into increased client transactions and increased revenues and profitability. For customers, this mission provides value by making veterinary medicine more accessible and customer friendly. Staff were happy because it provided them with an interesting challenge, learning prospects, and the possibility of increased compensation.

Step 4–Select Verifiable Goals

The team proposed that any staff members that could pass the region's Spanish Proficiency Exam would immediately be entitled to a recurring annual bonus and that the practice would reimburse all staff members for successful completion of an Elementary Spanish course offered at the local community college. The teams also proposed that all doctors in the practice take the Spanish course as well.

It was decided that, realistically, the first three months of the program would involve a steep learning curve but that after three months, the best tracking information would be customer acquisition (monitoring the number of new clients each week that selected Spanish as the primary language on the practice's New Client Information form. They already tracked owner satisfaction for all clients with a client satisfaction survey. It was thought that both were important in this case.

Step 5–Improve Capabilities

The first step was to research client needs and create a service that meets these needs. The second step was to provide those services to the clients. The third step was then to continue servicing the client after the visit.

Market research was done to identify the size of the market, client preferences, and price points for targeted services (e.g., vaccination, sterilization surgeries, etc.). This research was also intended to survey what new opportunities might be available in the market that are not being addressed, and how to preempt competitors in delivering those benefits to the marketplace.

It was also determined that the practice management software used by the hospital could not easily produce forms in Spanish, but there was a module that could be purchased to accomplish this function. It could be in place and functional within 3 weeks. The team also discovered that there were lots of Spanish language handouts available on the Internet and they selected several for the practice.

Step 6–Keep Score

BARKing the process included performance measurement for:
- New Hispanic Clients
- Client Retention
- Client Satisfaction
- Staff fluency
- Marketing and Promotion
- Computer Adaptation
- Return on Investment
- Return on Market Segment

Milestones were established, and everyone in the practice tracked the metrics on a regular basis. The consultant came in quarterly to help tweak the model, but the staff managed to keep the program on target by themselves. Only once did the veterinarians step in and try to micromanage the process, but the staff actually had everything under control and the consultant politely advised the veterinarians to "back off" and spend their free time considering other strategies.

Step 7–Continuous Quality Improvement

Teams evaluated the process on a continuous basis, making strategic improvements wherever possible. By the end of the first year, 7% of the client base was Hispanic and the segment return on investment was better than anticipated. Was it time to start considering a fluent Spanish-speaking veterinarian for the practice?

Summary

Breakthrough performance is only achieved by strategically selecting objectives, empowering employees to achieve goals, and constantly tracking the metrics of performance.

Recommended Reading

Ackerman, L: In, Business Basics for Veterinarians. ASJA Press, 2002

American Veterinary Medical Association: Employment, starting salaries, and educational indebtedness of year-2002 graduates of US veterinary medical colleges. J Am Vet Med Assoc, 2003; 222(3): 312-314.

American Veterinary Medical Association: Employment of male and female graduates of US veterinary medical colleges, 2002. J Am Vet Med Assoc, 2003; 222(5): 598-600.

Kaplan, RS; Norton, DP: The Balanced Scorecard. HBS Press, 1996, 322pp.

Badaracco Jr., JL: Leading quietly. Harvard Business School Press, 2002, 224pp.

Belasco, JA; Stayer, RC: Flight of the Buffalo: Soaring to Excellence, Learning to let employees lead. Warner Books, 1994, 355pp.

Giniat, EJ; Libert, BD: Value Rx for Healthcare. HarperBusiness, 2001, 243 pp.

Goleman, D; McKee, A; Boyatzis, RE: Primal Leadership: Realizing the Power of Emotional Intelligence. Harvard Business School Press, 2002, 352pp.

Harvard Business Review: Measuring Corporate Performance. Harvard Business School Press, Boston, 1998, 229pp.

Kennedy, Marilyn Moats; Mitchell, L: Office Politics for Dummies. Hungry Minds, Inc., 2002, 360pp.

SCHEDULING AND INVOICING

Kurt Oster MS, SPHR

Kurt A. Oster, MS, SPHR is a practice management consultant with Veterinary Healthcare Consultants, LLC—a national consulting firm dedicated to providing innovative and resourceful business solutions for veterinary professionals and humane organizations. Kurt is certified as a Senior Professional in Human Resources (SPHR), the highest level of certification offered by the Society for Human Resource Management. Prior to consulting, Kurt served as Hospital Administrator for a 16-doctor, 24-hour, full-service, veterinary hospital for six years. Additionally, he worked as an educator for a veterinary software firm for nine years. During this time he educated the staffs of over 325 veterinary practices on all disciplines of practice management. Kurt is the finance instructor for the American Animal Hospital Association's (AAHA) Veterinary Management Development School (VMDS) Level One and Advanced. He is a frequent lecturer and he has been published in the Veterinary Practice News and is regularly featured in AAHA's Trends Magazine. He may be reached via e-mail at kurt@vhc.biz

This chapter will focus on two of the most important tasks performed in a veterinary practice on a daily basis. The first topic to be explored is the management and analysis of your practice scheduling system (we do not call them appointment books anymore). The second topic will be the management of your invoicing procedures.

Scheduling

A discussion of scheduling systems must begin with a look at the basic units of time available. Traditionally, routine appointments for most veterinarians were scheduled at 15-minute intervals in an appointment book. These books were widely available and inexpensive. However, if you are still scheduling your appointments in a paper appointment book, you need to step into the information age and begin utilizing the scheduling system in your practice management software. Virtually all of the practice management software available on the market today has some type of scheduling capability. If yours does not, you need to replace it, today!

As veterinary software has evolved over the last couple of decades, two or more generations of scheduling systems have evolved. Even if you are using a less evolved system, many of the concepts discussed in this chapter can still be utilized through some creative workarounds, or by exporting your schedules to a different program (such as Microsoft Excel®) for analysis. Despite attempts by most of the larger veterinary software vendors, veterinary scheduling systems still lag far behind those used in other industries such as human medicine, dentistry and cosmetology. Currently, our industry stands in a bit of a catch-22. Vendors are not improving scheduling systems because many clients are not utilizing them. Clients are not utilizing scheduling systems because they are not full-featured. Although this stalemate has slowed the development of scheduling systems, the advantages of having a computer based appointment scheduling system instead of an appointment book are numerous.

Utilizing a software-based scheduling system allows team members to make appointments at any computer workstation within the building. This eliminates the need to physically carry the appointment book around the facility, as well as the need to place clients on hold while you run the length of the practice to pick up the telephone in the reception area to schedule an appointment. This limited access forced individuals performing tasks with a high probability that they will schedule an appointment such as reminder calls; to have to stay in the reception area to complete these tasks. If your practice calls clients to confirm appointments, schedule rechecks, or to update their pet's healthcare needs; you had a real customer service problem at your front desk!

Utilizing a software-based scheduling system allows multiple users to access the appointment book at the same time which will improve customer service and staff efficiency. Most contemporary scheduling systems refresh the appointment pages very quickly so the odds of two people trying to book an appointment with the same doctor at the same time are nearly impossible. The need to decipher illegible handwriting will be eliminated and those practices that typed out the appointment schedule each day for the doctors will be thrilled with their new found freedom.

Over the last decade, the 10-minute flex scheduling system has grown tremendously in popularity. Many practices have made the transition to the 10-minute flex system as they have migrated to more contemporary Windows® based practice management software. Utilizing a 10-minute flex scheduling system offers numerous advantages over the traditional 15-minute system.

A ten-minute flex system means the appointment book is formatted in ten-minute time slots. The system is said to "flex" because it allows the receptionist to choose the number of ten-minute slots reserved based on the needs of each specific type of appointment. Simple recheck appointments, suture removals, and some discharges are often scheduled for ten minutes. Most routine appointments and more involved rechecks are scheduled for twenty minutes. New client visits, two pets from the same client, second opinions and clients that have a reputation for talking a lot, are scheduled for thirty minutes. Appointments scheduled for exotic pets are often scheduled for 30-minutes as well, because most doctors do not see exotic pets frequently enough to have drug dosage and other information memorized. Many new exotic pet owners also require a large amount of education on nutrition, behavior and general husbandry.

Some practices refer to ten-minute flex scheduling as reality based scheduling because it takes into consideration the real amount of time required to complete the visit instead of mashing it into a rigid fifteen or twenty-minute slot. This "reality-based" approach allows individual doctors within a multi-doctor doctor practice to customize their individual appointment length preferences once they have completed the initial two to four week transition period. For example, some doctors will see two cats from the same client in a 20-minute slot, but request 30 minutes for two-patient appointments with at least one dog. Some doctors have a special interest and request 30-minute slots for seeing a skin case or an ophthalmic case. The ability to customize allows doctors and support staff members to work together to achieve maximum efficiency.

If you examine the individual components of the appointment experience, you learn that there are basic components that are a "fixed" part of each appointment. The doctor needs to introduce themselves to the client, ask for a chief complaint, take a history, perform a physical exam, explain their findings to the client, ask the client if they have any questions, etc. The end result is an average of approximately 10-12 minutes out of a 15-minute appointment is fixed functions of the appointment that must be completed each time. This means the doctor only has about 3-5 minutes of quality time with the client to educate them about the services their pet needs. Add a few extra minutes of family small talk and the marketing opportunity for this visit has vanished. Considering that most pets visit a veterinary practice less than twice each year and you can see how fleeting the moment is for educating the client.

Utilizing the 10-minute flex system, the "typical" appointment is 20-minutes. After you subtract the "fixed" portion of the appointment, the quality time left with the client jumps to an astonishing 8-10 minutes per visit. Ample time to discuss life stages wellness screening, dentistry, diet and the myriad of other health-care topics that you never seem to have time for. This expanded quality time is why practices with ten-minute flex scheduling traditionally have a significantly higher average client transaction compared to practices scheduling the traditional method of 15-minutes per patient. These practices also receive higher client satisfaction scores because in addition to being punctual the clients feel the doctors do a better job of communicating with them and answering their questions. Staff morale also increases because the practice generates higher revenues while processing fewer clients.

Typically, a practice takes two to four weeks to complete the transition to ten-minute flex scheduling. Initially, some appointments will be booked incorrectly such as forcing a twenty-minute appointment into a ten-minute slot. These errors can be reviewed each day, and the list of how long to book each type of procedure can continue to be refined. It is recommended that transitions be made "cold-turkey." Many practices have made the mistake of trying to run two scheduling systems concurrently through the transition period. This creates high levels of frustration within the staff which must work twice as hard to produce results. The transition to the new system is best made as quickly and completely as possible.

The second operational concern regarding the mechanics of how a practice handles appointments is the choreography the staff follows while working with the clients and patients and the level of tasks the doctor routinely perform. During appointments, doctors need to regularly delegate more responsibilities to the technicians. All practices need to evolve to a standard protocol utilizing fully trained exam room technicians.

To increase the amount each veterinarian is leveraged, the most common protocol in use in the industry is for each doctor to have a dedicated exam room technician assigned to him or her for the duration of the appointment block. This doctor/tech team will have two exam rooms assigned to them that they are responsible for managing (this protocol is also referred to as high density scheduling). This system allows the doctors time and expertise to be significantly leveraged. Some practices that run on this system effectively have expanded the same principle of leveraging to a doctor with a technician and an assistant to work three exam rooms during appointments. While the three-room system takes experience in order to work well (and is not for everyone) it does show how inefficient the old one doctor one room system can be. Unfortunately, many veterinary practices were designed and built before this protocol became commonplace. The result is that most practices lack enough exam rooms for doctors to utilize a high-density system at all times. If a change in your facility is in your future, determining the proper number of exam rooms is a critical component in the long term success of your design.

To properly schedule appointments in a ten-minute flex high-density system, the first appointment for the first room is scheduled at the beginning of the appointment shift. The second room has the first ten minutes of the shift blocked out in order to stagger the appointments (this stagger allows the room tech to get each of the clients in a room on time). As additional appointments are scheduled, care must be taken to ensure that the overlap of scheduled appointments should never exceed one ten-minute block each at the beginning and end of the appointment. A properly developed high density schedule will have some gaps between appointments. While we are striving for maximum efficiency, it is still impossible to be in two places at the same time.

The choreography of a high-density schedule begins as the exam room technician brings the client and patient into the first room. The technician can quickly verify vaccination status and other key information in the record as a double check to the receptionist. The technician can also reconfirm any chief complaints the client may have that will need to be addressed by the doctor. The technician also makes sure that a current weight and temperature are/were obtained and placed in the record (this has been made easier by the relocation of the scale). The technician may perform a pedicure at this time if needed (and if possible to complete it independently). The technician now exits the exam room as the doctor enters. The doctor can begin to gather a history and perform a physical exam. While the doctor is performing these steps on patient one, the technician can begin the process over with the client and patient scheduled for room two.

After the technician completes the preliminary work in room two, they can excuse themselves and return to room one. In room one; they will help the doctor with anything that requires two people to complete. This may include drawing blood, performing a pedicure on a difficult pet, or cleaning ears. The doctor and tech stay together in this room until these tasks are completed. If the pet is cooperative (or if the technician is talented) the doctor may leave as soon as he/she and the technician decide the technician can finish the remaining tasks alone. The doctor can also inform the client that the technician will give them instruction and/or answer questions on any of the topics that remain to be covered such as flea control, heartworm prevention, home dental care, medication administration, etc. If the doctor specifically states that he/she will have the tech handle any and all of these topics, it greatly increases the confidence the client will have in the technician. As soon as the tasks that require both staff members are completed and the doctor "wraps up" with the client, the doctor will go to room two to begin the history and physical exam. Upon completion of the final steps in the first room, the technician will escort the client to reception for discharge. The receptionist will assemble any medications and bring them to the client and finish cashing them out. Concurrently, the room technician will then clean exam room one and bring in the next client. Upon completion of weight and temperature and pedicure, the technician will return to room two to assist the doctor. When all tasks requiring both staff members are completed, the doctor will introduce the tech to begin the client education, then the doctor will return to room one to begin the history and physical exam on that patient. This staggered cycle will continue throughout the entire appointment shift.

High-density scheduling allows the doctor/tech teams to see an increased number of patients within a specified block of appointment time. While this choreography may sound complicated at first, it can actually be mastered in a very short period of time. The results are a well-educated client that has received a lot of individual attention, service and education. Utilizing this system results in more productive technicians that are happier because more of their skills are utilized instead of just wiping off tables and drawing up vaccines. The doctors are also happier and more productive because they can focus their time and expertise discussing more significant topics in veterinary healthcare with the clients such as dental care and wellness screening and delegate the more routine topics to the support staff. Simply put, the doctors perform doctor work; the technicians perform technician work resulting in happier clients, happier staff and increased productivity and profitability.

During on-site consultations, doctors are observed performing technician work far more often than should be acceptable. This lack of leveraging is a major contributor to the consistently poor productivity per veterinarian and/or per non-veterinarian employee that many practices suffer from.

Now that you have learned how to operate your appointments at maximum efficiency, it is time to evaluate the effectiveness of your appointment schedule. Establishing an appointment schedule that meets the wants and needs of your specific client base is a key component of your customer service strategy. After all, many practices lose sight of the fact that veterinary medicine is a service industry competing for the discretionary dollars of its clients. Being available when your clients want to see you is important. An appointment audit can help you measure how well you are meeting this need. An appointment audit is also a key factor in determining if you are able to meet the needs of your client base, or if it is time to expand your operating hours or the size of your practice. An appointment audit measures the percentage of available appointment offerings that were scheduled during a specific time period. Appointment audits are typically performed every three months.

To perform an appointment audit your scheduling system needs to be divided into specific blocks of time. The most common blocks are morning, afternoon and evening. Each day of the week is tracked separately, as are the results for each specific doctor (if you are in a multi-doctor practice).

To begin, select one specific block such as Monday morning and determine the number of possible appointments that could normally be scheduled into this block. For example, if your morning appointments are scheduled from 9:00am to 11:30am at 15-minute intervals, you have 10 possible appointment slots. If 7 of these slots were booked on the first Monday, it booked at 70% of capacity, 6 appointments would equal 60% and so on. If all 10 appointment slots were booked and the doctor saw an additional client at the beginning or end of appointments, that session booked at 110% of capacity. When the analysis has been completed for each of the 12 Monday mornings, the results should be averaged for a final value.

To complete the analysis, the final values for each time block should be plotted in a table similar to the example displayed below:

Dr. X	Monday	Tuesday	Wednesday	Thursday	Friday	Saturday
Morning	82%	65%	55%	67%	68%	98%
Afternoon	76%	32%	40%	58%	63%	N/A
Evening	102%	N/A	N/A	96%	N/A	N/A

Compare the average fill rate for each appointment slot against the list below. Appointment blocks with a fill rate of less than 50% are not a cost-effective use of staff time.

< 50% discontinue this slot, not cost effective to staff
50-65% Poor
66-84% Good
85-93% Excellent–essentially a full schedule, but an opening for an emergency, or enough time to catch up if running late.
> 94% need to increase available appointments to meet demand

In the above example, the Tuesday afternoon block should be discontinued. One or more of the other afternoons (hopefully Wednesday) can easily absorb the few clients that were coming in on Tuesday afternoons. Evening appointments need to be expanded, as do Saturdays. Since Saturday appointments are hard to staff, it may be easier to make Tuesday a short day and Wednesday a long day by adding a third evening of appointments.

In summary, appointments need to be available when clients want them and doctors need to increase the amount of quality educational time they can spend with clients. This can be accomplished by adopting a 10-minute flex scheduling system and delegating more tasks to exam room technicians.

Invoicing

Now that you have learned some techniques for improving the efficiency of your delivery of veterinary healthcare, you need to make sure that you and your team are compensated fairly for the work that you do. Many practices operate on thin profit margins—too thin. If you or your staff miss a few charges, your day might end without the practice turning a profit at all. To help you maintain your practice profitability, we will illustrate several common traps that practice owners and practice managers frequently fall into.

Computers began to appear in veterinary medicine in great numbers in the mid-1980s. The impact of computerizing a veterinary practice back then was dramatic. Invoicing clients was simplified and much more professional in appearance than handwritten superbills. Monthly billing statements were produced with a few keystrokes and managing multiple reminder contacts was a breeze. The initial gain in efficiency and productivity made computers one of the best investments in veterinary practice since penicillin, but has all that automation lulled practice owners and practice managers into a false sense of security? Could your staff be losing practice profits at "computer speed?"

Unfortunately, the information received from your computer program is only as good as the quality of the data that is going into the program in the first place. No matter how many ways your program can slice and dice the information, it can only process the data that someone has entered. The question becomes, who is monitoring the data entry? Staff members nearly become hypnotized by the number of reminder postcards printing to the point that they forget the double checks we had in place in our old manual systems and believe the "system" works flawlessly.

In the manual system, a new client completed a new client/patient form which was often kept in the medical record for reference. The form asked for client contact information along with the pet's description and prior medical history. Any line left blank was very noticeable. If the client did not have all of the information on the pet, a call would be placed to the pet's previous veterinarian. Sometimes, a client would bring a pile of old records to the practice which many receptionists would leave for the doctor to decipher during the appointment. The doctor would then make the necessary entries into the record. In the old days, you could not file back a record until after you completed the necessary reminder cards and placed them in the appropriate pile to be mailed out next year. Yes this was labor intensive, but if you followed the rule to never file back a record without creating a reminder card, you never missed a future opportunity to market goods and services to a new client. The only unfortunate side effect of this system was our emphasis on vaccination as a reason for clients to return to the practice. Rarely did practices emphasize the importance of the annual physical examination. This short sightedness is coming back to haunt many practices now as we move towards vaccinations every three years instead of annually. This however, will have to be a topic for a different chapter.

Today, many practices do not even use a new client form; they simply obtain the data verbally from the client. Some would even argue that eliminating the form improves customer service because "clients hate paperwork." Many of the practices that are using the scheduling system features of their software obtain basic client information over the telephone in order to book the first appointment. What's the potential problem with this perceived efficiency? After all, if the pet gets vaccinated, the computer will automatically generate a reminder, right?

The problem comes from those new pets that don't get vaccinated during their first visit to your practice. For example, assume a new client has moved into your practice area. They have a dog that has itchy smelly ears. They schedule an appointment and the receptionist enters enough data into the computer to get the client an ID number so the appointment can be scheduled. When asked about vaccination history, the client responds that their dog is current on vaccines and they will bring their dog's records with them from their previous veterinarian.

Upon arrival, the client asks the receptionist if they would like the old records. The receptionists tell the client to show them to the doctor during the appointment. The veterinarian reviews the records and dutifully fills in the blanks on the medical record, examines the dog and recommends medications for the ears. The doctor circles the appropriate charges on the travel sheet and sends the client back to the reception desk. The receptionist then enters the codes on the front of the travel sheet into the invoice and places the medical record in the file back box. Do you sense any potential for problems with this scenario?

The first potential problem with the scenario described above is that no one has gone back into the computer and entered the pet's vaccination history from the prior veterinarian. While it is true that the computer will create reminders after a vaccination is invoiced, there were no vaccinations given to this pet. The doctor filled in the vaccination part of the hardcopy medical record, but no one has completed this task in the computer. Thus, an active client with an active patient will never be asked to return to the practice. In my travels to practices as a consultant, I have seen practices fail to enter vaccination histories on as many as 20% of their new patients. The economic consequences of these omissions can be devastating to a practice's bottom line.

Many veterinary software programs even have built in features designed to help you catch these errors that practice staffs are not utilizing. Depending on the software package you have, you may see an "alert" or "flag" that critical data such as reminders are missing from a patient's file. These flags are designed to make you take action and fix the problem. However, reality is that most receptionists just enter right past the flag and never stop to read them because they perceive them as an unimportant distraction that keeps them from completing the task at hand. Other software programs have features such as missing reminder reports or other database queries that help you identify records missing important data. These reports are only helpful if it is someone's responsibility to run them at regular intervals and follow through with the necessary actions.

I have found that the easiest method to insure that all data is properly entered is to print a new client report each time you process an end of day. This important responsibility should be assigned to a specific staff member that is then held responsible for checking the completeness of each new client/patient record. Handled each day, the task is easy. Considering that in a small animal general veterinary practices as many as 70% of scheduled appointments come from reminder cards. Verifying a complete record is critical to the practice's bottom line and ultimately, its survival. Monitoring compliance is easy if you use your software's missing reminder report on a bi-weekly basis as a double check.

Missed reminder opportunities can be costly, but missed charges can be even more devastating to a practice's bottom line. A missed charge means that the work was performed or the product was dispensed, but the client was not invoiced and no dollars were collected. Therefore, the practice has incurred an expense with no corresponding income. I have seen missed charges in some practices run as high as $50,000 per year per doctor, but in my experience, the average is about $20,000 per full time equivalent (FTE) veterinarian per year.

Many practice owners and managers have falsely believed that if they compensate their veterinarians based on a percentage of their production that all missed charges will magically disappear. The reality is that production based compensation will certainly reduce intentional errors and omissions on the part of associates wishing to give a client a discount, but it does very little if nothing to remedy errors inherent in the design of the practice's billing system.

The most common trap practices fall into is believing if their cash drawer balances with their computer printout at the end of the day, that they are error free. In reality, a balanced cash drawer only indicates that your reception staff knows how to make change. To illustrate, carefully re-read the appointment scenario described above. Note that it states "the receptionist then enters the codes on the front of the travel sheet into the invoice." What happens if the receptionist is using a double-sided travel sheet? In many practices, a travel sheet has service codes on the front and inventory codes on the back. If the receptionist only entered data from the front of the sheet, the client received free medication because its codes were circled on the back of the sheet, but not entered into the invoice.

The trap comes from balancing the cash drawer. If the services on the front of the travel sheet included a physical examination, an ear cleaning and cytology for $70.00 and the receptionist collected $70.00 the cash drawer will balance. If you do not dig deeper, you will never discover that the $12.00 medication charge on the back of the travel sheet was missed. In most practices, if the drawer balances, the daily close out process is complete.

The first problem is the practice incurred the expense of the medication, which was dispensed for free. Losing $12.00 on an $82.00 invoice for most practices is the difference between profit and no profit. The second problem is that doctor on production that just discovered that they lost $12.00 of productivity by no fault of their own. The solution is to compare your travel sheets to your computer printout each day. It is a long report, but almost every brand of veterinary software has one, only the names are different. Some common names are "Itemized Audit Trail" or "Daysheet Report." If you can't find this report, contact your vendors support line and ask for it.

The above example illustrated a receptionist error, but doctors make mistakes too. A shrewd practice will carry this daily audit a step further and compare the hardcopy medical record to the computer printout before the record is filed back. This allows the reception staff to catch any doctor or technician omissions. You should never file a record in our practice without first comparing the medical record to the computer. The results of these audits should be recorded each day to determine if they follow any pattern. Often, it is a single doctor or a single technician that is struggling to keep track of charges. Sometimes, the results will point to a wider problem such as tracking surgical cases or all multi-day hospital stays.

Many practice managers have groaned when I have recommended this type of lost charge audit. Yes this is a sizeable task best performed by your most detail conscious staff member(s), but it can be a very profitable one. Many larger practices have a staff member who handles all inpatient charges and is also responsible for auditing outpatient charges as well. This position is usually referred to as the Chart Audit Technician (CAT). In a large multi-doctor practice, this staff member could be your most profitable team member.

You still don't believe your practice has a problem? Try this simple test; count the number of fecal examinations in your laboratory log book for one entire month, then check the number of fecal examinations listed in your computer's end of month production report for the same month. Do the two numbers match? If they match, share the celebration with your practice team. If they do not match, multiply the number of missed examinations times the current fee times 12 months and that is the number of net dollars your practice lost on fecal exams alone! I challenge practices to perform a thorough audit of all invoices each day. I recommend discontinuing when your billing system is working so well that you recover less than $100 in lost charges for the week. I have never seen a practice that has started auditing, reach that goal.

EQUIPPING YOUR PRACTICE

Karen Felsted CPA MS DVM CVPM

Dr. Felsted graduated from the University of Texas at Austin with a degree in market-ing. She spent 12 years in accounting and business management, six of it with the "Big-8" accounting firm of Arthur Young (now Ernst & Young.) During this time, she also obtained an MS degree in Management and Administrative Science (concentration: accounting) from the University of Texas at Dallas.

After graduating from the Texas A&M University College of Veterinary Medicine, Dr. Felsted began her career as a veterinary practitioner in both small animal and emergency medicine while maintaining her existing veterinary accounting and consulting practice. In 1999 she opened and became Manager-in-Charge of the Dallas office of Owen E. McCafferty, CPA, Inc., a national public accounting firm specializing in tax, accounting and practice management services for veterinarians. During this time she received her Certified Veterinary Practice Manager certificate. In 2001, she joined Brakke Consulting, Inc., where she continues to offer practice management consulting services to veterinarians. She also runs her own accounting firm specializing in financial services for veterinarians.

Dr. Felsted has been published in numerous national and international veterinary journals including Veterinary Economics and Texas Veterinarian. She has spoken at many local, national and international veterinary meetings.

Introduction

Three factors are essential to the practice of quality medicine and surgery:

- A doctor with a high level of knowledge and skills in veterinary medicine

158

- An appropriate range of high-quality equipment for both diagnostics and treatment
- An appropriate range of safe and effective therapeutic agents

If any one of these factors is missing or of substandard quality, patient care will suffer.

In this chapter, the second factor will be discussed—possession of an appropriate range of high-quality equipment for both diagnostics and treatment.

Most veterinarians make their most comprehensive purchase of equipment at the time they buy or start a practice. However, any successful hospital must be continually replacing and upgrading equipment as well as purchasing new technology if they are to continue offering the highest quality of care to their clients and their patients.

Whether a doctor is buying one piece of equipment or several, the principles are the same.

It must first be understood what the goal of the acquisition is. Will the new equipment improve patient care? For example, the purchase of an ultrasound may allow for more accurate diagnoses. Will the new equipment lower the operating costs related to the provision of services? A new blood chemistry unit may lower the direct costs incurred in running a blood profile because less maintenance is required for the unit. An automatic processor may improve staff efficiency and lower staff costs because the time needed to develop radiographs is less. Will the new equipment increase revenues? Use of a laser surgery unit may allow a practice to increase the surgical fees charged. Often, more than one of these goals is met with the acquisition of a single piece of equipment. For example, an IV fluid pump will often reduce staff costs related to monitoring fluid administration as well as improve patient care by more accurately ensuring patients receive the volume of fluids needed.

If a practice buys a piece of equipment that doesn't meet one of the above goals, the purchase usually falls into either the coat rack or toy category. The first category includes all the equipment purchased which is never used, sits in a corner, gathers dust and is used to hang coats on. The second category includes all the equipment purchased and used occasionally, but never consistently or profitably. Coat rack equipment purchases are a failure in all regards. Toy equipment may provide much enjoyment and satisfaction to the purchaser and is not necessarily a bad decision, but the purchaser must understand that instead of making a wise, profit-generating business decision, he or she is instead using part of his or her profits to purchase a fun item, much in the same way as they might use those profits to purchase a lake house.

Leaving aside inventory and office or janitorial supplies, most items purchased for a hospital fall into one of the following categories:

- Medical equipment and fixtures
- Office equipment and furniture
- Computer hardware and software
- Leasehold improvements

Collectively these items are often called fixed assets.

Medical equipment and fixtures

This category of equipment includes all the common items necessary to diagnose and treat patients' illnesses. Office-type equipment and furniture as well as computer hardware and software are covered in later sections.

Exam rooms often include stainless steel examination tables, stethoscopes, otoscopes, radiograph wall viewers, scales, etc. The prep/treatment area will include diagnostic equipment such as an EKG, an endoscope or ultrasound, and other equipment such as stainless steel tables, a vacuum cleaner, cold packs, dental unit, crash cart, etc. The hospitalization section of the hospital will include stainless steel cages, an oxygen cage, fluid pumps, heated cages, etc. The laboratory will have blood machines, a microscope, centrifuge and other equipment. The surgery area often includes items such as an autoclave, anesthesia machine, surgery table, surgery packs, pulse oximeter, gurney, laser surgery unit, surgery lights, heating pads, oxygen tanks, stool, stainless steel bucket, etc. In addition to an x-ray machine, this area of the practice will include processing equipment, a view box, lead gloves and aprons and x-ray film cassettes. The kennel generally includes stainless steel cages, stainless steel food bowls, a cage dryer, etc. The reception area usually doesn't include medical equipment though a walk-on scale is sometimes located here. Some equipment will also be required by OSHA regulations such as eye wash stations and protective equipment for the handling of chemotherapy agents.

As noted earlier, the most significant purchase of equipment in dollar terms often comes when a veterinarian buys or starts a practice. However, this may not be the time during which the buyer can exercise total choice in type of equipment, brand, or features. The buyer of the practice doesn't usually have much choice in what equipment he or she will receive as part of the practice purchase. Generally the purchase is a package deal, though there may be some room for purchase price negotiation if certain equipment is seriously outdated or in need of repair.

Veterinarians starting their own practice from the ground up theoretically have total flexibility in purchasing equipment; however, most doctors cannot purchase everything they'd like to have at the outset due to lender restrictions and limited personal capital. In these cases, it is necessary to decide which equipment and of what quality is essential to the start-up of the practice and which items can remain on the wish list until further money is available. The purchase of used equipment from veterinary or human medical companies or on an internet auction site can help reduce the initial capital outlay.

The decision to purchase an individual piece of equipment by a practice with a reasonable cash flow is often the time when the veterinarian can exercise the most choice in selection. "Selection" doesn't just mean picking the equipment one is most interested in learning to use with the features most desired. Selection includes performing the financial analysis necessary to determine if the equipment purchase will likely increase the profits of the practice.

Capital budgeting

The term "capital budgeting" involves all of the financial planning and analysis tasks associated with buying capital assets. Capital assets are those with a life of greater than one year and expected returns over a period greater than one year. The one-year cut-off is somewhat arbitrary but conforms to the concept of current and long-term assets and liabilities that is routinely used in financial statement preparation. Almost all equipment purchased by a hospital is expected to have a life of greater than one year.

The process of capital budgeting can be loosely divided into two sections—analyzing the acquisition of certain assets for profitability and, assuming that a transaction appears to be a sound one, determining if the cash flow necessary to finance the transaction will be available from the business or must be obtained elsewhere. Financing choices will be discussed later in this chapter.

There are many considerations, financial and managerial, associated with planning and implementing the purchase of assets of this kind. The decision to purchase some capital assets may be an easy one—for example, it may be clear that the practice needs a new anesthetic machine and even though this is a long term asset, its cost is not too great and the practice already uses this type of equipment daily; therefore, the decision is clear cut.

The purchase of more expensive assets and those not previously used in the practice, however, requires more planning and forethought than does the purchase of equipment or supplies with a much shorter life. As with any asset, it is important to understand why the new equipment is necessary. Mentioned earlier were the most common reasons: to improve patient care, to lower operating costs (either direct costs or via increased staff efficiency), or to increase revenues.

However, because the cost of certain capital assets is high, the positive results may not be seen immediately and other aspects of a practice may also be impacted by the purchase, the risk associated with their purchase is much greater. Clearly, a $500 piece of equipment that sits in the corner and gathers dust is not nearly as much of a problem as a $15,000 such item. For example, a veterinary practice may want to purchase an ultrasound unit costing $30,000. This clearly is much more expensive than an anesthesia machine and if this is the first such ultrasound to be owned by the practice, it may not be clear if there will be enough usage to justify the purchase. It is unlikely the payback on the machine will occur within the first year or two and other questions will also have to be addressed.

- What kinds of cases will benefit from an ultrasound exam?
- Are all the doctors in the practice committed to using the machine?
- How will the doctors be trained in its usage?
- Will outside interpretation of the images need to be made during the early months of usage? How much will this cost?
- Will additional support staff be needed if the ultrasound is used frequently?
- How will clients be educated as to the benefits of the new diagnostic tests?

- How will the machine be financed?
- Are there timing issues to consider in the acquisition?
- What fees will be charged for the exams?

There are a number of capital budgeting techniques that are extremely useful in analyzing the purchase of new equipment. These techniques can be used in contemplating the purchase of just one asset (for example, the ultrasound) or in comparing the benefits of two different assets (for example, an ultrasound versus a laser surgical unit.)

As with any analysis, good data are critical to good results. A number of variables will be used in these calculations such as the cost of the equipment, the additional annual costs associated with the asset (such as a service contract or supplies), the expected cost savings to be obtained from usage or the anticipated increase in revenues. If these items are not accurately estimated, the results of the acquisition analysis may be erroneous. For example, cost of equipment does not just include the sticker price. Other components of cost include tax, installation, training, and interest costs if the asset is financed.

Some of the more commonly used financial techniques are payback period analysis, net present value calculations, internal rate of return and breakeven analysis.

The <u>payback period</u> is the number of years necessary to breakeven on the purchase of the asset. After this point, the practice will start to realize a profit on the acquisition assuming the figures used in the analysis are accurate and reality conforms to the assumptions made in the analysis.

The payback period is calculated as:

$$\frac{\text{Total purchase price}}{\text{Annual net income (i.e. revenue minus operating costs for a year)}}$$

Example:

The Felsted Cat Clinic is planning to purchase an x-ray machine with a total cost of $16,000. The average fee charged to clients per view is $60.00. On average the practice takes 5 radiographs per week or 260 per year at a cost to the practice of $32.00 each. Costs to the practice include veterinarian compensation related to provision of the service, staff time, supplies, and maintenance.

Payback period = $\dfrac{\$16,000}{(\$60\text{-}32) \times 260/\text{year}}$

= 2.20

In other words, it will take 2.20 years to pay for this machine and before any profits will be made by the clinic on this service.

The payback period is not the only tool that should be used in analyzing an asset purchase. Acquisitions with the shortest payback period may not be the ones that are ultimately the most profitable to the practice. It is also important to remember that the time value of money has not been factored into this calculation. The net present value of money is based on the fact that a dollar today is worth more than a dollar tomorrow (or a year from now).

Net present value (NPV) analysis estimates the total cash outflows involved with the purchase of an asset compared to the total inflows. A positive outcome equals a profitable purchase. NPV analysis also incorporates the time value of money into the calculations. This concept was covered in significant detail in *Business Basics for Veterinarians* and it is recommended that you review this information.

The difference in value depends on the interest rate used in the calculation. Differences get larger with higher interest rates and longer payback periods.

While this calculation gives more accurate information, it is also more difficult to do and many small business owners will enlist the aid of their accountant or financial advisor in performing this calculation.

Continuing the example used above, the NPV analysis for the first three years of the life of the x-ray machine is as follows. The first chart calculates the cash flow related to the purchase as well as the income expected each year less operating costs and an overhaul of the machine in year 3.

Year	Cash out	Cash in	Net flow
0	$16,000 (purchase)		-$16,000
1		$7,280 (annual net income)	+$7,280
2		$7,280	+$7,280
3	$500 (overhaul)	$7,280	+$6,780
Total	$16,500	$21,840	+$5,340

The next chart calculates the discounted cash flow using present value factors. These discount factors can be found in charts, or in spreadsheet programs, or calculated with some basic algebra. Remember, if you didn't invest in this piece of equipment, you might have invested the money in something that would provide positive rate of return immediately on your money. For example, you might have invested in something paying you a 10% return on your investment. In that instance, forsaking investing $1,000 today means that getting $1,000 a year from now instead only has a present value of $909 ($1,000/1.1). [The 1.1 in the denominator reflects a discount rate of 10% (i.e., 1+10%=1.1)]

Year	Net cash flow	10% PV factor	Discounted net cash flow
0	-$16,000	1	-$16,000
1	+$7,280	.909	+$6,617
2	+$7,280	.826	+$6,013
3	+$7,280	.751	+$5,092
			+$1,722

After allowing for the time value of money, it is expected that use of the new x-ray machine will generate profits of $1,722 (in present value dollars, given a discount rate of 10%) after three years of use. If this analysis is done on a monthly basis instead of an annual basis, the payback period turns out to be 2.75 years instead of 2.2 years due to the time value of money.

This analysis could be performed over the full expected life of the equipment in order to estimate the total profitability. If this were done, any amounts expected to be realized from the sale of the equipment at the end of its life should be recognized as an inflow in that final period and any costs of disposal should be recognized as an outflow.

Tax effects and alternative financing can be included for even more precise analysis, but those calculations are beyond the scope of this chapter.

Internal rate of return (IRR) is another tool for analyzing the feasibility of an asset acquisition. This calculation can be difficult to do and, again, a practice owner may wish to enlist the aid of their accountant or financial advisor.

The IRR is the interest rate that equates the cost of the asset to the present values of the expected future cash inflows. This rate is a "break-even" rate and represents the maximum rate of interest that can be paid for financing without having the investment become unprofitable. Thus this figure can be compared to the cost of the capital needed to finance the acquisition to determine if the project makes sense. If the asset has an IRR of 10% and it will only cost 6% to borrow the funds necessary to buy the equipment, then the project will be profitable.

Breakeven analysis is a very useful tool for studying the relationships between revenues, fixed costs, and variable costs. It is particularly helpful in analyzing the consequences of starting or expanding a business or when acquiring significant pieces of new equipment.

The breakeven point is the level of sales that will just cover all costs, both fixed and variable. Variable costs are those that fluctuate directly with revenue. For example, variable costs in a veterinary practice would include anesthesia, drugs and supplies. If no patients are seen, none of these items are used and there is no associated cost.

Fixed costs are those that do not fluctuate with revenue over some range of this revenue. For example, the rent paid to lease the building in which a veterinary practice is located is a fixed cost. Even if no clients come in the door and no revenue is generated by the practice, the business still has to pay rent. Very few fixed costs, however, are fixed forever over the life of the business. A 2-exam room veterinary hospital may spend $1,500/month in rent payments for the facility. This amount will be the same whether the practice generates $300,000 or $600,000 in revenue per year. There will come a point; however, at which the building is simply too small to accommodate any more clients or any more revenue growth. In order to continue growing the business, facility expansion will have to occur and this cost will increase. Rent is a fixed cost over a very wide range of revenue (in this case from $0 to perhaps $900,000) but at some point the cost will change. It is important recognize that if there were no fixed costs, there would be no breakeven point. A practice would have no costs if it had no revenue.

Some costs that don't fluctuate directly with revenue but must be increased over shorter ranges of revenue than an item like rent are often called semi-variable costs—staff salaries would be an example in a veterinary clinic.

At the breakeven point:

Revenue=fixed costs plus variable costs

or

Revenue=total costs

Breakeven analysis can be used very effectively for new equipment decisions. For example, let's assume the Felsted Cat Clinic has been in existence for 5 years and has been doing very well. Dr. Felsted decides to buy a new x-ray machine and wants to know how many radiographs she will have to take in order to pay off this machine. The machine costs $16,000 and the average fee charged to clients per view is $60.00. Costs to the practice for each radiograph are $32 and include veterinarian compensation related to provision of the service, staff time, supplies, and maintenance.

Number of Radiographs	=	$\dfrac{\text{Fixed costs (\$16,000)}}{\text{Cost per radiograph (\$32)}}$
	=	500

Dr. Felsted must take 500 radiographs in order to pay for this machine and start making a profit. Since she takes about 5 radiographs a week (260 per year) she feels this machine can be paid for in a reasonable amount of time. It is important to note that this is a fairly simple example that excludes the time value of money.

While breakeven analysis is very useful in understanding the relationships between transaction volume, prices and costs, it does have some weaknesses. As with all analyses, reasonable estimates are essential. The linear assumptions made may not hold true in all cases; for example, as the volume of transactions increases, variable costs may increase or decrease on a per unit basis.

Office equipment and furniture

This category generally includes all the items necessary to perform the administrative functions of a practice. The reception area includes a reception counter, chairs, tables, copier, phone system, fax, safe, supply cabinet, calculators and other items. Exam rooms will include client chairs, doctor stools and possibly

TVs and VCRs. Offices will include desks, chairs, shelves, filing cabinets, a shredder, etc. Such items will also be found in other parts of the hospital. A kitchen or staff break room will often include a microwave, refrigerator, shelves, TV and table and chairs. The kennel area will include a washer, dryer, vacuum cleaner and often a time clock.

These items are generally not as expensive as the medical equipment nor are the brand choices as difficult to make. Most veterinarians do not need to spend a great deal of time in analyzing these purchases except to insure that they fit within the overall spending plan for the year involved.

Computer hardware and software

Selecting hardware and software isn't just about buying some pieces of equipment. It is about improving the document management system of a practice. A document management system consists of the various activities and procedures performed in a practice to organize and use the thousands of pieces of information that are produced by the practice or come into it via fax, letter, email, vendor catalog, etc. Some parts of the system may operate on a manual basis and some on an electronic basis. Every practice <u>has</u> a document management system even if it isn't a very good one! In most businesses, a computer system is the cornerstone of an efficient document management system.

Buying a computer system can be one of the most challenging purchases a practice must make. Not only is this a high-dollar transaction, but the equipment tends to become obsolete more quickly than other items in the practice. Additionally, many veterinarians aren't comfortable assessing their document management needs nor in choosing amongst the many hardware and software options available. However, operating an efficient, busy practice is virtually impossible without such a system.

The benefits of computerization include:

- Reduction of repetitive, time consuming tasks leading to increased staff productivity and reduced staff costs
- Reduction of storage space requirements and costs
- Quick, easy access to client and management data
- Reduced risk of information loss

- Increased security by limiting access to sensitive areas and by use of audit trails
- Reduced misfiling
- Increased accuracy
- Increased "usability" of information for management and marketing purposes

The term "hardware" includes more than just the computer system server, network and workstations. Related equipment such as printers (laser, photo, label, and other), scanners, battery backups, routers and other items are usually grouped into this category also. Practice software doesn't just include the practice management system that tracks client data and performs the invoicing and other functions. Many practices also have word processing and spreadsheet capabilities as well as an accounting program.

Whether a practice is selecting its first computer system or replacing the current equipment, it is important to perform a needs analysis before looking at individual software packages or pieces of hardware.

During the needs analysis, a practice should review all of its information processing procedures in order to understand the following:

- How does the procedure work now? (For example, how does the practice produce client invoices at the current time?)
- What is the output generated by the performance of the procedure?
- Do the people who have to perform the procedure know how to do it and find the system simple and efficient to use?
- Does the practice get accurate results?
- Is the procedure efficient?
- What problems does the practice have with the current procedure?
- What would we like to be able to do instead?
- Can the system or procedure produce information on a timely basis?
- Is the data protected from alteration or destruction?

Systems to be reviewed include:

- Client check-in and check-out
- Fee estimates
- Fee capture and invoicing
- Accounts receivable monitoring
- Reminder systems for immunizations and other procedures
- Appointment scheduling
- Patient medical records
- Prescription label preparation
- Preparation of health certificates
- Preparation of consent forms
- Preparation of release instructions
- Accounts payable
- Payroll
- General ledger entry
- Inventory control
- Accounts receivable
- Key performance indicator generation for management analysis
- Generation of marketing and administrative documents
- Online access
- Email
- Reference access (ex. VIN-Veterinary Information Network)

Generally, the more a practice computerizes its activities, the more efficient and effective will the data management be. "Paperless" practices are those that have maximized the use of a computer in their activities and minimized the manual procedures performed and the storage of hard copies of documents. The biggest difference between paperless practices in veterinary medicine and those that are not is that paperless practices keep all data related to the patient medical record in electronic format. More and more veterinary clinics are choosing this route and the decision will vastly impact the selection of computer hardware and software.

While few fully "paperless" practices exist and reducing the paper load by any level takes time, the advantages of such a move are many. These include:

- Electronic storage of all sections of the medical record including history, SOAP areas, laboratory results, radiographs, etc
- Improved efficiency through immediate and accurate access to records
- Improved record legibility
- Database search capabilities for medical and marketing purposes
- Audit capabilities—user can determine who entered each piece of information
- Improved security
- Exchange of electronic data via email such as digital x-ray images or reports to specialists
- Standardization of record keeping and vocabulary
- Electronic log capabilities
- Remote access to data

Computer hardware and software can be bought either separately or together. Almost all computerized practices use software designed specifically for the veterinary industry. Most of the major veterinary software companies offer hardware packages in addition to the software. The advantage to this method of purchasing is that just one company is responsible for installation, networking and support—this eliminates the hardware company blaming the problem on the software company and vice versa. The downside is that some software companies charge a very large mark-up on the hardware and better hardware prices can be obtained independently. However, there is a great deal of variability in pricing and at least one newer software company is pricing its hardware at the same cost as if bought directly from the vendor.

Evaluating hardware and software packages can be time-consuming, but this process should not be shirked. Not only will this be an expensive purchase, but the resulting system will be used constantly and is critical to smooth operation of the hospital.

Many vendors advertise in the major veterinary periodicals or have booths at veterinary conferences. All are willing to provide information about their systems, provide demonstrations or send "demo" disks. All will provide references of happy clients. In addition to this basic research, spend as much time as possible talking to users and observing the systems that seem best for the practice. Talk to as many colleagues as possible and identify users who are not necessarily on the manufacturer's reference list. Involve both doctors and staff members in this process. The American Animal Hospital Association periodically publishes a very useful survey of software systems in Trends magazine. As with many purchases, all computer systems are not created equal and price is not generally a good indicator of the value to be contributed to a practice. While lower cost systems will generally have fewer features, higher priced systems may not be the best choice for a particular practice if all the features will not be used or they are not the ones the practice needs.

Key areas to consider in evaluating hardware/software vendors and their systems include:

1. Technical support including cost, response time, work to be included, courteousness of personnel and upgrade frequency

2. Frequency and comprehensiveness of upgrades

3. Hardware service contracts including cost, response time, work to be included and availability of loaner machines

4. Size of vendor company and length of time in business—a new one-person software company may offer a very attractively priced package; however, a practice may not be able to find support for the software if anything happens to the owner of the company.

5. Willingness to provide all promises in writing and all financial information in clear, easy to read format

6. Space, electrical and safety requirements for the system

7. Written statement as to location of and access to vendor software codes should the company go out of business

8. Flexibility in creating reports

9. Speed of system

10. Simplicity and ease of use in various areas

    • Creation of client record

    • Scheduling appointment

- Creating estimates
- Creating client education material
- Medical records and logs
- Inventory module

11. Backup time and procedures
12. Reputation of company and software
13. Price
14. Cost and type of training to be provided
15. Integration with accounting packages
16. Data conversion cost, time and limitations
17. Use of search features to create customized data reports
18. Simultaneous access to records

Installation and conversion to the new computer system is as important a task as the purchase. The vendor should work with the purchasing practice to layout a schedule for the various installation, data conversion and training activities.

The practice can do much to help this process along. Strong leadership is essential during any significant change and computer conversions certainly fall in this category. If the practice owners and leaders are not fully committed to the computerization change, there is a good chance the practice will not receive much of the potential benefits anticipated.

Staff members should be involved early in the process. The people who will be using the equipment and software often have a great deal of knowledge and insight about the improvements a new system could bring to the practice. Early involvement also helps bond them to the decision to make this change. Users with various levels of computer capabilities and various computer duties should review the systems being analyzed and asked to give their opinions.

Training should start early and it should be recognized that this process will continue long after the formal vendor training sessions are over. In-house sessions should be held periodically to improve everyone's skills.

Leasehold improvements

A leasehold is a contractual agreement between a lessor (the owner of the property) and a lessee (the one leasing the property) that allows the lessee to use specific property for a specific period of time in return for periodic cash payments. The contractual agreement itself is called the lease. Veterinary practices use these kinds of agreements both to lease facilities and equipment.

Leasehold improvements are a common feature in practices renting their facilities from a third party. These are additions or changes made to the leased space and paid for by the lessee. The lease agreement generally spells out the conditions under which a lessee may make such changes to the facility. These improvements almost always become the property of the landlord when the lease term is up. In some cases, the lessee must remove all improvements and restore the facility to its original condition before vacating the premises.

A simple way to determine if an addition to a practice is a leasehold improvement or equipment is to look at its portability and the damage that would be done to the facility when the item is moved. A stand-alone storage cabinet that can be easily moved to a new location is clearly a piece of equipment and remains under the ownership of the lessee. Built-in cabinets that could not be moved without significant effort and damage to the building are a leasehold improvement and become the property of the lessor.

Typical examples of leasehold improvements include rearrangement of walls, construction of new doors or windows, electrical work and additions to heating, ventilation or air conditioning systems.

A build-out allowance may be negotiated as part of a lease; this represents some amount of money that the lessor will contribute towards finishing the space to the lessee's requirements. In many cases, the actual costs of the build-out will be greater than this and must be paid for by the lessee. It may also be possible to negotiate several months "free rent" at the beginning of the lease to allow for the time necessary to complete the changes to the space before the lessee can use it for economic gain.

Time is a very important concept in leasehold improvement situations. The shorter the lease term (including options to renew) or the shorter the time period the lessee plans on remaining in the leased space, the less value leasehold improvements have.

For example, if a practice owner rents a facility for five years and does not have an option to renew, it would not be financially advantageous to choose the most expensive cabinetry and flooring materials. It is very possible that these improvements could last well over five years, but the original lessee may not be the one to enjoy them. The landlord may decide to lease the space to another party after five years or the lessee may decide to move to a different location. If the lessee is going to pay $50,000 for cabinetry that has a reasonable lifespan of ten years, moving from the leasehold after five years and turning that asset over to the landlord does not make financial sense. If money is borrowed to make the improvements, the lender may only grant a loan term equal to the lease term with possible consideration of options to renew. Deductibility of this asset for federal income tax purposes is determined by the Internal Revenue Service and is generally 39.5 years; however, the amount remaining may be written off when the premises are abandoned if this occurs before the end of the amortization period. This means the practice owner will have to make principle and interest payments on the loan much faster that they are allowed to amortize the asset for tax purposes. Leasehold improvements may be amortized over a different period for financial statement purposes, but most practices prepare their financial statements using the same basis as that used for tax return preparation.

Advice from the practice attorney, CPA and consultant are very useful when planning significant leasehold improvements in order to make the best operational and financial decision.

Financing alternatives

Generally there are three ways to obtain an asset:

- Cash purchase
- Purchase using bank or other lender financing
- Lease

A cash purchase is attractive in that it is simple and leaves the practice unencumbered with debt. Additionally, no financing charges are incurred. Cash is, of course, not available for other purposes later on down the line and cannot be put into investments which may have a greater return than the interest rate charged for the financing. It is critical to recognize that owner financing has a cost just as does outside financing. That cost is the foregone investment income that could have been generated from the investment of that cash. Financing a purchase may also help a new entity build up a credit rating.

Bank or lender financing is useful for practices in need of equipment, but without the cash reserves to outright purchase it. Terms and interest rates at several institutions should be compared before making a decision as to which financial institution will be used. The practice will obviously incur costs related to the financing in the form of interest and a large amount of debt on the books may limit the practice from future borrowings or place it in a cash flow situation which is hard to get out of. A down payment is frequently required on the equipment.

Leases are perhaps the most complicated method of financing and the one least understood by small business owners. Leases can be attractive alternatives if a practice is low on cash because a down payment is not required and monthly payments may be lower than with purchase financing. Lease agreements may be less complicated and include fewer requirements than financing documents.

With a true lease, a business pays a specified amount per month for the use of a piece of equipment for a period of time. The lessee does not own the equipment and at the end of the lease term (or potentially before if desired) returns the equipment to the lease company and has no option to purchase it. This is called an operating lease. The leasing company estimates the value of the equipment at the time it is returned and adds an interest factor in determining the monthly lease payments. Both of these values can significantly impact the amount of the lease payments. The monthly payments are generally lower than with purchase financing because the equipment user is only paying for the decline in the value of the equipment to the point at which it is returned.

Some leases, however, are more accurately characterized as installment loans, but are called leases. These are capital leases and for financial statement and tax return purposes are treated as the purchase of equipment using a loan.

It is important to compare the costs of leasing equipment not only with those of outright purchase but also amongst the different kinds of leases. Again, it may be helpful to have an accountant involved with this analysis because the IRS has certain guidelines that determine whether a lease is an operating or capital lease and the tax and other calculations can be complicated. Some of the issues to consider include:

- Depreciation ramifications of each alternative—it is obviously to a business's benefit to get the biggest tax deductions possible as early as possible as seen with capital leases or outright purchase options

- Monthly cash requirements—operating leases usually have a lower monthly payment

- Interest rate—this may not be clear if you're just quoted terms of "$300/month for 36 months" and the interest rate may be much higher than market rates

- Purchase options at end of lease—this is one of the most important items in determining the type of lease

- Obsolescence of equipment—an operating lease may be more advantageous for equipment that becomes obsolete quickly or a practice will want to replace soon

- Sales tax—in a lease, sales tax is generally calculated on both the principle and interest portions of the lease payment whereas in an outright purchase, tax is paid only on the equipment value

- Early termination penalties/cancellation clauses

- Signing or documentation fees

- Personal property tax payments

- Responsibility for maintenance and insurance

- Cost of equipment at the beginning of the lease

- Value of equipment at the end of the lease

- Insurance requirements

Traditionally, leases have often been less attractive from a truly financial viewpoint, but bargains do exist—either very low interest rate or free supplies are included. Some more unusual leases also exist that may be attractive—for example, a practice leases a blood machine from a vendor and the payments are waived each month a certain amount of drugs and supplies are purchased. These are particularly complicated to analyze and account for, but can represent a good deal in certain circumstances. In making the decision to purchase or lease equipment, both the practice's financial position and the cost of each option must be reviewed.

As discussed earlier, buying a chair for a practice is a relatively simple process and doesn't require too much thought or analysis. However, large expenditures such as those required for a computer system or advanced diagnostic or treatment equipment should be analyzed closely to determine if the benefits to the practice will exceed the costs. The tools and concepts discussed in this chapter should help ensure practices are able to make a wise choice.

PROFESSIONAL PROMOTIONS AND PUBLICITY TECHNIQUES

James Humphries, B.S., D.V.M.

Dr. Jim Humphries is a veterinarian, media spokesperson and communications consultant in Colorado Springs, Colorado. He was the animal health reporter for NBC Dallas-Ft. Worth for 10 years, and has been a contributor to CBS The Early Show for over 13 years. Jim has given over 4,000 interviews and completed 23 national media tours for the animal health industry. He now consults with a variety of businesses and industries in the area of media relations and training. He is the author of a new web resource for small business and medical practice promotions and publicity, www.Publicity123.com.

Introduction

Promoting and publicizing your veterinary practice is becoming increasingly important because of economic pressures and increasing competition from many directions. However, many professionals are reluctant to undertake such an effort because of the traditional feeling that professional practices should simply make their services available and clients or patients will arrive at the front door. There is also a strong feeling that it is unprofessional or crass to "toot your own horn". The attitude is very pervasive that advertising, promotions, and publicity may be suitable for other types of small business, but it is not for the professional practice.

Yet when professionals undertake dignified and professional efforts to publicize and promote their practices, they grow at record rates. Potential clients enter the front door "half sold" because of the practice's exposure in the mass media or their ethical support of community programs. Today, a public relations plan that includes various forms of promotions and publicity are essential in the economic growth and long-term health of a veterinary practice.

An Important Trend In Advertising and Publicity

In the past, American companies have traditionally allotted about 70% of their advertising budget to traditional advertising. Typical advertising in the print category includes the yellow pages, signs and flyers, outdoor signs, newspapers, magazines and coupons. The electronic category includes time on targeted radio and television programs, and recently the Internet as an advertising medium has grown rapidly.

The remaining 30% of the typical ad budget has historically been spent on public relations and promotional efforts. These include the typical coffee mugs, pens, ball caps and other "give-aways", and have also included special events and contests, media tours, sponsorships, celebrity endorsements, and even PR stunts.

However, over the past decade a noticeable shift has occurred. A full 10% of advertising dollars have shifted from traditional advertising to public relations and promotions. This significant amount of money accounts for billions of dollars and has caused advertising agencies to create or expand their public relations and promotions departments to hold on to or capture that new business.

Why has this happened? The reason for the shift away from traditional advertising is simple: promotions, public relations and publicity are less expensive and can generate as many or more consumer impressions as paid advertising. Shrinking advertising budgets have forced companies to find more cost effective means to promote their product or service. They have found that well-done promotions and publicity can accomplish powerful results.

What is the lesson in this for your veterinary practice? Promotions and publicity are an important part of advancing any business. Your animal hospital may be much smaller than the corporate giants, but publicity is just as important, and it is not difficult or expensive. You can promote and publicize your own practice, simply and effectively, even on a very tight budget.

Another very important point is that you, as the doctor, are the very best spokesperson you could possibly have. No one else understands your business like you do. No one else understands your industry and what makes your hospital or practice unique in that industry. You and your hospital team are the best story you have to tell! All you have to do is to learn to effectively package and deliver your story to the media and you'll have more clients than you ever imagined.

Let's take a brief look at some essential definitions of publicity and public relations.

The Elements of Publicity

<u>Advertising</u>: *The activity of attracting public attention to a product or business, by announcements in print, broadcast, or electronic media.*

Advertising can be fairly passive and one-way, and may not specifically ask for an action from the consumer. To reach a broad-based audience, advertising requires many outlets, constant repetition and a good-sized budget. Advertising yields results, but it must be done properly to be effective. Many small businesses undertake an advertising campaign only to see little results in the first phase, then drop the program out of fear or disappointment.

With the exception of a telephone book listing, "advertising" was long thought a dirty word in the medical and legal professions. Traditionally professionals of all types enjoyed automatic foot traffic and referral business after simply announcing their business open. For decades it was considered unnecessary and undignified for a professional to advertise or publicize his or her services.

Today's practices rarely open and simply wait for patients or clients to find them. All businesses and practices that wish to grow and thrive in today's economy and competitive environment must pay attention to consumer outreach. Many call it professional marketing or even public awareness, but it is the same important *activity of attracting public attention by announcements in the print, broadcast, or electronic media.*

<u>Marketing:</u> *The act or process of selling.*

If advertising attracts attention, then marketing is the activity of selling a service. Our profession has used the term in place of advertising because it is more palatable to our professional sensibilities–but truly, marketing is selling. It can encompass a broad range of aspects from the appearance of your hospital and staff to the type of displays in your reception room. Every time you discuss options with a client and suggest one over another, you are marketing.

Subtle and professional marketing can also include wellness visit reminder cards, on-hold messages, reception room displays even the logo on your staff's smocks. Such marketing can be taken a bit farther with some planning and creativity. Hospital signs on vehicles, brochures at pet stores and humane shelters, newsletter articles in allied fields and neighborhood weekly papers.

Publicity: *The act of delivering information with news value as a means of gaining public attention or support.*

When a doctor opens a new hospital, or acquires new diagnostic or surgical equipment and then finds ways to spread the word, he is engaging in publicity. The goal of this publicity is to have more clients hear about the hospital in general (public attention) and then come into the hospital and become a client (support). Satisfied clients may begin to spread the word about the operation and this achieves even more publicity for the hospital. Managing this new public interest is the key to turning it into business success.

Public Relations: *The art of developing reciprocal understanding and goodwill between a business and the public.*

You may be a fantastic veterinarian, but an inefficient hospital, uncaring staff or a rundown facility in a poor location will spell disaster in attempting to develop goodwill with your clients. Many factors, some large and some very small, can affect your relationship with the public in general, and consequently, with clients seeking veterinary care! You should always pay close attention to everything that will impact your relationship with the public.

Remember, most consumers act on their *perception* of who you are and what you do. A business can artificially create a perception that is not true and generate new business. At the same time you can be the victim of "bad PR" or perception if you let sloppy employees, an ugly facility or uncaring people go unchecked. You may deliver great service, but the perception may be adverse and you will loose clients.

Promotions: *Contributions to the growth and advancement of a business; the act of encouraging a trial or persuading an action.*

Your hospital grows as a result of advertising, marketing and public attention you have generated. You have persuaded clients to try your hospital and that has advanced your business-that's promotion. Promotion can go even farther with direct efforts such as cooperative events held with pet stores, humane shelters where you draw public attention and then actively promote your hospital with promotional items and offers. Promotional items would include refrigerator magnets with your contact information, free ID tags, leashes or other "give-aways" with your hospital information attached. Promotional offers also work well in actively "persuading an action"; examples include coupons for a free examination, shampoo or other service. The idea of course is to get the clients to "try" your hospital and experience your facility, great staff and caring attitude. This should have the desired effect of establishing the new clients as a long term Class A client. In other words, promotion is a result of good advertising, marketing, publicity and public relations.

There are two other very important relationship categories that must be addressed: client relations and media relations!

Client Relations: *The art and science of managing the relationship a business has with its consumers.*

Managing the relationship you have with your clients doesn't happen automatically. A positive relationship with your clients requires a conscious, concerted effort toward ever improving communications with, and the satisfaction of, that valuable set of people.

The promotions-smart veterinarian never assumes a client will automatically return for another visit. The doctor makes sure the client understands what has happened, feels like they have received more than they expected and have all their questions answered. The client should feel special and a part of that unique group of people that make up your clientele.

Remember, consumers primarily act on their perceptions. Excellent service and relationship management is what keeps them. Make sure clients leave first feeling sure their perceptions were correct and secondly sure of their decision based on their experience with your service and compassion.

Media Relations: *The art and science of managing the interactions an individual or business has with the public media.*

If you wish to promote your practice, even in the smallest way, you should develop some form of relationship with your local media. Relations with the media are interactions that you should manage in order to have the best possible outcome for a media story and future story possibilities. Becoming known to the media; being easy to produce, news-savvy, responsive, and a good source of stories is the first step in establishing a workable relationship for all types of media. This type of relationship with the media is one that will benefit your business many times in the future.

Media Training

Basic training in the art of media relations and the mechanics of "giving a good interview" has become mandatory for business executives and professionals.

For your practice you want newspaper coverage that reflects what you've actually said and television reports that use your carefully crafted message points. That's what media training can do for you. You will learn how to avoid being taken out of context, how to steer clear of the traps set by overly aggressive reporters and how to get your message across *no matter what they ask!*

This takes training because giving sound bites and making sure your quotes are accurate is a very specialized type of communication. If you include the media in your public relations outreach efforts, sooner or later, it will be your turn in the hot seat. Media training prepares you to excel in all media encounters, from routine interviews on stories you have generated to crisis communications issues where your reputation is on the line.

Today's media is quick to judge who's right and wrong and they hate to admit their mistakes-and they make a lot of mistakes.

I'm not being overly critical; all you have to do is check out stories you know something about. It's appalling how many mistakes and half-truths there are in everyday stories. The news media will always be attracted to controversial and sensational issues, but when they all begin to jump on the hot story bandwagon and have fast approaching deadlines, fairness and accuracy are often out the window.

Veterinarians who do well in interviews are not born with that skill. They were media trained to use techniques that produce success and decrease the media's tendency to get the facts wrong. They treat media encounters as opportunities to communicate their message, promote and publicize their hospital and not something to dread. This only comes with media training and experience.

In our profession, media training is often offered at many of the national meetings. I highly recommend attending a half or full day session.

Promotion and publicity is an ongoing process

Advertising and marketing agencies call promotions and publicity "campaigns" because they know that they are ongoing processes. Each project and concept builds on previous exposures, very much like advertising.

However, an advertising or PR agency may not be your best choice. An agency needs time to learn your business. You could spend your first six months and thousands of dollars teaching an agency about who you are and what the important issues are within your profession. You can start effective and professional self-promotion projects on your own. I suggest you spend your initial time and money on your own promotional projects–not an agency-and you'll be dollars ahead.

As much as you may hate to admit it, a successful business and professional career requires you to constantly sell yourself. Everything you do in your office or in the community builds name recognition and credibility. Clients like to do business with, and refer friends to, names they know. Therefore, one of your primary goals in self-promotion is to build your name, and the name of your hospital, so that it's "top-of-mind" in your community.

Well-done self-promotion should become an integral part of your business life. If you execute your publicity well, you'll never need an agency because it will naturally become a part of your business. Whether you intended it or not, you will become something of a "celebrity"—a person who is known in your community—and our society, and your clients, love celebrities!

Essentials In Promoting A Veterinary Practice

Alert The Press!

Reporters love to cover local events. So begin now to cultivate relationships with the news media. Become a quote source in your specialty area and be available for talk shows, sound bites and even submit articles for publication.

When you have some special technique, skill or success, call the media. Submit an article to print and electronic media in your community about your special area or idea. You may be amazed at the reaction.

Tell print editors and radio and television producers these things:
How does your story idea affect their audience?
What is the local angle? The press LOVES the local angle.
How is it different, unique or special?
What's NEW about this?

What's the result? First, you may receive media attention-perhaps a story on you or your practice. Second, the media may begin calling on you as an expert in animal health care. Third, you may receive other media attention such as feature stories from other stations, local news, or even national news. The net result will be name recognition, more clients and perhaps even a second career in writing or hosting a talk show.

After devoting the time it takes to get media coverage, don't forget the reason you did all this…. publicity for your practice! Media air time or print space that does not mention your name or your practice is a waste of your time. If you don't plan in advance to include your message points, important quotes, sound bites, and comments about your knowledge and expertise, you are only contributing to a story–not building your practice. Always use the media to position yourself and your practice for a promotional opportunity.

Of course the media knows you are doing this! Don't for a moment think they don't know what you're up to. However, almost every producer will let you get away with a little promotion, especially if you are a good interview and a good source of information for their audience. But don't be a walking commercial–you'll get sent to the advertising sales department and never be seen again on the news. Strive to be full of useful and helpful information for the viewers or readers and you will become a valuable expert guest that will be back regularly.

Relationships with the media are the life-blood of your publicity and promotion campaign. The relationships you develop should be ongoing and should grow with each exposure. Be of value, be fun and easy to produce and you will have developed a priceless tool for your practice.

Develop a great logo

Your hospital name, logo and slogan are essential ingredients that will follow you throughout your professional career. They are crucial to your image. In fact, some of your promotions and media attention may even center on your name, logo, and slogan. This is especially true with unique services like a mobile veterinary hospital. The best logos are simple, clean and professional. Logos that do not work well include: cartoon type, cutesy, obscure, complicated line drawings or anything that won't reproduce well. If you are in the process of developing a logo for your practice, I strongly suggest you spend the time and money to get the help of a professional graphic artist who has experience in logo design.

If your logo is well established, but you believe it's time for a change, consult a graphic artist, make the improvements, then make a splash with the new event and you might even get some media attention!

Produce your own press materials

Every practice owner who wants to approach the media needs some basic press materials. One essential ingredient is a press kit or media kit. Your media kit will have to be many things to many people. In addition to the media, you might use it for business contacts, proposals, loan applications and even major hires. Therefore, it must tell your story concisely, clearly, and quickly!

A good media or press kit doesn't have to be elaborate or expensive. In fact, basic and inexpensive usually works just as well. You simply need a glossy portfolio type folder you can buy at any office supply store. Use computer-generated labels, professionally printed labels, or a picture of you or your hospital and glue it to the front. Inside, place the following:

- A news release about you, your hospital, or your event

- A photo of you and your staff (with lots of pets)
- Your bio—keep it to one page if possible
- Letters of praise or testimonials (keep them brief and concise)
- A history of your practice, no more than one page
- Any letters you have from prior media appearances
- Potential interview questions (radio/TV only)
- Any published magazine or newspaper articles
- Your business card

These items are the basics. You can add items as your unique situation requires, but do keep it simple. Less is better than more! What the press is looking for is straightforward, honest, to-the-point information that will capture their attention in a matter of seconds.

Don't make the mistake of sending your full media kit to everyone on your media wish list. The nice thing about developing your media kit is that you can use various elements from it in a variety of situations. When you first approach the media, send an introductory letter or a press release. If a media contact expresses interest, then send your media kit as a follow-up. Only when someone asks for more information, should he or she should get your great, concise "story in a folder".

One thing radio and television people like is the unusual. You might try including a list of little-known facts about pet care in your kit. Trivia and "factoids" create intrigue and memory links which viewers and listeners like. If you're not sure how to write factoids, watch television news shows! Almost every news show is full of them.

Write some "how-to" articles and give them away

One of the easiest, least expensive, and most effective things you can do right now is to write a series of "how-to" articles and send them to your local paper, neighborhood weekly, or community newsletter. You can even distribute them as a giveaway or brochure in local shops. Make sure your practice name, phone number and web address is on each piece.

Don't have time? Get someone from your staff, your resident frustrated journalist, to do it. Have them research a topic and write an article. Then you can review it and edit it to assure correct content. In this way, your team can produce a series of very nice and helpful articles or brochures that become promotional tools for your business. Collect these and keep them up-to-date. You may find you use them more than you ever imagined.

Write a series of "tip sheets" for clients and the media

Tip sheets, or fact sheets, are one-page how-to articles for attention-deficit people. These sheets often go with clients after a procedure or service. They help clients understand and quickly get the main points of a subject without reading an entire article.

Tip sheets can be very helpful and full of information that you have spent years learning. After you have amassed a series of them, they can be organized into more expansive articles or even a small book. That small book, published inexpensively in your community, can make you a celebrity in your area of expertise. The media loves a "promote-able" celebrity. Take that fame and turn it into media appearances and, consequently, into new clients.

Tip sheets are also great "leave-behinds" at seminars and other public events. Your press kit might include some of your best "tip-sheets" because they are so media friendly.

Media people have very little time to review material. A well-written tip sheet can act as a radio or television story summary sheet. With a tip sheet, a reporter or producer can tell in a matter of seconds if your story will make a good 2-3 minute segment on the news. That's why the media loves them. For example, if you can give the local morning news producer "Seven Ways Dog Lovers Can Save $100," you have a winner! "The Top Injuries in Dogs and How to Prevent Them" can't miss.

Here's how to produce a tip sheet:

- o   On ONE sheet, offer 5-12 short statements that explain how to do something—usually how to save money or solve a problem-or teach and inform. (Holidays or special seasons are great opportunities for a survey of your clients. Offer the results of your survey and the tips you learned from the work.)

o   Be sure to use a "headline" and make it catchy. (For example-
Don't Let Deadly Bugs Pester Your Pet!)

o   Always include your contact information for credibility and so
that readers make the connection with you and your hospital!
Don't forget to include your web site address.

Always ask the print media to acknowledge you if they use your information. At
the bottom of your tip sheet for media include a short statement such as: Dr.
John Billinger, The Pet Doctor, is available as an interview resource to the media.

Give a local seminar

Many veterinary practices find that offering an educational seminar is a great way
to reach the public, attract new clients and stimulate media interest. Here are
some simple steps to follow:

- Find a meeting hall, community center or barn and reserve a date.
- Write six really great "how-to" or informational tips.
- Incorporate your tips into a one-sheet advertising flyer for your seminar.
- Photocopy 500-1,000 copies and begin distributing them at pet stores, feed
  stores and other parallel businesses.
- Send a press release about the event to the local media.
- Rent a good public address system and LCD computer projector to deliver
  an informative talk on your practice specialty.
- Hand out business cards, brochures and fact sheets, all printed with your
  hospital name, contact information and web address.

You will be surprised at the media interest and response from new clients. You
might even get invitations to speak at other events.

Build your web site

Your hospital needs a web presence. To develop your own web site, start by looking at lots of Web sites. Use search engines to find other practices around the
country. Be inspired by what your colleagues are doing, and then use your own
unique situation and creativity to construct your own site.

There are many ways to construct a Web site. Computer programs are available that allow you to do the work yourself. If you're not computer-savvy, or don't feel that adventurous, you will want to find a web site designer to do the job for you. Ask friends and colleagues for recommendations. Search the web for sites that impress you. You can usually find out who designed the site by looking near the bottom of the home page. Email several different web designers to get quotes for your site.

How much will it cost? You don't have to spend a lot. You can build your own site inexpensively with a program such as Microsoft FrontPage®. There are also many individuals and small companies who can build an inexpensive site for you. Either way, it is possible to have an inexpensive, yet effective, presence on the World Wide Web in short order. You can also spend a fortune on a Web site, but don't be lured into a razzle-dazzle site right away. See if your basic site works for your business before you begin to add a lot of electronic goodies that cost much more.

At first you may start with a site that's basically an electronic brochure, describing your hospital and your services. As soon as you can, you should begin to add lots of great content and functionality to make your site really worth visiting. Your site is a great place to archive articles and tip-sheets, and announce upcoming seminar topics. If you are participating in an upcoming event, promote it on your web site and link to any co-sponsors' sites. If you are appearing in the local media, link to the newspaper or radio and television station's web sites–that's great credibility.

Eventually, you may even create an online pressroom. Here, members of the media can see your picture, read your press releases, and learn about your hospital. You can archive past news stories you have done and promote new story ideas. Your online pressroom should help the media make a quick decision about using you as an expert quote source or a news story contributor.

Your next step is to make sure your web site gets seen. The most basic way to have your site publicized is to do it yourself. With all the attention you are getting from media appearances, seminars, articles and newsletters; you have a ready-made forum to cross-promote the site. Include your web address on your stationery, business card, and on every piece of promotional material you create. Your web site manager can use a variety of Internet tricks to generate traffic coming to your site, including the proper use of search engines, email newsletters and reciprocal agreements with other sites.

Volunteer your services

One of the best ways to foster goodwill within your community is to volunteer your services. Through volunteering your time, you will meet people, develop relationships and share ideas with other business people. You will discover many areas where your practice can benefit from this effort.

For example, you may send technicians to the local shelter to perform health screenings or parasite checks. Shelters need the help and they are more than happy to send new puppy owners to your practice. This is also a great place for your tip sheets and how-to articles.

Give something away

One of the best promotional strategies is to give something away. Sampling of products is a proven marketing concept that puts the decision to try a product squarely in the hands of the consumer. It is such a useful strategy that large corporations consistently spend millions of dollars to mail sample-size packages to consumers, simply to get them to try a product.

Veterinarians should give clients something that will create a feeling of gratitude and loyalty. Dentists know the value of giving away samples of dental floss and toothbrushes. I never have to worry about finding my dentist's phone number because I just look at my toothbrush!

Sounds great, but what can a veterinary practice give away? Be creative! You can have everything from leashes to reminder magnets imprinted with your name, phone number, logo and web address very inexpensively. Just go to your on-line search engine and type in "promotional items". You'll find hundreds of companies that will customize all types of promotional items for you. As a veterinarian you also have many samples of diets, treats and other products that should be regularly given away. Each item should have your business card or brochure attached.

Here is where the veterinary product industry can help. Take every sample, magnet, leash, coffee cup and pen they will give you. Find a way to personalize the item with your information and give them away to clients as fast as you can.

In addition to product sampling, giveaways work well with informational items with content related to your practice. Booklets, cassette tapes, videotapes, and other inexpensive media can make informational giveaways that can inform clients about your hospital. Be creative and start immediately giving things away!

Start a monthly newsletter

In the old days, producing a newsletter meant lots of printing, folding and mailing. While newsletters are an effective informational, promotional, and sales tool, many busy practices don't have the time or resources to print and mail one.

Enter the wonderful world of email. From the very beginning of your business— even if you don't yet have a Web site—you should be collecting email addresses so that you can send out an e-newsletter. Monthly or quarterly, write a fun, informative, and useful newsletter and send it to your email list. Use it to promote special offers and seasonal items, send medical alerts, offer vaccination and heartworm reminders, announce new product promotions, or offer free giveaways.

Include a short case study about an interesting case or specific technique, news bulletins of interest to your clients, or breaking news in pet care. Attach some helpful related links. This different, "news" spin on a newsletter may help you come up with content and help keep the reader's interest.

If the recipient knows you and has offered their email address, you don't have to worry too much about being lumped into the "junk" email category. However, you do need to offer a way for the recipient to be taken off your list. Always include your contact information, a link to your Web site and links to sites that are helpful to your audience in general. Have your Web site manager help you with this.

Recycle corporate promotions

Many businesses miss the opportunity to use corporate promotions to their full advantage. Every veterinary hospital buys products and pharmaceuticals from the industry's manufacturers. These large corporations continually promote new products, services or programs. They have the budgets to hire professional advertising and promotional agencies to do award-winning creative work.

Corporate promotional campaigns are usually centered on a real disease threat, trend or common pet care condition. These issues make excellent focal points for you to generate topical client and public awareness campaigns. Also they usually make good media stories. Ask for the program's media kit and search through to find useable elements for you to carry the story to <u>your</u> media with <u>your</u> local angle.

Press releases, brochures, samples, reminder cards, calendars, and any number of other promotional items come to your practice by the hundreds. These items are often free to you for using, promoting or distributing a product or service. Too often, all this great creative work and fun, useful items are stuffed into a closet or back room never to be used. That is a shame.

You can use corporate promotional materials to generate media interest and publicity for your practice. Place your business name, phone number and web address on all brochures, pamphlets, and other corporate promotional items and give them freely to your consumers.

Take the press releases (and other elements from corporate media kits) and re-write them, using your hospital and your case examples in order to generate local press coverage for your practice. Turn corporate press releases into tip sheets, fact sheets, or seminar topics. Call your local media and offer your take on the story idea.

By doing these things, you exhibit to your clients that you are on the cutting edge of new developments. You have also taken a larger issue and localized it to your community. The media will see you as an up-to-date expert who can put the local angle on your profession's news and trends. This makes you someone they will begin to turn to for expert quotes and commentary.

Give a fresh look to every corporate promotion that comes into your hospital. Use each good one to the greatest extent you can. It's free publicity and all you have to do is make it your own.

Get to know your peers

It takes time and effort to meet your community peers, but the dividends can be amazing. Promotion-minded professionals are always looking for ways to network and build working relationships with their peers. Special events, Chamber of Commerce functions, trade shows, and club meetings are good places to start. At these events, you will meet people who are interested in making relationships that are helpful and synergistic. People at business functions tend to be very approachable and you'll find they like to "talk shop" and learn what others have to offer.

Learn where such events are held and make it a point to attend regularly. Business organizations are a good starting point. Look also for professional or trade associations, social or religious organizations, civic and community groups.

Many veterinarians find that in these settings, they can softly and gently promote their practices, which may be more palatable than more obvious types of promotion. These groups provide a rich field of potential clients and contacts. They are inexpensive to be involved in and encourage you to talk about your profession.

The peers in your community can be a valuable source of direct and referral business. People naturally refer their friends and clients to people they've personally met and have confidence in. You will stimulate this instinct in your peers when they get to know you and find out about your practice. This can generate many high quality referrals that you may never have received otherwise.

Establish and refine your hospital's "message points" and plan on repeating them over and over. Here's an example:

Our hospital is unique as we have:

- late evening hours for working families
- a state-of-the-art intensive care facility
- laser surgery/color ultrasound
- a visiting dermatologist.

You don't have to run the entire list of goodies you have in your practice; simply select three of four things that make your hospital unique and proudly tell others about it. Soon, you will be very comfortable networking in this way, and you'll have fun! You may make friends that will last a lifetime. Give out lots of business cards and remember, these people are interested in knowing who you are and what you do. Approached positively, these meetings can fill your appointment book with valuable clients!

Build your PR network

When you are your company's PR department, you will learn valuable lessons and gain experience that will pay off many times in your practice history. You can also build on and profit from your expertise and celebrity status within the community.

However, as a single person PR department, you are limited by the "touch principle." You can only promote and publicize to as many people as you can personally touch. That's a limitation you can correct by building your PR Network.

You may not realize it, but you already have a PR network. Leave 2-5 business cards, brochures or fact sheets with your doctor, dentist, accountant, lawyer, pastor, insurance agent, and anyone else you do business with. You'll find they understand and admire your self-promotion skills.

Your family and staff should always carry your business cards and know the central theme (message points) of your business so that when they are talking with friends and other business people, they can help spread the word. However brief or chance the encounter, such duplication of your efforts will pay off. Businesses are built on referrals and class-A clients. Eventually, you want a file cabinet full of mostly class-A clients. These often come the old-fashioned way, through personal contact and referral.

Pay special attention to those people or businesses that are complementary to yours. Make reciprocal arrangements to include their promotional material in with yours.

"I Don't Think This is for Me". Overcoming Promotion Fears and Objections

Reluctant Promoters

Most professionals don't want to stand on the proverbial street corner and shout how great they are, what wonderful service they offer, and what a fascinating job they have. It's a natural reaction to hope someone else will do that for them. Some of this thinking is the belief that public attention should just come automatically. Some of this feeling is the fear of rejection, and some is just plain busyness. Although most veterinarians would like some attention and "spotlight" shined on their practices, they may believe that what they do is simply not special or unique enough to warrant media or public attention.

In reality, what you do is VERY special. The art and science of veterinary medicine is extremely interesting to the public and the news media. But if you don't take the time to tell them–who will?

The "reluctant promoter" attitude is especially prevalent in the medical, dental and veterinary professions. Such professionals spend many years in college learning their craft, but get little training in business, marketing and publicity. Additionally, many professionals have an idealistic anticipation of an automatic line of clients waiting at the front door–just because they have opened a practice.

Perhaps in "the old days" that may have been true, but in today's competitive business environment, it is mostly NOT true. It takes approximately ten years to be at the break-even point after investing $500,000-$750,000 in a practice or business. So why are you waiting for clients? Especially when a little professional publicity can bring them in? P.T. Barnum was a master of promotion. One thing he said is worth quoting here; "A terrible thing happens without publicity…NOTHING!"

It's Hard To Be At Center Stage

Self-promotion is the art and science of putting yourself at center-stage. The leading role is the one you know best. Shining the spotlight on yourself is an intensely personal venture. Once you get past the fear and reluctance of promoting yourself, and begin to see results, it will become a fun process that will follow your business life from now on.

The bottom-line to self-promotion is *self*. You know your business or profession best. With a little thought you will be able to determine what sorts of promotion and publicity will work best for you.

One of the first steps in overcoming the initial fear of self-promotion is to do something subtle or low-key like a community service sponsorship or event. After you see the results of small projects, you can graduate to more overt and direct promotional projects.

The Busy Practice

Some veterinary hospitals find themselves in a different situation-too much business. For these practices there is a unique way to use publicity.

1. Examine your client database. You will probably discover that about 20% of your clients are responsible for 80% of your business. These are the kind of clients that make practice fun-you know the ones.

2. Promote and publicize in ways to attract MORE of these types of clients and begin purging all the others! While this is radical thinking, many busy practices are doing just that. Concentrating on your best clients helps keep the doctors and staff happier and less stressed. This translates into treating clients and patients better, because practice becomes enjoyable again.

This can only be done if you have the courage to focus on the 20%, and then make a commitment to publicize and promote your practice to attract and retain more of this type of client.

Using publicity and promotions to build community awareness and even celebrity-style recognition will build people's trust in your abilities, and that puts you on the map. Clients will come to your practice because they have read your articles, seen you on the news, heard you on the radio, or seen you helping people at your sponsored events. That's priceless advertising! Further, it's effective public awareness that drives new clients.

INVENTORY MANAGEMENT

Kurt Oster MS SPHR

Kurt A. Oster, MS, SPHR is a practice management consultant with Veterinary Healthcare Consultants, LLC–a national consulting firm dedicated to providing innovative and resourceful business solutions for veterinary professionals and humane organizations. Kurt is certified as a Senior Professional in Human Resources (SPHR), the highest level of certification offered by the Society for Human Resource Management. Prior to consulting, Kurt served as Hospital Administrator for a 16-doctor, 24-hour, full-service, veterinary hospital for six years. Additionally, he worked as an educator for a veterinary software firm for nine years. During this time he educated the staffs of over 325 veterinary practices on all disciplines of practice management. Kurt is the finance instructor for the American Animal Hospital Association's (AAHA) Veterinary Management Development School (VMDS) Level One and Advanced. He is a frequent lecturer and he has been published in the Veterinary Practice News and is regularly featured in AAHA's Trends Magazine. He may be reached via e-mail at kurt@vhc.biz

The primary emphasis of this chapter is to help improve the overall efficiency and profitability of inventory operations in practice. The subject begins with a brief but relatively thorough introduction to inventory management as it pertains specifically to daily operations in a veterinary practice. Once knowledge of "ideal" inventory options is gained, the chapter will introduce several techniques for troubleshooting inventory problems.

The first challenge in understanding inventory management as it pertains to veterinary medicine is the usage of standardized terms. The first terms to be defined are found on a Profit and Loss Statement from practice operations. Most practices have an account for "Drugs and Supplies." Drugs are usually defined as any form of medication that may be directly administered to a patient. Examples of drugs might include cephalexin capsules or acepromazine tablets. Supplies, on the other hand, are those inventory items consumed by the practice in the performance of a service. Examples of supplies might include a syringe or a catheter. Supplies may also represent inventory items required to process and/or dispense drugs such as drug vials.

The definitions outlined above will be used throughout this document. However, it should be noted that some practices also use these terms to make a distinction between items that may require the collection of sales and/or use taxes. Discussion of sales tax laws is beyond the scope of this chapter; a tax professional should be consulted if the practice has any questions or concerns in regards to sales and/or use taxes.

The Big Picture

For most practices, a single account line for drugs and supplies is an acceptable level of detail in the Profit and Loss Statement. Larger practices (sales in excess of one and one-half million dollars per year) may wish to analyze inventory costs in greater detail. Typically, a more detailed analysis of inventory costs would parallel profit centers within the practice. Examples of profit center detail would include radiology costs, surgery costs, hospital costs, dental costs, etc. Noteworthy exceptions to this rule are laboratory costs and diet costs. Most practices (regardless of size) will give these profit centers separate accounts if their respective sales exceed 3.0% of practice gross revenues. Laboratory costs may be further divided into in-house and sendout costs if the practice has a large in-house laboratory operation.

Specifically tracking diet costs is common because diets have a very small markup percentage and hence are items with low profit margin. Diets are also the most susceptible inventory item to "shrinkage" in the veterinary practice. Most practices also do a poor job of tracking diets sold to clients versus diets used in house to feed hospitalized pets or boarders. Diet costs are easier to track than other items in the practice because typically the most prevalent lines come from proprietary distributors. This simplifies bookkeeping procedures because it eliminates the need to categorize invoices on a line-by-line basis as is required with most other forms of profit center analysis.

Laboratory costs are frequently monitored on a separate basis for two reasons. The first reason is the laboratory is the greatest single source of missed charges in most practices. Despite enormous efforts to correctly establish profitable laboratory fees, many practices continue to lose money in their laboratory due to missed charges. Missed charges generate expenses because the work has been performed, but no income has been received (insights on how to capture lost charges are included in the chapter on *Scheduling and Invoicing*). Tracking in-house laboratory costs is also monitored in order to factor in fee setting decisions for the laboratory. Practices in the past have established fees by using ancient rules of thumb such as "two times send out cost" which do not accurately reflect true costs involved in running the laboratory.

In order to simplify the process of tracking laboratory costs, most practices will place a weekly order for laboratory supplies in a separate telephone call to the distributor so the entire week's laboratory supplies arrive on a single invoice. As with diet purchasing, this simple step of placing a specialized order means the total of the entire invoice may be posted to the in-house laboratory account and no additional "dissection" of the invoice is required on the part of the bookkeeper.

Many practices also separate send out laboratory charges from the in-house lab. This is also simple to facilitate due to the specific invoices received each month for testing services. These invoices can be posted directly to the laboratory send-out account. It is a wise precaution to utilize these invoices in two separate audits. The first audit is against the send out laboratory logbook to make sure that all of the tests listed on the invoice were actually sent to the lab. Practices regularly report billing errors on the part of the laboratories they use. The second audit should compare this invoice to the computerized billing records of each of the patients listed to make sure they were actually charged for the services listed. Some practices have missed laboratory charges in excess of $3,000 per month due to faulty billing processes and a lack of audits.

Balance sheets also contain important information regarding inventory. Generally, most veterinary practices produce accountant-prepared financial statements once each year. An important piece of this process is to obtain a complete, accurate and timely value of all inventory on hand. This requires a physical count of all inventory items (drugs and supplies) multiplied by an accepted cost (usually the average cost) of each of the items. Several important measures of inventory management performance can be calculated from this data.

The first indicator that can be calculated is the number of inventory turns each year. Within reason, the greater the number of inventory turns the better the management (and hence profitability) of the inventory. Turns indicate how often the total value of the practice inventory is being consumed as the practice provides goods and services to its clients and patients. The equation for calculating the number of turns is the cost of goods sold (from the Profit and Loss

Statement) divided by the average value of standing inventory. For example, if the cost of goods sold was $71,400 and the average inventory represents $21,000, then "turns" can be calculated as follows:

$$\frac{\text{Cost of Goods Sold}}{\text{Average Inventory}} \quad = \quad \frac{\$71.4K}{\$21K} = \quad 3.4 \text{ Turns}$$

In the above example, the practice turns over its entire inventory 3.4 times each year. This would indicate a veterinary practice that is doing a very good job of managing its inventory since the typical range for small animal practices is 3.2 to 3.4 turns per year. Why is this important?

Inventory turns are one of the most important concepts to understand in inventory management. To illustrate—assume you have $10,000 cash in your hand and you want to invest it to earn some money (return on your investment). If you purchase $10,000 worth of inventory and sell it for $12,500 over the course of a year, you have made $2,500 in gross profit for the year or a 25% return on your initial investment. Now a 25% return on investment isn't a bad return in almost any market, but could you do better? What if you took only $5,000 of your money and purchased inventory that you sold for $6,250 in six months. You could reinvest $5,000 of those dollars again, sell it for another $6,250 and make ($1,250+$1,250) $2,500 dollars in one year off of an initial investment of $5,000, which equals a 50% return on investment. Could you still do better?

What if you invested $2,500 in inventory and over a 3-month period sold it for $3,125. If you reinvested $2,500 of those dollars over again three more times during the year, you would generate $2,500 gross profit off an initial investment of $2,500 which is equivalent to a 100% return on investment. Therefore, the more times your inventory turns over, the bigger your return on investment. This also translates to a smaller amount of your capital being tied up in inventory sitting on your shelves. At the beginning of this scenario, you had $10,000 cash in your hand to invest. If you determined that you can turnover your inventory four times during the year and will therefore only need to invest $2,500 in drugs and supplies; that leaves you $7,500 cash to invest in something else such as new equipment for your laboratory, or perhaps some computer upgrades.

A higher number of inventory turns is an admirable goal until the increased number of turns represents an increased frequency of shortages. A lower number of turns frequently represent a "we must never run out" philosophy, which ties up valuable capital in standing inventory.

Once the number of turns has been calculated, that information can be used to calculate the number of days of inventory on hand. The formula for this calculation is:

$$\frac{\text{\# of days in a year}}{\text{\# of turns}} \quad = \quad \frac{365}{3.4} \quad = \quad 107.4 \text{ days on hand}$$

This equation illustrates the fact that a practice with a number of inventory turns on the high end of normal typically has 107 days worth of standing inventory on hand.

These two formulas are the primary measurements of efficiency in inventory management in the veterinary practice. Knowing these values is very important for establishing a baseline in order to be able to measure the effectiveness of any changes that are made to current inventory management. It should further be noted that these indicators are only valuable if the numbers used to calculate them are accurate. Some veterinarians do not accurately count quantities on hand; others do not have current cost figures available to calculate realistic shelf values. This may be of significant concern for these practices because inventory technicians have not entered receiving costs into their practice computers on supply items for a considerable length of time (potentially as long as 3-4 years).

Also, some veterinarians may report less than accurate inventory values to their accountants in order to improve their tax position. In order to properly evaluate changes to the inventory system, the numbers used in these calculations MUST be accurate.

The final and most prevalent benchmark indicator for practices to utilize in the management of inventory is the cost of goods sold as a percentage of gross revenue. This is a simple number to calculate, but there can be a wide margin of error in its application. It is a difficult number to benchmark because there is an enormous potential for variance even amongst small animal practices. We have seen practices stock from 400 to 1,100 different inventory items. Some practice sell lots of ancillary items such as collars and leashes while others sell almost no such items. The inventory pricing structure as well as the service pricing structure of a practice can greatly influence the final number calculated from this report. Monthly variances can be high depending on such factors as when and how delayed billings are handled. If a practice purchases a large quantity of heartworm preventative in January on a delayed billing until June, the cost of goods sold could be artificially low in April and May and artificially high in June when that large invoice is paid. The best way to use this number is for internal comparisons over as long a period of time as possible (such as on a semi-annual, or annual basis).

It's All in the Details

The remaining discussion of inventory management will focus on a level that is much closer to where the inventory technician functions on a daily basis. The information needed for decision-making at this level should all be available to the technicians without requiring clearance from the Practice Manager or the practice owner (such as access to the financial statements might).

Inventory items that are invoiced directly to clients are easier to manage than supply items. Virtually all veterinary practice management software systems on the market today will track sales statistics generated automatically by invoicing the client. This data is usually reported in month-to-date and year-to-date sales statistics. This data can be used to determine the most effective reorder point and reorder quantity for each item. The reorder point is the point at which the computer will remind you to order the item. For those items that normally turn over very quickly, most practices set the reorder point at approximately a two-week supply. If possible, the reorder quantity is usually about a two-week supply as well, or the smallest container size that must be purchased if the container size is greater than the two-week quantity.

For example, if the sales reports indicate that the practice typically sells about twenty 200mg amoxicillin tablets each week, the computer would have a reorder point of approximately 40 or 60 tablets. This would allow the practice to have enough safety stock to cover an unusually large usage of the product. It would also allow enough time to reorder from a different distributor if the first distributor has the item on backorder. Ideally the practice would order 40-60 tablets if it was possible to do so. In reality, the smallest unit the practice can purchase would probably be a 100-tablet bottle. In this example the practice is forced to purchase a five-week supply of this item. However, this 35-day supply is considerably less than the 107 days of standing stock we said was average for a typical small animal practice. This is because there are a number of inventory items that the practice must stock in order to be prepared for acute emergencies that turnover very slowly. Examples would include medications for heartworm treatment or an ethylene glycol test kit. These items may take a year to turnover (if they don't expire first). Therefore, when the turnover times of all inventory items within the practice are combined, the result is average turnover time of 107 days.

Every item that is received by the practice should be entered into the inventory receiving option of the veterinary software. This step triggers three important functions. First, it increases the shelf count in the computer in order to remove the item from the computer's want list. Second, it provides the computer with current cost information in order to update the selling price (if the computer is configured to do so). Lastly, it updates the computer's purchase records. This is an important function for supply items that do not get directly invoiced to clients. This purchase history can be used to approximate a two-week purchase quantity when placing the order. For example, if you only have one box of 1-inch 20 gauge needles in stock and the computer shows that you purchase an average of 4 boxes of these needles each month, it tells you that you only have a one-week supply of needles on-hand and that you should purchase 2 or 3 more boxes.

In most small animal practices, approximately one-third to one-half of the inventory items are items that can be directly invoiced to clients. The remainder of inventory items are supply items. Supply items must therefore be logged into the computer in order to create a purchase history if that history is to be used for helping estimate purchase quantities. This purchase history will also help during those times when shopping for a lower purchase cost is indicated. The only other alternatives are working off of the technician's memory, or utilizing a manual system of shelf tags.

The computer should always be used to track all of those items invoiced directly to clients. The computer will tirelessly count how many items have been purchased, how many have been sold and when the time is right to order more. Virtually all tablets, capsules, shampoos, drops and ointments can be tracked in this manner. Ancillary items can also be tracked in this manner as well as flea, tick and heartworm products.

Tracking premium diets offers a unique set of problems. The majority of diets are sold to clients and tracked directly by the invoice. Unfortunately, some diet is also used in-house to feed hospitalized patients. The worst possible method for handling this challenge is to set up the practice as a client in the computer and invoice the practice. If sold at cost, the selling of diet will create false sales that will result in false and artificially high sales data. This method will also create a false accounts receivable obligation as well. An alternative that some practices try is to invoice the items to the practice at zero cost. If invoiced to the practice for zero dollars, the computer will record a lot of transactions at zero dollars, which will cause the average client transaction to be reported artificially low. Both methods will create an artificially high transaction number, which will skew the results of a number of practice health indicators.

The correct method of dealing with this issue is to utilize the return to vendor option in the software's inventory capabilities. This option is where an incorrect or expired item would be returned back to the vendor for credit. The practice simply sets itself up in the computer as a vendor and completes a return to vendor transaction for any diet that is brought into the ward for in-hospital use. At the end of the month a vendor purchase history report can be run which will indicate the quantity and dollar value of all inventory consumed by the practice.

Practices that have an actual central storage location will enter all **supply** items into the computer in this manner to record **supply** usage. Examples would be returning to vendor a box of needles. The box will be placed into the treatment room for use; when the box is emptied another box will be "returned" to the practice. This allows the want list feature of the software to always have an accurate shelf count on file so it can signal the technician when items need to be ordered.

It is extremely important to note that when an order is received from a vendor and entered into the computer, it does much more than update the quantity on hand and the purchase history. Receiving the item also allows the computer to compare the current cost with the average cost, or last cost (depending on which software package is in use) and determines whether or not a price increase should be recommended.

Price increases are determined by multiplying the receiving (purchase) cost times the predetermined markup percentage. For example, if an item once cost 20 cents per tablet and the practice utilized a 100% markup percentage, the tablets would sell to clients for 40 cents each. If the total cost were to rise to 22 cents each, the new selling price would be 44 cents each. Practices that do not allow the computer to automatically raise prices risk drastic reductions in revenue. In the above example, failing to raise the per tablet selling price to 44 cents would result in the loss of 10% of potential product revenue until a new price is determined. This can have a devastating impact on a practice's bottom line if the practice fails to pass along cost increases. The extra couple of hours each week it takes to have a technician enter purchase data into the computer is one of the most cost effective uses of support staff. Most practices could pay full time wages for this single function and still make a profit. ALL INVENTORY

PURCHASES SHOULD BE ENTERED INTO THE COMPUTER IN A TIMELY MANNER.

When establishing a fee structure for inventory control with the practice software, there are three common components. They are: per unit pricing; minimum price, and; dispensing fee (sometimes called a filling fee). These fees play a critical role in making the pharmacy a profit center for the practice instead of a source of red ink.

A minimum price is the minimum dollar amount that an inventory item is allowed to leave the practice for. Minimum prices tend to be used very little these days since most practices are computerized. Minimum prices were very popular when invoices were done by hand and the staff could remember this simple rule of thumb to get the client processed and out the door. Most practices stocked considerably fewer medications then, and most were fairly inexpensive. Some practices had fee structures as simple as "all pills are 10 cents each with a minimum purchase fee of five dollars." Those days are gone! Contemporary practices may stock hundreds of pharmaceuticals with costs ranging from less than one cent to several dollars per pill. Proper pricing must be delegated to the computer.

A dispensing fee is a fee that recovers the labor and other costs associated with getting the medication(s) out the door with the client. Virtually every veterinary management software program allows for the utilization of a dispensing fee. The fee is automatically built into the total price that the client sees on the invoice. It does not appear as a separate itemized charge as many doctors initially fear.

Depending on the local market, dispensing fees currently run in the range of $6-15.00. When a medication is invoiced, the dispensing fee plus the per-unit prices are combined, then checked against the minimum price (if one has been set). The computer will then invoice the client whichever amount is higher. For example, if a medication costs 10 cents per tablet and is marked up 100% it will sell for 20 cents per tablet. Let's also assume that the practice has a $6.00 dispensing fee and a minimum price of $10.00. If the doctor prescribes one tablet twice daily for five days, ten tablets will need to be dispensed. The price to the client will be 20 cents per tablet, times ten tablets equals $2.00, plus a $6.00 dispensing fee equals $8.00. The computer will compare this $8.00 total to the minimum price of $10.00 and charge the client the greater amount (in this case, the $10.00). In this example, it doesn't seem like the dispensing fee adds much value, however, very few tablets cost 10 cents.

Let's repeat the prior example with a medication that costs the practice 65 cents per tablet. Utilizing the same 100% markup, this medication would sell for $1.30 per tablet. Dispensing 10 tablets would total $13.00. If however a $6.00 dispensing fee were in use, the medication would be priced out at $19.00. This total would then be compared to the minimum price of $10.00 and the computer would charge the higher price, which is $19.00. Therefore, without a dispensing fee the practice would lose six dollars on this and every similar transaction. Specifically, the practice would lose money on any inventory transaction where the total tablet price was greater than $4.00, because the minimum price would no longer be making up the difference in the total fee.

The above example utilized a markup percentage of 100% (otherwise known as doubling the cost). Most practices today utilize a markup in the range of 120-150% for most pharmaceuticals. This means it takes very little medication to get to the number where the practice is losing revenue by not charging proper and complete inventory fees. A 100% markup is acceptable for those items that have attained commodity status within practices that are very competitive such as flea and tick medications. However, most pharmaceuticals typically mark up in the 120-150% range depending on how quickly the product is expected to turnover. Items that are expected to sit on the shelf longer need to recover greater storage costs and additional return on the invested capital. True "shelf sitters" need to be marked up even higher. It is not unusual for practices to add 10% per month to items for each additional month they are expected to sit on the shelf before they are utilized. Examples include such items as orthopedic pins and plates. A surgeon is required to keep these items on hand, yet it may be 6 months to a year before they are used. A markup in the range of 150-200% is not unusual for these items.

If you have a fee schedule in place, but are unsure of the markup percentage used to create this schedule, the following formulas may be helpful. To determine a markup percentage of an item, the formula is:

$$\frac{(\text{selling price}-\text{purchase cost})}{\text{purchase cost}} \times 100\% = \text{the markup percent}$$

Therefore, if an item is priced at $2.00 and it cost the practice $1.00, the markup is:

$$\frac{\$2.00-\$1.00}{\$1.00} = \frac{1}{1} \times 100\% = 100\% \text{ markup}$$

If your practice utilizes a multiplication factor to set fees, such as product cost times 2.5 equals the selling price, the formula to determine the markup percentage is as follows:

Multiplication factor–1 X 100%=the markup percentage

In the above example of 2.5, the result would be:

2.5–1=1.5 X 100%=150% markup

The revenue generated by the markup percentage covers the costs associated with the ordering and storage of the medication including the costs associated with the inventory technician. This revenue also covers the compensation of the veterinarian who prescribed the medication. Combining wages and benefits, veterinary compensation alone will usually approximate 25% of the price charged.

The dispensing fee is created to recover the costs associated with getting the medication packaged and into the hands of the client. These costs are commonly referred to as the costs of transaction (COT). In order to understand the costs involved in the transaction it is necessary to understand how labor should be billed in the veterinary practice. The lack of a proper dispensing fee is probably the single greatest problem with inventory operations I see at veterinary facilities!

Labor in a veterinary practice can be divided into two categories-hard labor (sometimes referred to as direct labor) and soft labor (sometimes referred to as indirect labor). Hard labor is defined as the actual tasks performed by the employee to assist a client or a patient. Examples of hard labor would be answering the telephone or counting out tablets. Soft labor costs are those tasks that support the hard labor. Examples of soft labor would include hiring staff members, training, performing reviews, attending staff meetings and payroll functions. The generally accepted norm in veterinary medicine is hard labor and soft labor existing in a ratio of one to one. Simply put, for every one minute of work performed, there is one additional minute of extra labor to support that work. If a practice does not factor soft labor costs into its fee structure, it will lose money on each task that is performed.

For example, if a technician is being paid $10.00 per hour and the practice wanted to keep staff wages at 20% of gross revenue, then the technician would bill out at $50.00 per hour ($10.00/0.2). If a task such as flushing a catheter takes

3 minutes, there is an additional 3 minutes of soft labor involved for a total of 6 minutes. Six minutes is 1/10 of an hour so the total fee would be $5.00 (1/10 hour at $50.00 per hour).

This means that a $7.00 dispensing fee designed to recover the COT allows staff members paid at the rate of $10.00 per hour 4.2 minutes to complete the tasks involved in getting medication ready for a client. This is calculated as follows:

4.2 minutes of hard labor+4.2 minutes of soft labor=8.4 minutes
8.4 minutes/60 minutes per hour=0.14 hours x $10.00/hour=$1.40
$1.40 as staff labor cost (which is typically 20% of revenue)=$1.40/0.2=$7.00

Using a simple refill as an example, in 4.2 minutes the staff must, at a minimum, complete the following tasks:

1. Answer the telephone and speak to the client
2. Pull the pet's medical record for the doctor
3. Locate the doctor and ask them to look at the record and approve the refill
4. Type out a prescription label for the medication
5. Measure the medication (such as counting out the pills) and place it in a dispensing vial
6. Prepare an invoice for the client
7. Greet the client
8. Complete the invoice and collect payment from the client
9. File the medical record back where it belongs
10. Cash out that transaction as part of the end of day process

Any time the staff takes longer than 4.2 minutes to complete the above transaction components, the practice loses money on the transaction. Practices that are not charging a reasonable dispensing fee are absorbing these costs every time they complete a pharmacy transaction. The result is a pharmacy that becomes a drain on profits instead of a profit center.

The solution is simple. If a practice sets a reasonable markup (100-150%) along with a reasonable dispensing fee, then drug and supply costs become a variable expense that practice owners should rarely ever have to worry about because increases in drug costs will always be passed along by the computer and increases in labor costs will always be passed along to the client in an increased dispensing fee.

It is important to note that when extrapolated to extremes, any rule that can be made can be broken. Most practices will not charge a dispensing fee when one or two tablets are dispensed. Examples of this exception may include Droncit®, Cestex®, or an acepromazine tablet used for sedation. Most practices will simply charge a larger than average per pill charge such as $4-5.00 per pill instead of causing sticker shock for dispensing what may be perceived as a $10.00 pill.

During consultations, there is always significant discussion regarding the overall efficiency and cost effectiveness of the inventory control system. In order to have a meaningful dialogue with practice owners and practice managers an understanding of basic accounting procedures and terminology is essential. This is covered in greater detail in *Business Basics for Veterinarians*, and readers are encouraged the review this material.

On the larger scale, inventory is generally considered to behave as a variable expense. A variable expense is an expense that increases in direct relation to the amount of work that is performed. In theory, if the hospital did not see any patients it would not consume any inventory so there would be no associated inventory expense. If the hospital treated two hundred cases over a specified period of time, the inventory expense incurred should be roughly twice the amount that would be incurred if the hospital treated one hundred patients during that same time period.

If a proper fee structure is established for inventory (markup percentage and dispensing fee), the practice should almost never have to concern itself again with inventory as an area of financial concern. As items are received into the practice, they are marked up to a proper selling price and are sold. The revenue generated from the sale should pay for the inventory consumed and provide the practice with a reasonable profit.

The resulting expense for inventory consumed during a period of time is reflected in the Profit and Loss Statement. Expenses may be stated in both dollar amounts and percents. Stating expenses in percentages is valuable for analysis for it makes comparisons easier between similar practices and/or different time periods. The practice norm for inventory expense as a percentage of gross revenue in small animal practice is typically in a range near 17.5% (including diet costs while excluding laboratory costs).

Traditionally, veterinarians have tried to make their practices more profitable by controlling expenses. Contemporary financial thinking favors driving additional income, rather than attempting to control expenses. This contemporary theory is based on three factors. First, veterinary practices have high fixed costs (this concept will be discussed in greater detail later), so once breakeven sales volume is reached, many dollars will go straight to net due to the low percentage of variable costs associated with veterinary practices. Second, the amount of potential available for expense control is minimal compared to the potential for increasing income. The best most practices can hope for is a 5-10% reduction in expenses, but some practices have raised revenue per pet as much as 200-300%.

The final factor influencing the decision to drive income is the cost associated with trying to decrease expenses such as inventory. Typically, a technician would be assigned to telephone shop in an effort to locate drugs and supplies at a lower cost. As illustrated previously, if a technician is paid at the rate of $10.00 per hour, that technicians billing rate would be $100.00 per hour. Rarely does telephone shopping result in a total cost reduction greater than that expended to generate the savings. Simply put, why spend two dollars to save one?

If however, the numbers reported (for inventory costs as a percent of practice gross revenue) indicate a significant variance from the norm, they must be investigated. There are five possible explanations for inventory costs to be above guidelines. They are: product mix; undercharging; bookkeeping error; increased safety stock; and shrinkage. Let's examine each one of these possible explanations separately, understanding that the true cause is often a combination of these factors.

Product mix may be a significant factor at practices that do a large volume of diet sales. Most small animal practices do sell at least some prescriptions and/or premium diets. These diets typically have price markups in the range of 25-43% of purchase cost. This markup is significantly lower than the 100-150% markup that is typical for pharmaceuticals. This means that as diet sales increase as a percentage of total sales, the cost of goods sold as a percentage of total sales will increase as well. The mix of service receipts versus product sales also impacts these percentages. A practice with a large retail area would be expected to have a higher percentage of inventory sales than a practice with little or no merchandise sales. If the inventory-to-service mix skews closer to inventory than a standard small animal practice model, the cost of inventory as a percentage of gross will also increase. This is especially true if lower margin items such as diets cause the skew.

To test this hypothesis, most practices will track diet purchases and sales as separate entries in their chart of accounts rather than blending the data into a single drugs and supplies category. The generally accepted value that mandates a separate account for diet is 3.0% of gross revenue. If diet sales are exceeding this amount, management should look at diet sales and expenses separately from total drugs and supplies.

The effects of flea and tick products in the product mix can also be significant, for several reasons. The first reason is the actual classification of the products. Some practices have continued to categorize flea and tick products as ancillary items to be consistent historically when flea and ticks sprays and collars were sold in competition against pet stores and department stores. Veterinarians sold approximately 2% of the national market share of these items. More recently, with the advent of the so-called flea and tick super products, veterinarians have gained enormous market share with some estimates as high as 30%. Many veterinarians have also re-classified these new products as pharmacy items. Both the increased sales and re-classification may cause deviations from historical and/or standard expense norms.

The second possible factor responsible for the perception of high inventory cost is failing to properly charge for supplies consumed, inventory sold, or services provided. The topic of inventory pricing has already been discussed in great detail. Pharmaceutical markups should be in the 100-150% range, accompanied by a dispensing fee (currently ranging from $6-15.00).

However, inventory fees alone are not the only fees that affect inventory costs as a percentage of gross revenues. If a practice has not utilized a proper methodology to determine their service fees, this will impact their expense ratios as well. Reality is, it is more likely that a practice with an unusually high inventory cost as a percentage of gross income is more likely to be suffering from abnormally low service fees rather than low inventory fees. The result is a syndrome in which the practice is actually "under grossing" rather than "over expensing."

The third most common factor in higher than expected inventory costs can be bookkeeping error. The timing and allocation of delayed billings is the most common problem. A reasonable allocation for the amount of inventory used should be expensed in the Profit and Loss Statement concurrently, or figured into the true costs of inventory when making management or analysis decisions. Due to the industry-wide increase in delayed billings the possibility of bookkeeping error should always be investigated.

The fourth reason for higher than expected inventory costs can be an increase in safety stock. Safety stock is the amount of inventory represented by the reorder point. Therefore, if Amoxidrops™ are reordered when the practice has 6 bottles on the shelf, the safety stock is six. This means that it is a safe assumption that the practice will sell less than six bottles before the new stock arrives, so there is little or no risk of the practice actually running out. Properly managing safety stock levels is a critical piece of the inventory manager's responsibility, but they are seldom allowed to make these decisions alone.

A staff member with primary inventory responsibilities should have enough experience to know which items turn over quickly and which ones do not. They should be committed to maintaining as small a standing inventory as would be practical while minimizing the potential of running out of a given item. That having been said, a typical small animal practice typically stocks between 600 to 800 items. If an inventory manager is performing their job at 99% efficiency, the practice will typically have 6-8 items out of stock at any moment in time. Therefore, having several items out of stock is actually a sign of well-managed inventory.

Obviously, some items are more critical than others. Examples of critical inventory would include euthanasia solution, anesthetics and vaccines. Running out of one of these critical items can bring a practice to its knees. It can also cause a practice owner or almost any practice employee to savagely attack an inventory manager. The common response of inventory managers is to then raise the safety stock levels of all items in the building in an attempt to prevent ever being out of stock again in order to avoid future negative consequences. The result is a considerably larger amount of stock on hand. Maintaining these higher levels of stock can become extremely expensive. Generally, the personality traits that create great inventory managers such as attention to repetitive and boring numbers and details are the same traits that make them overly sensitive to negative feedback. Veterinarians, or other staff members that berate a technician when the practice is out of stock on a particular item, often create a technician that will overstock inventory. This is commonly referred to as "defensive purchasing."

The challenging exception to this rule is diet inventory. Studies have shown that if a client cannot obtain the desired type and size of premium diet they are seeking twice within a six-month period, they will discontinue the diet, or purchase it elsewhere. Due to the odd purchasing cycles for dietary products, practices that sell a lot of diet are required to keep a large amount of diet on hand to avoid stock outs. This is another reason to track all values related to diet separate from the rest of the practice inventory. At a superficial level, many practice owners and managers do not recognize the value of diet sales to a practice if they only look at the relatively small markup percentage. However, for many practices, diets are extremely profitable due both to their high number of turns as well as their ability to bond clients to a practice.

The final reason for unexpectedly poor inventory performance results is shrinkage. Shrinkage (or theft) is much more common in the workplace than most employers suspect. Some items are stolen from the workplace solely as a matter of convenience. These items would include pens and post-it© notes. However, theft of inventory on a larger scale generally indicates an underlying problem within the practice. Frequently, shrinkage can be explained by a human resources theory called the equity theory. Simply put, the equity theory implies that employees perform at a level they believe is *equal* to the quality and quantity of the compensation and recognition they receive. If an employee is being paid $10.00 per hour, but feels as though the work he or she is doing is worth $12.00 per hour, they will attempt to *equalize* the imbalance. These employees may attempt to balance the equation by decreasing their work output to what they believe is a $10/hour level, or they may attempt to increase their level of compensation. Attempts to increase their level of compensation often include stealing inventory, or embezzling cash. Shrinkage is also an indicator of low employee morale. Practices experiencing a high level of shrinkage should consider a human resources consultation.

LEGAL ASPECTS OF VETERINARY MEDICINE

Frank Muggia JD

Mr. Muggia is a graduate of Middlebury College and Boston University School of Law. For the past 13 years, he has been serving the veterinary community with representative clients across the country. Mr. Muggia's national practice has him trying cases in State and Federal Courts throughout the country including New York, Massachusetts, Georgia and Florida, and advising clients throughout the country.

Mr. Muggia has become one of the most well respected attorneys in the United States in the field of veterinary law; whether buying or selling a practice, resolving partner and employee conflicts, effectuating a solid and comprehensive business plan, or litigating restrictive covenants. He is well published in the area and lectures nationally within the veterinary industry, in addition to being listed as an approved consultant by the American Animal Hospital Association. He can be reached at www.MuggiaLaw.com

Introduction

With all the time one spends studying in veterinary school, it is surprising that there is no instruction on the legal aspects of veterinary care. After all your hard work, you land a job. You are then presented with an Employment Agreement and Restrictive Covenant. If you are lucky, you have heard of these documents but you do not know what they mean, nor do you have an appreciation for the potential long-term adverse effect they can have on your career.

You are paid a base salary with some benefits, but likely have no appreciation for the typical benefits that are paid to veterinary associates around the country, in your area; nor are you in an ideal position to negotiate for additional benefits.

When you are first practicing medicine, chances are you do not know the corporate structure of the company you are with, nor do you have an appreciation for the time, effort and expense associated with establishing a business and running the same. Because you have not had formal training in corporate structure and in partnerships, it puts you at a disadvantage when it comes time to advance your career beyond that of Associate Veterinarian.

There are five simple subject areas that will put you in an exceptional position with respect to the legal aspects of your career. They will allow you to understand Employment Agreements, depth and scope of Restrictive Covenants, and put you in a position to negotiate for your growth at the practice and your financial security.

Employment Agreements

An Employment Agreement is the document which outlines the terms and conditions of your employment with the practice. So it is fair for both employee and employer, from an employee's perspective, you want to make sure the duties and responsibilities are spelled out clearly. Will you have any management or administrative responsibilities? How will vacation, holidays and weekends be handled as well as night and emergency calls? What is the exact description of your responsibilities? Are they on a full-time or part-time basis?

Associate Veterinarians often believe all they have to negotiate with the practice is their base salary compensation. This is only a small fraction of what belongs in your Employment Agreement. It is critical that you lay forth your expectations. What additional benefits will be provided to you by the practice such as health insurance, disability and malpractice insurance?

Insofar as you want to be in a position to promote the practice and build a client base, will the practice be providing you with an expense account or entertainment account? Is it your expectation that the practice will pay all professional dues, license fees and organization fees? Furthermore, if you have a mobile practice, what are the terms and conditions under which you will be provided with a company car?

Every practice you work for is going to want you to stay on the cutting edge of technology and therefore it is fair and reasonable that they provide continuing veterinary education of at least $1,000.00 to $1,500.00 per year.

You will discuss your ability to participate in a 401K or pension plan, depending on the type of structure held by your employer.

Once the compensation terms have been considered, it is important to address the term of your agreement. Will the initial term be one year, five years or some-where in between? There is certainly a benefit to a one-year term, because you will learn so much in that first year that perhaps you will be a better position to negotiate a better deal in moving forward.

The down side is the practice owner can also change their opinion or perspective of you and it can result in your looking for work. Most Employment Agreements will carry an initial ninety-day probation period followed by a two to three year employment term.

It is important to consider how the agreement can be terminated. For instance, if you resign from the practice, pass away or become mentally incapacitated, that may be construed as a termination. However, if the practice is going to use some type of mental or physical illness or chemical dependence as a basis to terminate you, it is important that you have an opportunity to cure your alleged default. This means that if the practice believes they have grounds to terminate you, they must give you written notice of the alleged grounds for termination. You would then have an opportunity to cure those grounds. If you solve the problem within thirty days, your employment continues, but if you do not, you may be subject to termination.

Make sure the controlling law for your Employment Agreement is the law of the state in which you are practicing. With multi-state and national practices, you can be practicing in Indiana and be bound by California law. Not only does this pose a practical problem for your local attorney, but you may be forced to litigate out of state, and that puts you at a great disadvantage. Many lawyers recommend that Employment Agreements contain an arbitration provision so you can avoid lengthy and expensive litigation. Arbitration is simply a procedure whereby the parties voluntarily agree to have a neutral determine the dispute short of any Jury, Judge, trial or lengthy and expensive discovery.

The above forms the fundamental basis for an Employment Agreement. There is no question there may be other terms and conditions unique to your situation that you would like to incorporate into your Employment Agreement, but you now have a clearer sense of the objective when executing an agreement.

Restrictive Covenant/Non-Competition Agreements

When you sign an Employment Agreement, quite often it will contain Non-Competition or Restrictive Covenant provisions and it is critical that you fully understand these types of documents before you sign them. Restrictive Covenants are designed to limit the ability of a departing employee from competing within a certain geographic area for a certain period of time. However, there is a common misconception about these agreements within the industry.

A Restrictive Covenant is not designed or intended to punish an employee. To the contrary, a Restrictive Covenant is designed to protect the goodwill of the business for which the employee was working. The question becomes, if a doctor leaves a practice, how long will it take the practice to replace this particular individual so they may protect the goodwill created by the investment in the departing doctor and the departing doctor's practice.

When a Court looks at a Restrictive Covenant, they generally don't ask themselves what the effect is on the departing individual; their focus is on whether the geographic and temporal limitation are fair and reasonable to protect the legitimate business interests of the practice.

If you had a two-year limitation around a fifteen-mile radius of a practice, this means that if the doctor leaves the practice, for two years that doctor will be unable to compete in any capacity with the practice s/he departed, within a fifteen-mile radius of that practice. In most states, that radius is as the crow flies.

If that departing veterinarian wanted to challenge the Restrictive Covenant, he or she would have to prove to the Court that either two years or fifteen miles was unreasonable and was not narrowly tailored to protect a legitimate business interest (e.g., the company's goodwill), or the public interest has been violated.

Before you sign a Restrictive Covenant, you should read it over very carefully, and of all the papers you may have to sign in your practice, have an attorney review the same regarding the scope and depth of the limitations.

Typical provisions you will find in a Restrictive Covenant are as follows:

    a)   You will be unable to invest in a competing business.

    b)   You will be unable to hire employees from the practice that you left and unable to solicit employees of the practice.

c) You will be unable to advertise in a newspaper or publication with circulation and/or sales in the town in which the practice was located and in a town or city contiguous to the practice's location.

d) You will be unable to use any of the confidential information of the practice, which would include, without limitation, their customer list, billing practices and marketing philosophy.

Should you breach or threaten to breach the Restrictive Covenant, most of these agreements contain a provision that would allow the practice to go to court and obtain a Preliminary Injunction. To recover on the Preliminary Injunction, the practice would only have to prove that there was a contract, that you either breached or threatened to breach the contract, that there was a likelihood of success on the merits, and that if the court did not enter an injunction prohibiting you from your conduct, there is a likelihood of irreparable injury. This means that your competition will damage the practice. If the Court finds that the balance of equities are in favor of the practice, an injunction will be entered and you may even be facing the obligation of paying attorney's fees to the practice that you left.

It is a disturbing trend in the industry that Associate Veterinarians, fresh out of veterinary school, are required to sign Restrictive Covenants that are overly broad and debilitating to the veterinarian. You leave veterinary school, you get a job, you buy a house, you settle down, and then you find out that it is not the right practice for you. However, the limitation that you agree to is such that if you want to continue to have gainful employment, you can't continue to live where you have established your family.

Be very careful about any Restrictive Covenant and when you consider it, ask yourself these questions:

If I leave this practice, (1) is there somewhere else I can go without violating the agreement; (2) can I stay here if I want to maintain my practice; (3) can I maintain the nature of my practice; (4) will I be able to make a living?

If you had to answer any of these questions in the negative, you need to reconsider whether or not this Restrictive Covenant should be executed.

Buy/Sell And Partnership Agreements

When your transition into practice goes well, you may have the welcome opportunity to become a partner in a business. The days of serving as a partner on the basis of a handshake are over. It is critical, when you enter a partnership, that you memorialize and understand your expectations in writing.

Eventually, virtually every partnership will result in divergent perspectives or focus and the Buy/Sell Agreement and/or Partnership Agreement will assist you in ensuring a fair and effective resolution in any dispute that arises.

Once you establish the simple standards of who owns what percentage, there are a number of topics that require your ongoing consideration. How are capital contributions going to be handled and what will you get in return for these contributions?

Enter into an understanding on how employees will be hired and fired and how disputes over practice policy will be resolved.

Have you considered how the partnership interest will be handled in the event of death, divorce, dissolution, bankruptcy or disability? Arrange a standard whereby the corporation can either buy back shares, or the ongoing partner will have the right, but perhaps not the obligation, to acquire those outstanding shares.

Succession planning requires forethought. If you are successful in building a practice that doubles or triples in value, and your partner desires to retire, will you have the cash available to buy out the interest? Should your partner suddenly die, the only way you may have the capital necessary to acquire the interest is if you have cross-life insurance policies.

If your partner desires to retire, the Buy/Sell and/or Partnership Agreement will have a mechanism whereby that interest will be purchased.

The Buy/Sell and Partnership Agreement are designed to ensure that while you see eye-to-eye and agree on the direction of the company, the mechanisms for smooth business operation are agreed upon.

Should a dispute arise, this agreement should facilitate a prompt and inexpensive resolution.

The key to a successful business is to make sure that the Buy/Sell and/or Partnership Agreement is in place at the inception, that each partner is represented by counsel in making their decisions, and that the parties comply with corporate formalities in the years to come.

Informed Consent

As a new veterinarian, the enthusiasm to provide treatment, test your experiences and satisfy clients is tested on a regular basis. Before you undertake the responsibility as a doctor, make sure you have a clear understanding as to the practice's informed consent policy.

Informed consent is the concept whereby a pet owner satisfactorily and intelligently understands the procedure to which their pet is going to be subjected. The law recognizes that you, as the doctor, have the superior knowledge base and understanding regarding risks associated with the care you provide. Informed consent mandates that you determine a mechanism by which you can educate your clients so that they have a clear understanding of those risks in layman's terms.

Study your company's informed consent policy and their written documentation. If there is any ambiguity or confusion in your mind regarding the informed consent waivers, then question the practice owner and take steps to revise and modify the documents.

You do not want to unnecessarily expose yourself to litigation, particularly when the informed consent documentation can assist you in the litigation process.

Ultimately, if your competency is called into question during a legal proceeding, you want to ensure that an executed informed consent document can be presented into evidence to demonstrate that you sufficiently and adequately explained the risks and hazards associated with a procedure and that the pet owner thoroughly and clearly understood those risks.

The informed consent documentation is your last defense against litigation.

Corporate Structure

Many practices are not incorporated and are simply owned by individuals under a doing business as ("d/b/a").

Generally, when a practice is owned in your individual name, if there is litigation, you can be held personally liable. This means that a patient could potentially obtain a verdict against you that would expose the equity in your home, your retirement plans, investment accounts and the like.

Veterinarians should consult with their financial advisor to work with them to determine the appropriate tax structure for a new corporation based on their objectives, demographics and practice.

An attorney will then take the accountant's recommendation and establish the appropriate corporation. While there are many corporations of which you may be aware, such as limited liability corporations, professional limited liability corporations, sub-chapter S and sub-chapter C corporations, they are not all alike. Consult with your expert to ensure that the proper structure is put in place for you.

Even if you take the step to set up the appropriate corporation, your job is not complete. Unless you are a tenant at the particular practice, quite often the practice owner also owns the real estate. Because pain and suffering awards are limited in the United States when it comes to animal care, your biggest liability exposure as a veterinarian may be the premises liability for the real estate upon which the practice is located.

Rather than own the real estate in your own personal name, it may be in your best interest to set up a separate corporation to own the real estate or a Realty Trust. This corporate structure will insulate you from personal liability.

Your attorney can then set up Lease Agreement between the corporation and the real estate entity. This will achieve not only personal liability protection, but depending on how well structured the organization is, there might be tax benefits as well.

Conclusion

Veterinarians are among the most honorable professionals in the world. The service you provide is invaluable and the energy, compassion and the ethics with which you deliver the services are unparalleled.

Do not let the legal ramifications of practicing veterinary medicine inhibit or limit your excitement about your practice. Understand Employment Agreements before you sign them and study the nature of the Restrictive Covenants before you agree to them.

In negotiating a deal for yourself, you always want to deal from a position of strength. As badly as you want to work at a practice, that practice also wants you to work for them. You are profitable for them and you promote their goodwill. Make sure the contracts you enter into with the practice are fair and reasonable.

As you transition from a new graduate into an established marketable professional, make sure that you understand the legal ramifications of your transition as well. Look to protect yourself from personal liability, establish a proper corporation, educate your patients on the risks of the activities that you undertake on behalf of their pets and comply with corporate formalities.

Ultimately, you will consider succession planning and exit strategies. By complying with corporate formalities, and educating yourself on the above topics, you will be in the best possible situation to transition from novice veterinarian, to seasoned medical professional, to retired, yet financially secure, veterinarian.

VETERINARIANS & INDUSTRY–PARTNERS IN VETERINARY HEALTH CARE

Elizabeth Bellavance DVM MBA

Dr. Bellavance graduated from the Ontario Veterinary College in 1991 and returned to school in 1995 to complete an MBA. She has several years of experience in mixed animal practice. Currently, Dr. Bellavance provides project management and consulting services to the veterinary industry while completing a CMA (Certified Management Accountant) designation.

Introduction

Industry plays an essential role in the practice of veterinary medicine. The continued development and distribution of industry products and services have improved the quality of medicine veterinarians can offer their patients. Companion animals are living longer and healthier lives. Livestock production is more efficient and the safety of our food supply is improved.

In addition to providing necessary products and services to veterinarians, industry adds value to the profession in many other ways. Industry contributes millions of dollars each year sponsoring continuing education events for veterinarians. Financial support for research and special projects are generously provided. Contributions in the form of time, expertise and equipment often go unnoticed.

The purpose of this chapter is to provide exposure to the many ways industry members contribute to the betterment of the veterinary profession. The chapter will also address the need for veterinarians and industry to maintain an ethical relationship that instills trust and respect in the animal owning public. The first part of this chapter will concentrate on the advantages of having close ties with industry and the final section will deal with some of the potential disadvantages that must be effectively managed to keep that partnership positive and ethically sound.

There are hundreds of companies in the animal health care industry. Unfortunately, it is impossible to acknowledge all companies and their contributions in this short chapter. Ask your industry representatives about their activities that promote the veterinary profession. They will be more than grateful you asked and willing to share their contributions.

Education

Industry is very active in supporting education in the veterinary profession. This support takes many forms including sponsorship of continuing education events, educational resources, scholarships, and in-clinic sales presentations.

Educational Events

Animal health companies spend hundreds of thousands of dollars each year supporting veterinary educational events. Not only is industry's backing visible at the large international veterinary conferences, but it is also visible at the smaller local and regional conferences.

The North American Veterinary Conference has over 100 industry sponsors contributing hundreds of thousands of dollars to this event alone. Without the support of these sponsors, Dr. Colin Burrows, the Executive Director of the conference, estimates registration fees for participants would have to increase $150 to $200 per individual.[15]

The Western Veterinary Conference (WVC), which attracted North America's largest number of veterinarians in 2003, averaged approximately $300,000 in direct financial support. This figure does not include indirect sponsorship of hospitality events and concert entertainment. Dr. Stephen Crane, Executive Director

---

15 Dr. Colin Burrows, Executive Director, The North American Veterinary Conference, *pers. comm.* 5/16/2003.

of the conference, also acknowledged the time, expertise, and equipment donated to the many wet labs conducted at the conference.[16] Industry funding and support has allowed the WVC to offer the lowest registration fee for conventions of this caliber around the world. The registration fee for the world-class event was $175 in 2003. Industry's support of this conference is particularly noteworthy, given that the WVC has very strict anti-commercial policies in place.

Trade shows provide a wealth of information on the latest and greatest products and services available. Don't omit this important learning opportunity at veterinary conventions. Plan ahead and spend time visiting exhibitors. Your practice and your patients will benefit from the time you spend in the exhibit hall.

Scholarships and Awards

Veterinary schools across North America have hundreds of scholarships and awards available to them on an annual basis. Most of these are granted to students in financial need or students showing academic aptitude for a particular area in animal health. Animal health companies provide a significant proportion of this funding.

Resources

The on-line version of the Merck Veterinary Manual, published by Merck CO, Inc., represents a joint effort between Merck and Merial Limited. The Merck Veterinary Manual, in existence for over 45 years, provides the veterinary profession with a comprehensive and practice reference source. The on-line version offers a search function that allows quick and easy access to over 12,000 health care topics and over 1,200 illustrations. The on-line version is provided free of charge as a service to the veterinary profession and can be found at: www.merck-vetmanual.com.

The Compendium of Veterinary Products (CVP), published by North American Compendiums, Inc. is the most comprehensive and useful source of information

---

16 Dr. Stephen Crane, Executive Director, Western Veterinary Conference, *pers. comm.* 5/28/2003

on veterinary products. This reference book includes detailed descriptions of over 4700 products including pharmaceuticals, biologicals, pesticides and feed additives. Bayer Animal Health has generously sponsored the production of this resource for the past 14 years. Adrian Bayley, publisher of the compendium, indicates the cost of producing this resource could never be built into a realistic subscription price for the veterinarian. Bayer funds have made this possible. In addition, financial support from Bayer has made the CVP available to AVMA members on-line.

Value Added Educational Services

Almost all animal health care companies offer some form of service that improves the ability of practices to generate revenue and provide high quality medical care to their patients. These value added services often involve efforts designed to educate veterinarians and support staff on a particular health topic and a particular product or service.

Obviously the ultimate goal of the animal health company is to sell more products and services. However, veterinary practices can benefit from the offerings as well. Veterinarians should choose value added services they believe have the greatest potential for improving their ability to practice quality medicine. The revenues will naturally follow.

Presented here is a very small sampling of the types of value-added programs available from industry.

Hill's Pet Nutrition provides on-line staff training to all members of the veterinary healthcare team. Training is provided free of charge. The objectives of the learning modules are to understand and communicate information regarding pet nutrition. Another objective is to understand the benefits that can be derived from communicating this knowledge in practice. Dr. Marty Becker, Dr. Robin Downing and Fritz Wood are well-known professionals involved with this educational effort. For more information visit their website at www.hillspet.com.

Burns Veterinary Supply provides staff training and other practice management advice. The company offers seminars and in-house programs to practices and utilizes independent consultants to support their activities. Burns can be contacted through their website (www.burnsvet.com) or by phone at 1-800-922-8767.

Merial has produced a Zoonotic Education Kit for veterinarians, technicians and other support staff. This educational program is approved for CE credits and discusses the zoonotic risk of roundworm and hookworm infections. The kit contains a CD-ROM, video, study guide, and a zoonotic disease pocket reference. Educational charts and graphs are also included. Experts in the field of zoonotic disease provide guidelines to facilitate discussions between hospital staff and pet owners on zoonotic disease. The prevalence of zoonotic parasites is included as well as legal aspects of zoonotic diseases. For further information, contact Merial at 1-888-637-4251, www.merial.com

Sales Representatives—an educator role?

Many, if not most veterinarians will agree that sales representatives play a role in educating the veterinary profession. They are often the first to introduce veterinarians to new products and services before they appear in scientific publications. In doing so, they ensure veterinarians have access to the latest medical care for their patients. Sales representatives provide both the benefits and risks of using their products. The information provided by sales representatives is potentially biased and veterinarians should objectively evaluate the material supplied to them.

Some clinics do not allow sales representatives to have access to the veterinarians. If this is the case, one of three scenarios is likely occurring:

1. You are practicing in the dark ages and you need to become more aware of new products and services offered by industry.

2. You have a reliable 'gatekeeper' at your practice that filters the information for you and provides you with the essentials.

3. You are a reading buff who spends Saturday nights reading all available peer-reviewed literature in veterinary medicine. Perhaps not on Saturday night, but you get the picture.

A special note on gatekeepers: Ensure you have entrusted the gatekeeper role in your practice to a reliable, ethical, educated individual. If your gatekeeper is wearing and utilizing all the latest promotional paraphernalia supplied by industry, you may not be receiving the most accurate information. After all, personality and gifts play a role in sales. This will be discussed in more detail later in the chapter.

Should you rely solely on sales representatives for information on products and services? Studies in human medicine reveal that relying solely on information supplied by sales representatives can be problematic. In a 1995 study[17] reported in JAMA, 11% of pharmaceutical sales representatives made statements about drugs contradicting information readily availability to them. Most physicians failed to recognize the inaccurate statements. Veterinarians must critically compare the information they receive from sales representatives to information presented in reliable scientific publications.

Research

Animal health companies spend millions of dollars each year on their own research and development activities as well as providing funding for other research projects. Many educational institutions and veterinary associations receive funding from animal health companies for their research projects. Veterinarians and animal owners are able to reap the rewards of this research.

The Making of an Antibiotic

The process of bringing an antibiotic to market is a long and expensive one. According to the Animal Health Institute, a U.S. trade association representing manufacturers of animal health care products, the process takes an average of 10 years. The average cost of bringing it to market is $40 million.

Preliminary and pre-clinical trials are conducted to test a compound researchers believe has antimicrobial properties. If the results of these trials are favorable, the company conducts clinical trials under the oversight of the U.S. Food and Drug Administration's (FDA) Center for Veterinary Medicine (CVM). If the trials indicate the drug is safe and effective, an application is submitted to the FDA for drug approval. Approval processes are stringent and pharmaceutical companies

---

17 Ziegler MG, Lew P, Singer BC. The accuracy of drug information from pharmaceutical sales representatives. JAMA 1995 Apr 26;273(16):1296-8

must provide adequate clinical trial data that supports the drug's safety, quality and efficacy.

Special Projects

There are hundreds of special projects that benefit the animal health industry. Many of these projects would not exist if it were not for the financial support provided by animal health companies. The following are a few examples of industry's involvement in this type of initiative.

National Commission on Veterinary Economic Issues

The National Commission on Veterinary Economic Issues (NCVEI) is the most significant project undertaken to improve the economic health of the veterinary profession. If you are a practice owner and you are not familiar with this organization, YOU need to familiarize yourself with the services it provides.

The National Commission on Veterinary Economic Issues (NCVEI) was formed in response to a 20-year economic downward trend in the veterinary profession. Two significant studies contributed to this realization.

The Brakke Study was commissioned by the American Veterinary Medical Association and funded by Bayer Animal Health. The KPMG Mega Study was commissioned jointly by the American Veterinary Medical Association (AVMA), the American Animal Hospital Association (AAHA) and the American Association of Veterinary Colleges (AAVC). The combined cost of the two studies was $1.75 million.

The initial thrust of the National Commission on Veterinary Economic Issues was to determine the cause of the downward trend. The organization then began to develop interactive website tools to assist veterinarians in practicing better medicine and better business.

NCVEI's interactive website, located at www.ncvei.org, contains a wealth of information for veterinarians. On the website, you are prompted to submit information regarding your clinic operations. The website analyzes your numbers and compares your numbers to both national and regional averages. It then provides recommendations on how you can improve the operational aspects of your practice.

The interactive tools answer many questions about the economic health of your practice. For example, you can determine if your profit margins need to be increased or if your practice is operating efficiently. Assistance is also provided to help you determine how much adjustment to income is necessary to allow for the purchase of a new piece of equipment or, to hire an additional employee.

The types and number of tools to assist with practice management continues to be expanded upon. Immediate plans are to incorporate the ability of a practice to compare its performance from year to year, offer evaluation tools for equine veterinarians and introduce a staff utilization tool. The food animal industry will also benefit from the organization in the future.

It would be impossible for the NCVEI to have developed the scope of tools to date without the financial assistance of industry. Corporate sponsors of this very special project include Bayer Animal Health, Novartis, Merial, Hills, Pfizer, Veterinary Pet Insurance, Fort Dodge and Care Credit. At the end of 2003, these sponsors will have contributed almost $2 million to the NCVEI. Additional funding totally almost $½ million has been supplied by the AVMA, the Western Veterinary Conference, and the Canadian Veterinary Medical Association.

Expertise from members of the animal health industry has contributed significantly to the quality and variety of services NCVEI is able to offer veterinarians. Howard Rubin, the Executive Director of NCVEI, states that corporate sponsors have generously volunteered their time and services as well as their finances. For example, marketing and business development experts helped determine the price pet owners are willing to pay for services, and provided assistance in how best to match staffing needs with services offered.[18]

The importance of the National Commission on Veterinary Economic Issues to the animal health industry will only continue to grow. Again, if you are not familiar with this organization and you are not using the services they provide, YOU should be! Visit their website at www.ncvei.org or call 1-847-925-1230.

---

18 Howard Rubin, Executive Director, National Commission on Veterinary Economic Issues, *pers. comm*, 5/8/2003, 5/29/2003

Petfinder.com

Petfinder.com is an on-line searchable database of over 100,000 pets available for adoption from over 5,000 shelters across the US and Canada. Last year, the site helped more than 500,000 pets find new homes. Potential adopters are able to search for a pet by size, breed, age, sex and location. Photographs and descriptions of the pets are available. An on-line selection tool helps match adopters preferences with an appropriate breed.

Betsy and Jared Saul of Tucson, Arizona began the development of the website after a New Year's resolution to help homeless animals. The mission of Petfinder is to increase public awareness of the availability of high-quality adoptable pets and to increase the overall effectiveness of pet adoption programs across North America.

Petfinder appears to be successful in their mission. Shelters have found the site to be very beneficial. Many shelters attribute 50% or more of their adoptions to Petfinder.com. Some shelters are reporting a decrease in the number of animals euthanized and some have reported a decrease in the Number returned after initial adoption.

The service is free to both the shelters and the adopters. Shelters must register to become a part of the service. Pets that are adopted through Petfinder.com are eligible for 2 months of free pet health insurance. The available of this free service is made possible by the generous sponsorship of Nestle Purina, PetCare, PETCO Animal Supplies, PetHealth Inc., PETCO Foundation, Merial, Bissel, and American Society for the Prevention of Cruelty to Animals.

International Association of Assistance Dog Partners

The International Association of Assistance Dog Partners (IAADP) is a non-profit organization representing the needs of all dog partners including guide dogs, hearing dogs and service dogs. The primary goal of the organization is to provide a comprehensive resource of information regarding the assistance dog community. A website is used to disseminate this information and is located at www.iaadp.org.

With the help of industry, this organization is able to offer some remarkable services to its membership and the general public.

National Pet Care Centers, a corporate group of practices with 70 locations, has agreed to provide veterinary services to assistance dogs for a 20 percent discount. Avid® Microchip ID Systems, Inc., an international pet identification company, provides replacement microchips for dogs and access to its pet locator database.

The Veterinary Care Partnership program provides financial aid to members of the association for canine medical care. The financial assistance is available to those who cannot afford veterinary services by their own means. The program is supported by grants from Bayer Animal Health, Fort Dodge Animal Health, Nestle Purina, The Iams Company, and Nutramax Laboratories, Inc.

Through grants provided by Bayer Animal Health, the IAADP has created the Veterinary School Outreach Project. The purpose of the project is to educate veterinary students and veterinarians about the needs of clients with disabilities. In particular, the program addresses the needs of guide, hearing and service dogs. Representatives from IAADP travel to various veterinary Schools throughout the United States. Topics discussed include techniques for making disabled clients feel welcome, medical needs unique to assistance dogs and advice on counseling clients needing to retire or euthanize their assistance dogs. Bayer grants also support speaker presentations at various veterinary conferences throughout North American.

Benji's Buddies$_{(tm)}$ Fund

The American Humane Association recently launched the Benji's Buddies$_{(tm)}$ Fund. The Benji's Buddies Fund is a partnership between American Humane, Bayer Animal Health and Benji$_{(tm)}$. Benji is the canine movie and television star who was once an abandoned, neglected stray living on the streets before he was rescued by animal control and adopted by Benji creator, Joe Camp. The fund provides financial assistance to shelters to offset the medical costs of treating abused or neglected animals before they can be placed in caring homes. The Benji's Buddies Fund was established through a generous $30,000 donation by Bayer Animal Health. For more information on the Benji's Buddies Fund, you may contact American Humane at 866-242-1877 or www.americanhumane.org.

American Veterinary Medical Foundation–Animal Disaster Relief

The American Veterinary Medical Foundation (AVMF), founded in 1963, is comprised of veterinarians, animal health companies and private individuals. The foundation provides almost $1 million annually to various projects that facilitate the ability of veterinarians to help animals. Financial support is given for animal disaster relief, animal health studies, and veterinary financial assistance.

The Animal Disaster Relief program provides treatment for animals used in search-and-rescue operations and provides aid for animals involved in catastrophic events such as floods, tornados, hurricanes, fires, and earthquakes. The AVMF is able to respond to federal agencies and provide assistance within a 24-48 hour period.

The AVMF provided aid for the search and rescue dogs at the World Trade Center disaster in 2001 as well as the Oklahoma City Bombing in 1995. In addition, the AVMF provided support during numerous natural disasters including the Louisiana Flooding in 2001, the New Mexico Wildfires of 2000 and Hurricane Floyd in 1999.

A Disaster Relief Emergency fund reimburses the expenses of veterinarians who volunteer in times of need.

The AVMF is supported by many individuals, organizations and animal health companies. Major corporate and organizational supporters include Abbott Laboratories, American Association of Equine Practitioners, American Association of Feline Practitioners, American Society of Laboratory Animal Practitioners, American Veterinary Medical Association, Auxiliary to the AVMA, Bayer Animal Health, California Veterinary Medical Association, Cornell Feline Health Center, Fort Dodge Animal Health, Geraldine R. Dodge Foundation, Hill's Pet Nutrition, Inc., International Fund for Animal Welfare, Intervet America, Inc., JLT Services Corporation, Ohio Animal Health Foundation, Petland, Inc., Pfizer Inc., Ralston Purina Company, The American Kennel Club, The Cleveland Foundation, The Gracie Foundation of Three Dog Bakery, The Iams Company, Veterinary Centers of America, Waltham USA, Inc.

AAHA! Driving Excellence in Veterinary Practice[SM]

AAHA! Driving Excellence in Veterinary Practice[SM] is a traveling educational exhibit sponsored in part by educational grants from the following companies: Hill's Pet Nutrition, Inc., Merial Ltd., Novartis Animal Health US, and Pfizer Animal Health.

The exhibit has been custom built into an 18-wheel tractor-trailer. The tractor trailer expands to display a state-of-the-art veterinary practice including an examination room, client consultation room, in-patient area, laboratory area, diagnostic imaging area, staff training area, business office and pharmacy.

The exhibit educates veterinarians and their staff about the latest clinical and technological practices available as well as the best business practices. A multimedia presentation is used to enhance the educational experience.

AAHA! Driving Excellence in Veterinary Practice^{SM} is traveling across the country visiting veterinary medical association meetings and colleges. The exhibit also promotes the veterinary profession to pet owners.

Product sponsors of this effort include AAHA MARKETLink, Dan Scott & Associates, Inc., dbl.7 LLC, Digicare Biomedical Technology, Inc., Highland Medical Equipment, IDEXX Laboratories, Inc., Karl Storz Veterinary Endoscopy-America, Inc. Snyder Mfg Co., 3M Animal Care, VetPlan LLC, Gates Hafen Cochrane Architects, and Brede Exposition Services. For more information contact AAHA at 1-800-252-2242 or visit their website at www.aahanet.org.

Vaccine-Associated Feline Sarcoma Task Force

The Vaccine-Associated Feline Sarcoma Task Force (VAFSTF) was formed in response to the increased incidence of soft tissue sarcomas occurring at vaccination sites. The task force provides funding for research projects involving the epidemiology, etiopathogenesis, treatment and/or prevention of sarcomas. Since its inception, VAFSTF has approved over 15 studies.

In addition to providing research funding, the task force develops and distributes information to veterinarians and the general public on the issue. VAFSTF has published initial vaccination guidelines and produced a client information brochure for cat owners.

The VAFSTF, formed in 1996, has received over $800,000 to carry out its functions. The following associations and corporate sponsors have contributed to this project: the American Animal Hospital Association Foundation (AAHAF), American Association of Feline Practitioners, American Veterinary Medical Association, Cornell Feline Health Center, Veterinary Cancer Society, Ohio Veterinary Medical Association Foundation, Pfizer Animal Health Group, Fort

Dodge Animal Health, Novartis Animal Health, Schering/Plough Animal Health, Intervet America Inc., Merial Animal Health, Biocor Animal Health, Bayer Animal Health, Synbiotics Corporation, and individual donors. Additional information on this task force can be found on the AVMA website: www.avma.org/vafstf/default.asp

Maintaining an Ethical Relationship

There is cause for concern when the temptations of industry's gifts either knowingly or unknowingly affect the prescribing patterns of a medical professional. The public entrusts veterinarians and physicians to make medical choices in the best interest of the patient.

Problems in the Human Healthcare Field

In recent years, the interactions between pharmaceutical companies and physicians have gained a great deal of unfavorable media attention. The press has shed a negative image on both parties by exposing kickbacks to physicians prescribing a particular company's product.

In 2001, TAP Pharmaceuticals Inc. paid $875 million in the largest healthcare fraud settlement in history. TAP pled guilty to charges based on fraudulent pricing practices and marketing conduct.

TAP induced doctors across the country to push their products in exam rooms and provided rewards in various forms to the doctors. TAP sent cooperative physicians on extravagant trips to expensive resorts, provided free medical equipment and even forgave debts owed by some of the physicians. An unusually large number of free drug samples were provided to doctors who billed Medicare and patients for the product and pocketed the difference. There are several other cases where the marketing practices of industry and behavior of doctor's have come under investigation by federal authorities.

The pharmaceutical industry spent $15.7 billion dollars promoting prescription products in 2000. There were 83,000 sales representatives making one-to-one calls on physicians. The total value of free drug samples distributed as promotional items in the same year was $7.9 billion.[19] That amounts to a lot of *influence* in the market.

The public has become increasingly aware of the kickbacks provided to, and accepted by, physicians. These activities serve to erode the trust present in client-patient relationships.

In response to the problems, organizations representing doctors and industry became active in addressing the issues. The Pharmaceutical Research and Manufacturers Association (an association of research based pharmaceutical and biotechnology companies) adopted a professional code of ethics in 2002. The code of ethics details appropriate interactions for sales representatives in dealing with physicians. Following the code of ethics is voluntary. In 2001, the American Medical Association launched a campaign to educate physicians and sales representatives on ethical interactions with the goal of reducing gifts that are considered unethical.

What can the veterinary profession learn from the mistakes made in the human health care industry?

The AVMA has not received any complaints of this nature from the public about veterinarians.[20] The AVMA states in its Principles of Veterinary Medical Ethics'..."the choice of treatments or animal care should not be influenced by considerations other than the needs of the patient, the welfare of the client, and the safety of the public."

You may feel you are immune from the influence a gift may have on your prescribing behavior. However, several studies[21] have proven that prescribing methods and medical judgment are affected by such gifts. Doctors are more likely to prescribe a

---

19 A research report by The National Institute for Health Care Management, Research and Educational Foundation, Prescription Drugs and Mass Media Advertising, 2000 http://www.nihcm.org/DTCbrief2001.pdf

20 Arthur V. Tennyson, VMD, Assistant Executive Vice President, AVMA, *personal communication* 5/8/2003

21 Wazana A. Physicians and the pharmaceutical industry: is a gift ever just a gift? JAMA 2000 Jan 19;283(3):373-80 and

Coyle SL; Ethics and Human Rights Committee, American College of Physicians-American Society of Internal Medicine. Physician-industry relations. Part 1: individual physicians. Ann Intern Med 2002 Mar 5;136(5):396-402

company's drug based on previous interactions with the company, regardless of any demonstrable benefit!

In recent gallop polls, veterinarians have ranked above doctors, judges and policemen in ethics and honesty. If we wish to uphold this high standard, we will need to be proactive in managing our relationships with industry.

The interactions of industry representatives with veterinarians should focus on:

- informing veterinary professionals about products and services,
- providing scientific and educational information, and
- supporting medical research and education.

Advice for maintaining a responsible relationship with your industry partners follows:

- Establish protocols and rules for dealing with sales representatives from all segments of the veterinary industry including manufacturing, pet food, etc.
- Educate employees on ethical relationships and provide examples of potentially unethical marketing practices

Examples:

- Do not accept gifts that provide a personal benefit to you or other staff members such as tickets to a sporting event, t-shirts, baseball caps, etc
- Only accept gifts that benefit your practice or your patients (e.g., client education material such as posters, handouts, etc.)
- Consider establishing a no-gifts policy at your clinic

Given the goal of industry is profitability and the primary ethical goal of practicing veterinarians is to provide optimal patient care, there will be conflicts of interest. Managing these conflicts to the benefit of both parties is possible by establishing and following guidelines in your practice.

Conclusions

Industry plays a critical role for the veterinary profession. They produce new and innovative products and services that assist veterinarians in their ability to offer the latest in patient care. They disseminate information about these products and services to the profession. In addition, animal health care companies provide the veterinary profession with significant contributions in the form of financial support, time, and expertise. These contributions have many added benefits to the veterinary profession. They enhance the educational experience of veterinarians and provide humanitarian services to animals and animal owners that would otherwise not be available.

When your sales representative visits, ask him or her to provide you with an overview of their involvement in special projects, continuing education and research. Acknowledge their contributions to the profession. If their contributions go unnoticed by the veterinary profession, they may see no benefit in continuing to provide such support. Ensure their continued support of the profession by acknowledging that support.

Maintaining ethical relationships between veterinarians and industry is essential to the continued success of both parties.

ABOUT THE AUTHORS

Lowell Ackerman DVM DACVD MBA MPA

Dr. Lowell Ackerman is a Diplomate of the American College of Veterinary Dermatology and in addition holds an MBA from the University of Phoenix and an MPA from Harvard University. He is involved in clinical practice as a clinical assistant professor at Tufts University School of Veterinary Medicine as well as helping to develop the business skills curriculum there. In addition, Dr. Ackerman is affiliated with Veterinary Healthcare Consultants, LLC–a national consulting firm dedicated to providing innovative and resourceful business solutions for veterinary professionals and humane organizations. His primary business interests include leadership, team building, customer relationship management, strategic planning, Total Quality Management, profit center development, veterinary fee issues, marketing, promotion, action planning, and performance measurement. Dr. Ackerman developed the BARK^{sm} system for performance evaluation of veterinary practices.

Dr. Ackerman is the author/co-author of 75 books to date (including Business Basics for Veterinarians) and numerous book chapters and articles. He lectures extensively, on an international basis. Dr. Ackerman is a member of the American Animal Hospital Association, the American Veterinary Medical Association, the Association of Veterinary Practice Management Consultants & Advisors, the American Society of Journalists and Authors, and the Association of Veterinary Communicators.

Elizabeth Bellavance DVM MBA

Dr. Bellavance graduated from the Ontario Veterinary College in 1991 and returned to school in 1995 to complete an MBA. She has several years experience in mixed animal practice. Currently, Dr. Bellavance provides project management and consulting services to the veterinary industry while completing a CMA (Certified Management Accountant) designation.

Mark Davis

Mark Davis has been a veterinary practice manager and a practice management consultant for the last eight years in general, specialty and emergency settings. He is a graduate of the AAHA Veterinary Management Institute and has worked in California, Hawaii, Maryland, the District of Columbia and Virginia. He currently resides in Norfolk, VA

Tracy Dowdy, CVPM

Tracy Dowdy is a career consultant who is dedicated to helping veterinarians and all those who work with them reach new levels of success in all aspects of their business. She gained experience in the personnel industry working with Fortune 500 companies before entering the veterinary field. Since Tracy's father is a veterinarian, she has had years of opportunities to gain knowledge about the profession throughout her life. In 1995, Tracy joined Advanced Animal Care Centre located in Bedford, Texas. Within three years of leading the practice in a new, client and service oriented direction, the practice tripled in gross revenues and received a Hospital Design Merit Award (June 1998) and the Practice of Excellence Award (June 2000) from Veterinary Healthcare Communications, the publishers of Veterinary Economics magazine.

In March of 1998, Ms. Dowdy started Veterinary Management Solutions to help veterinarians and practice owners achieve the same success she was able to provide to Advanced Animal Care Centre. Ms. Dowdy has consulted with over 100 practices nationwide in the areas of financial growth, staff retention, client service and many other aspects of practice management.

Ms. Dowdy has built on her management and training experiences to create her own, unique hands-on approach. By working alongside veterinary teams and their leaders, she helps them develop a practice that is service and client centered by setting and training to standards of service, empowering the healthcare team, building effective and efficient workflow systems, improving communications, conduct, and appearances, creating a culture of emotional wealth sharing, and ultimately moving the entire practice to higher levels of personal and collective enjoyment as well as improved financial success.

Tracy has been published in local and national veterinary journals and has spoken at local, regional and national veterinary meetings. She is available to speak on topics such as leadership, client service and staff training at national and regional conferences. Ms. Dowdy is a Certified Veterinary Practice Manager and a Charter Member of the Association of Veterinary Practice Management Consultants and Advisors.

Karen Felsted CPA MS DVM CVPM

Dr. Felsted graduated from the University of Texas at Austin with a degree in marketing. She spent 12 years in accounting and business management, six of it with the "Big-8" accounting firm of Arthur Young (now Ernst & Young.) During this time, she also obtained an MS degree in Management and Administrative Science (concentration: accounting) from the University of Texas at Dallas.

After graduating from the Texas A&M University College of Veterinary Medicine, Dr. Felsted began her career as a veterinary practitioner in both small animal and emergency medicine while maintaining her existing veterinary accounting and consulting practice. In 1999 she opened and became Manager-in-Charge of the Dallas office of Owen E. McCafferty, CPA, Inc., a national public accounting firm specializing in tax, accounting and practice management services for veterinarians. During this time she received her Certified Veterinary Practice Manager certificate. In 2001, she joined Brakke Consulting, Inc., where she continues to offer practice management consulting services to veterinarians. She also runs her own accounting firm specializing in financial services for veterinarians.

Dr. Felsted has been published in numerous national and international veterinary journals including Veterinary Economics and Texas Veterinarian. She has spoken at many local, national and international veterinary meetings.

Jim Humphries BS DVM

Dr. Jim Humphries is a veterinarian, media spokesperson and communications consultant in Colorado Springs, Colorado. He was the animal health reporter for NBC Dallas-Ft. Worth for 10 years, and has been a contributor to CBS The Early Show for over 13 years. Jim has given over 4,000 interviews and completed 23 national media tours for the animal health industry. He now consults with a variety of businesses and industries in the area of media relations and training. He is the author of a new web resource for small business and medical practice promotions and publicity, www.Publicity123.com.

Thomas Lynch MA

Thomas A. Lynch, MA is the founder of Veterinary Healthcare Consultants, LLC–a national consulting firm dedicated to providing innovative and resourceful business solutions for veterinary professionals and humane organizations. Earlier in his career, Tom served as Hospital Administrator for a large, 24-hour, full-service, veterinary hospital. Additionally, he served as a member of the adjunct faculty at a private New England college where he taught business courses including Principles of Management, Principles of Marketing, and Small Business Management. Tom holds undergraduate degrees in business management and marketing, and a master's degree with a specialization in management and a concentration in veterinary practice administration. He has been published in the Journal of the American Veterinary Medical Association, Journal of the Veterinary Emergency and Critical Care Society, Veterinary Product News, Veterinary Economics, Veterinary Practice Staff, and DVM Newsmagazine.

Frank Muggia JD

Mr. Muggia is a graduate of Middlebury College and Boston University School of Law. For the past 13 years, he has been serving the veterinary community with representative clients across the country. Mr. Muggia's national practice has him trying cases in State and Federal Courts throughout the country including New York, Massachusetts, Georgia and Florida, and advising clients throughout the country.

Mr. Muggia has become one of the most well respected attorneys in the United States in the field of veterinary law; whether buying or selling a practice, resolving partner and employee conflicts, effectuating a solid and comprehensive business plan, or litigating restrictive covenants. He is well published in the area and lectures nationally within the veterinary industry, in addition to being listed as an approved consultant by the American Animal Hospital Association. He can be reached at www.MuggiaLaw.com

Kurt A. Oster MS SPHR

Kurt A. Oster, MS, SPHR is a practice management consultant with Veterinary Healthcare Consultants, LLC–a national consulting firm dedicated to providing innovative and resourceful business solutions for veterinary professionals and humane organizations. Kurt is certified as a Senior Professional in Human Resources (SPHR), the highest level of certification offered by the Society for Human Resource Management. Prior to consulting, Kurt served as Hospital Administrator for a 16-doctor, 24-hour, full-service, veterinary hospital for six years. Additionally, he worked as an educator for a veterinary software firm for nine years. During this time he educated the staffs of over 325 veterinary practices on all disciplines of practice management. Kurt is the finance instructor for the American Animal Hospital Association's (AAHA) Veterinary Management Development School (VMDS) Level One and Advanced. He is a frequent lecturer and he has been published in the Veterinary Practice News and is regularly featured in AAHA's Trends Magazine. He may be reached via e-mail at kurt@vhc.biz

INDEX

0-595-28711-5

CPSIA information can be obtained at www.ICGtesting.com
Printed in the USA
BVOW080546271112

306513BV00002B/181/A